BILLINGS FOOD

The Flavorful Story *of* Montana's Trailhead

STELLA FONG

AMERICAN PALATE

Published by American Palate
A Division of The History Press
Charleston, SC
www.historypress.net

Back cover, top: Garlic and potatoes sold at Good Earth Market.
All images by Stella Fong unless otherwise noted.

First published 2016

Manufactured in the United States

ISBN 978.1.46711.786.9

Library of Congress Control Number: 2015956828

Notice: The information in this book is true and complete to the best of our knowledge. It is offered without guarantee on the part of the author or The History Press. The author and The History Press disclaim all liability in connection with the use of this book.

For Joe, my husband, who always cooks up delicious ideas and adventures.

CONTENTS

Contents

FOREWORD

Taking an honest look at Billings, Montana, through the lens of a true foodie, culinary teacher, writer and Southern California transplant, Stella Fong delivers a thorough guide to the burgeoning importance of good food in Montana's largest community. Reading her descriptions of eateries, from fine to funky, throughout the neighborhoods of Billings is like visiting with a good friend. Her recommendations are effusive, knowledgeable and diverse.

My favorite imagery in the book is that of the Saturday farmers' market in summer—cold and windy in the morning but packed with customers who all are game to buy from farmers who grow food within a 120-mile radius of Billings. If anyone needs proof that the local food movement is on the rise in Billings, Fong offers the facts from the Yellowstone Valley Farmers Market, which has grown from one hundred customers in 1986 to three thousand in 2015, from three vendors to around sixty today. The delectable description of the sights and smells of the market captures a food-flash of downtown Billings with an array of A-to-Z choices, from apiary-fresh clover honey to a box of zucchini blossoms. I am already planning a visit next season and am prepared to drive the 120 miles from my house just to beat the crowds.

Highlighting the locavore movement at Montana's Trailhead, this book covers everything from beef to brewpubs, markets to Main Street, in a community where a diverse culinary scene has been growing over three decades. Noting the value of fresh, organic and natural in restaurants that serve breakfast, lunch and dinner and highlighting culinary leaders past and present, the author also gives a strong nod of gratitude toward Montana's farmers and ranchers who supply food to markets and restaurants in the community. In this no-frills ode to the culinary landscape of Billings—or, as Fong cleverly dubbed it, "the foodscape"—there is an approachable passion for eating well.

Seabring Davis
Author of *A Montana Table: Recipes from Chico Hot Springs Resort*;
Food Lovers' Guide to Montana; *A Taste of Montana*; and
Big Sky Journal's editor in chief and "Dining Out" columnist

ACKNOWLEDGEMENTS

I want to thank all the people who have so enthusiastically talked about Billings' food—sharing their favorite restaurants and telling of where they secure the best products to cook and to savor.

I thank the chefs and entrepreneurs who told their stories of desires and dreams of where they want the foodscape to evolve in Billings. I thank them for their passion and their persistence in bringing deliciousness to Montana's Trailhead.

Many thanks to Seabring Davis, author of *A Taste of Montana: Favorite Recipes from Big Sky Country*; *Food Lover's Guide to Montana*; *A Montana Table: Recipes from Chico Hot Springs Resort*; *Big Sky Journal*'s editor and "Dining Out" columnist. She has supported my craft and my love of food, art and people.

I thank those who helped me with my research, tasting and exploring restaurants around town: Renee and Dave Coppock, Sharon Forman, Suzi Rietz, Margit and Bill Thorndal, Sue Balter-Reitz and Paul Reitz and Bill and Mary Underriner.

Thanks to Sean McDaniel and Renee Coppock for being my eyes for detail, proofreading the words for *Billings Food*. I thank friends who have been the spirits of confidence and cheer. Thanks to Bess Fredlund, Robin Kline, Darla Jones, Kari Knierim, Barb Andersen, Bill Cochran, Lori Smith and Terrie Chrones. Always, I thank Deb Goffena for her artistic eye, her help with photographs and her support with research.

Also, thanks to Artie Crisp, Hilary Parrish, Jenni Tyler and Maggie Heatley at Arcadia Publishing and The History Press for their help and support.

Acknowledgements

Mostly, I thank my husband, Joe, who has inspired me to always seek new flavors and adventures. His help with research for this book was invaluable, along with assistance with editing and, of course, his countless words and spirit of support.

INTRODUCTION

Billings is bootstrapping the local food scene and standing tall. There is a growing confidence in the city's culinary identity while developing its own flavors and incorporating foods from around the world. The city's palate is evolving beyond the boundaries of the Treasure State while giving notice to the nearby ingredients that provide Montana's Trailhead with its distinctive identity. It is high time that our city is noticed for the many culinary treasures that can be found here.

Nearby ranches run cattle, and fields of wheat sway in nature's breath. It is no wonder that beef dominates the plate or that beer is brewed and wheat thrashed. The Yellowstone River is a massive nutrient artery providing home to fish and silty soil for morel mushrooms and spring asparagus, free for the picking. Huckleberries, buffalo berries and chokecherries grow freely, yielding fruit with just Mother Nature's care. Local chickens range freely and lay colorful eggs, while local lamb finds its way to restaurant menus. Game is bountiful here with elk, deer and turkey and, of course, the occasional bison. To spice up these treasures, wild sage, mint and juniper berries provide the optional finishing touches.

The tastes and food styles from the West, and globally, have infused into indigenous fare. With chefs such as James Honaker, Jeremy Engebretson, Tim Freeman, Carl Kurokawa, Ben Harman, Howard Shen, Marlo Spreng and so many more, new ideas and ways of cooking are appearing on the table. They bring their backgrounds and knowledge, stimulating our palates with food that showcases naturally, with little adornment.

Chefs are paying heed to the food that comes from Montana. Neighboring growers are taking advantage of our unique environment while working within the limits of our growing seasons. The knowledge they have gained has allowed local chefs to take advantage of the fresh produce now available. The residents of Billings reap the harvest with Community Supported Agriculture (CSA) programs that allow for weekly supply of in-season fresh produce. The Yellowstone Valley Farmers Market provides an avenue for securing fresh local bounty and, even more, the opportunity to interact with those who create the food we eat.

In recent years, Natural Grocers and Lucky's Market have settled into Billings to provide fresh organic and natural food options. Good Earth Market, Mary's Health Foods, Montana Harvest Natural Foods and Bonanza Health Foods have been anchors of the health foodscape. Though often viewed as alternative food options, their messaging and principles have influenced many to integrate healthier options into everyday living, and they now are becoming mainstream. Greater demand has produced more options for healthy eating and cooking.

These markets also sell gourmet items that previously required mail ordering or bringing back in suitcases from faraway locales. Boutique shops such as the Yellowstone Olive Company, Amaya Oriental Market, City Vineyard and many other retail outlets offer enough ingredients from around the world that I can now source items locally for most of my cooking supplies.

In *Billings Food*, I have endeavored to reveal a broad swath of the culinary establishments, personalities and events that shape Montana's Trailhead. Residents should be proud of what is offered here and should be optimistic about the future of our culinary heritage. Because of the limited number of words I was given to write about the food in Billings, I have unintentionally left out eateries and food sources that have contributed to the ingredients that make our town flavorful. Also, the establishments included in this book have had their beginnings here in Billings.

Historic Restaurants of Billings is a good companion to this book, allowing me the opportunity to write about the historical underpinnings of restaurants and the food scene's past. It acts as a bridge to yesteryear, as well as including those chefs and entrepreneurs who continue to influence the culinary landscape of our city.

A lot has changed since my move to Billings over sixteen years ago. There is vastly more variety in the way of restaurants, flavors, tastes and availability. With so much to be proud of in Montana's Trailhead, the future of food holds great promise. It will be exciting to watch it unfold and grow.

Chapter 1

YELLOWSTONE VALLEY FARMERS MARKET

The wind is blowing and temperatures are in the fifties this Saturday morning in the middle of August. The bell has already been rung to signal the start at 8:00 a.m. of the Yellowstone Valley Farmers Market, Billings' seasonal open-air market. Completed is the ritual of the clanging of the cowbell while Donna Miller navigates counterclockwise around the information booth. At 8:30 a.m., the crowds are manageable compared to other days since the market began the third week in July. It is unseasonably cold today. Perhaps customers do not feel the urgency to arrive early to beat the heat. We all clutch our coats in a protective shiver, but the rain from last night and this morning are welcomed, as smoke from nearby fires has clouded the skies, making the air heavy.

The Yellowstone Valley Farmers Market is the biggest in Montana, selling fresh produce, fruits, herbs, flowers, plants, frozen meats and a variety of foods such as caramel apples, grilled cheese sandwiches and homemade crèpes. As a free event, it brings people of all ages downtown. Its aim is "to operate a world class Farmers Market that contributes to the success of local food growers and producers, and create a vibrant community gathering." For over thirty years, it has brought freshness and flavor to Billings.

The market began in 1986 with the efforts of Laura Mitchell and Mary Underriner. The first idea arose in 1982, when Mitchell had just planted three hundred apple trees with her husband, John Ross, for Ross Orchards with the purpose of making cider. (Currently, Red Lodge Ales Brewing Company is making Apple Ale with its apples.) At the time, Underriner was

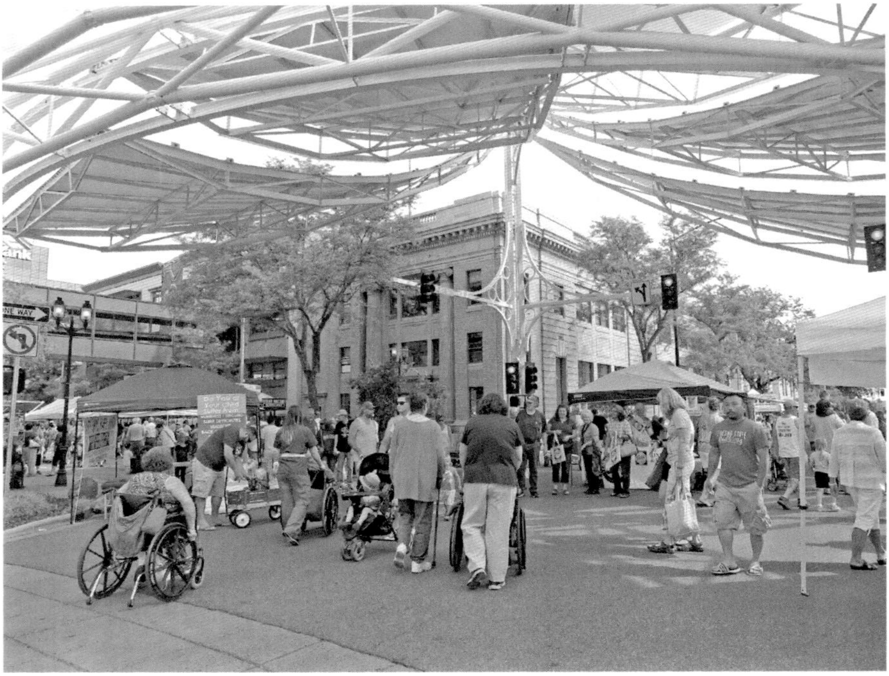

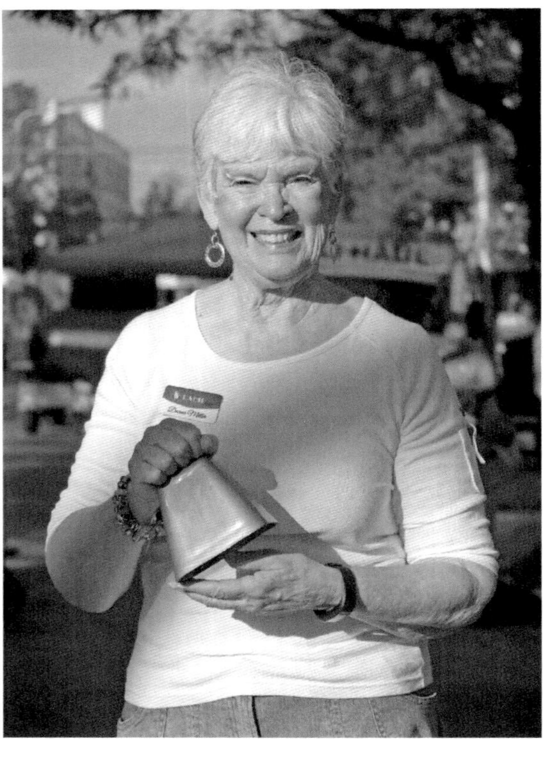

Above: Shoppers at the Yellowstone Farmers Market under SkyPoint.

Left: Donna Miller rings the bell for the start of the Yellowstone Valley Farmers Market.

working at the chamber of commerce as director of membership services. Mitchell called Underriner and said, "We need to put together a farmers' market. We need to do something for economic development." Then the work started. They got into their cars and, with the help of Dwayne Jelinek, drove into the Clarks Fork Valley and into Huntley and Shepherd, knocking on doors to find farmers interested in participating. "We had four markets the first year," Mitchell continues. "Three vendors participated in the First Federal and Loans parking lot" near the current-day Dude Rancher Lodge, with about one hundred customers arriving to buy goods. Underriner tells of how they promoted the first markets with free advertising from the *Billings Gazette* and the placing of posters around town. The market later moved to various locations, including the parking lot of the Billings Clinic and the current parking lot for Riverstone Health. To this day, Satorie Farms, one of the first sellers, still sets up its produce booth every Saturday. Now, in 2015, the Yellowstone Valley Farmers Market has come a long way.

Market Masters Kelly Weber and Penny Smith work together to oversee the fifty to sixty season pass holders, many of whom occupy the same spots every Saturday. Their work also involves teaming up with a nine-member board of directors. The vendors pay a flat fee to sell at the market and must follow a set of rules. In the rules it is stated:

> *The sale of items at the market is restricted to the sale of locally grown produce, plants, flowers, and locally prepared food items that have the market approval. "Locally" is defined as grown within a 120-mile radius of Billings, MT. Non-local produce can be sold with approval from the market under a different fee structure. Non-local produce can only be sold if it is not available from a local producer. No animal food or live animals may be sold.*

For Weber, she says, "This is a fun job for twelve weeks a year." During the rest of the year, she works as head custodian at a grade school in town. The time between the third week in July and the first week in October requires more intense and immediate work, yet planning for the market begins in January. Though impossible to really count, Weber estimates that roughly three thousand people come to the market on a given Saturday.

My husband and I always enter on the north side of Broadway, near the Alberta Bair Theater. The market basically encompasses North Twenty-eighth and Twenty-ninth Streets between First and Third Avenues North. We walk toward the market's heart, located right under SkyPoint. On the

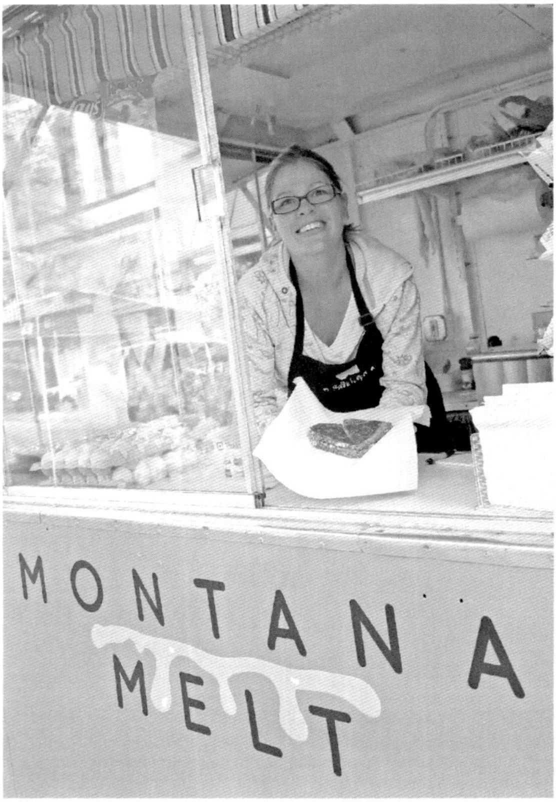

Left: Danielle Amundsen, co-owner of Montana Melt, presents her gourmet brie apple grilled cheese sandwich.

Below: Mike and Cara Schaer, owners of Log Cabin Bakery and McCormick Café, have been a steady presence at the Yellowstone Valley Farmers Market.

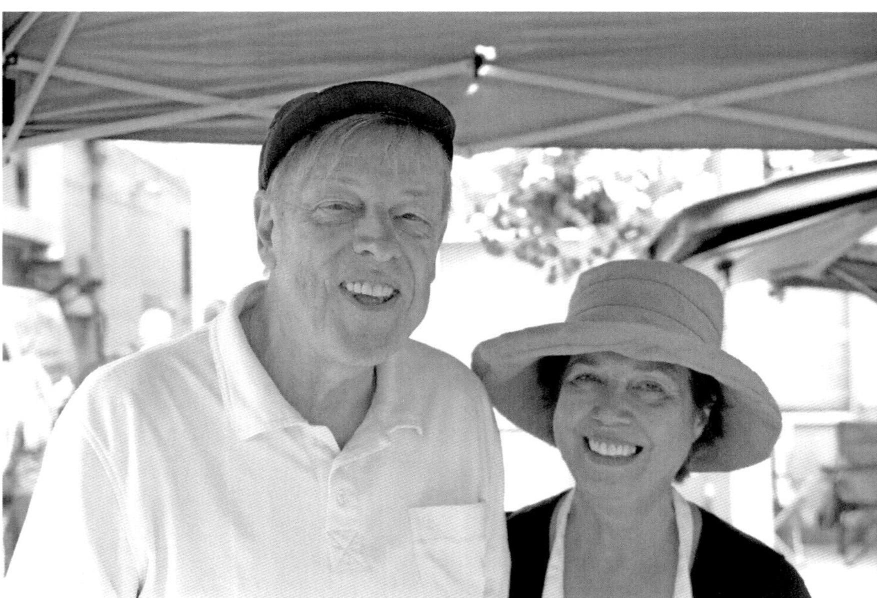

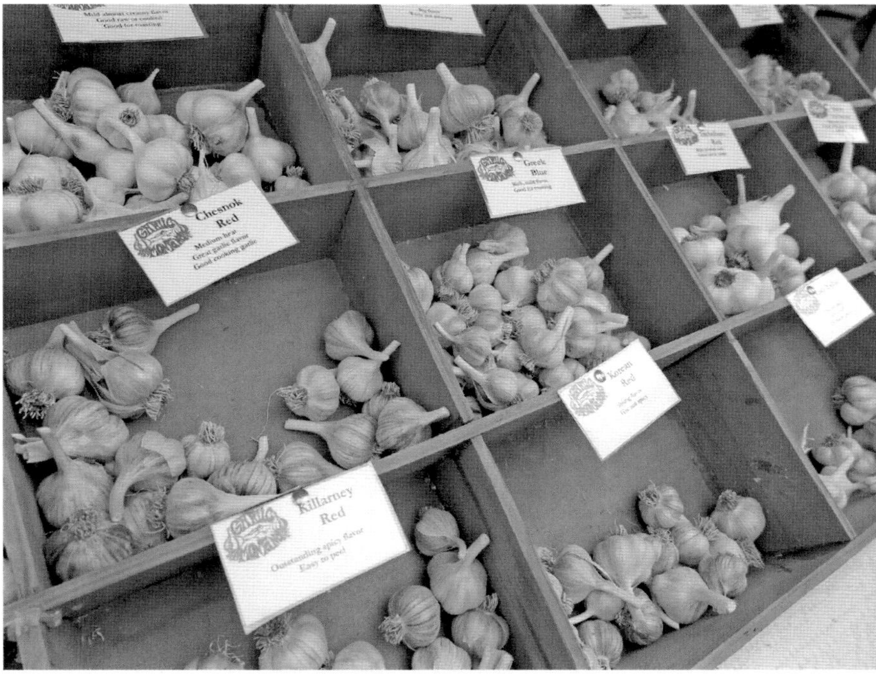

Garlic Montana, a small family business in the Bull Mountains, offers a variety of garlic.

street is the information booth, as well as the docking station for wagons for loan to carry wares for anyone interested. Today, a guitarist plays music that heightens the beat of the crowd.

On our way over, I always peek at Cena Anderson's booth with a long cart filled with fresh herb plants. Here I have purchased the thyme, basil and lemongrass I have growing at my house. Dominating the east corner just under SkyPoint are fresh fruits and vegetables sold by the Hutterite colony from Martinsdale. My first stop is Log Cabin Bakery's booth on Second Avenue North to secure a fresh crèpe with squeezes of lemon juice and dusted with powdered sugar. Already there are a handful of people in line.

As I round the corner, the smell of sweet kettle corn mixes with the aroma of fresh frying mini-donuts. On North Twenty-ninth Street, I secure Korean Red and Siberian bulbs of garlic from Garlic Montana. At the Montana Melt food truck, I pick up my second course of breakfast: a grilled brie cheese, sliced apple and honey sandwich. Back on North Twenty-eighth Street, we stop at Danly Farms and buy several organic heirloom tomatoes, a box of zucchini blossoms and a bag of chopped kale. Next door at Kenny's

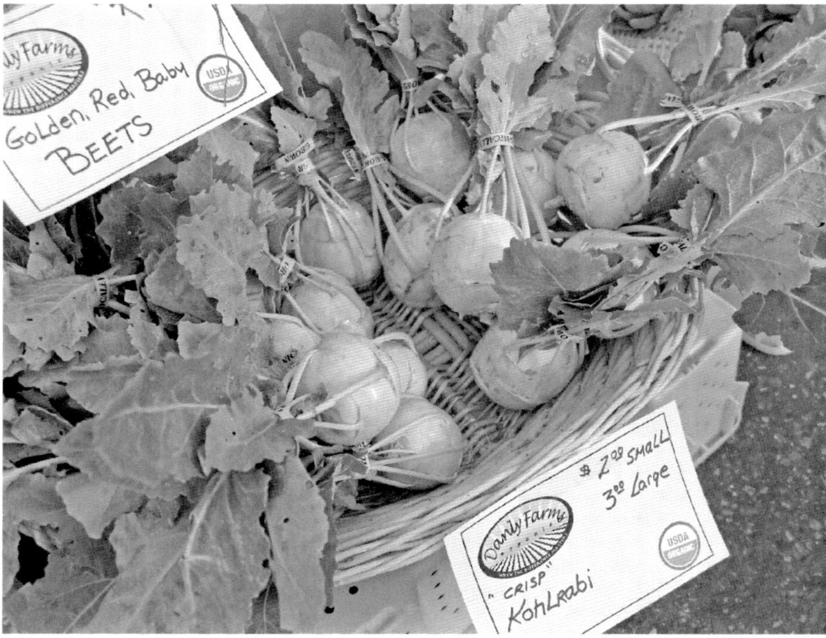

Danly Farms kolhrabi on sale at the Yellowstone Valley Farmers Market.

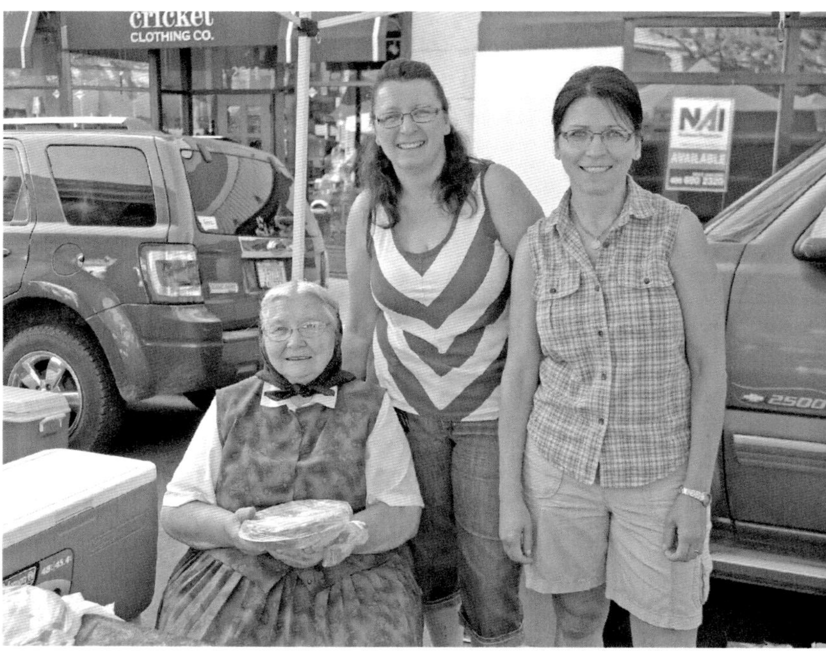

At Becky's Berries at the Yellowstone Farmers Market with (from left) Katie Hofer (baker of fruit pies), Ann Stahl and Becky Stahl.

Double 'D Salsa, we grab a container of mango-pineapple salsa. We walk by Wholesome Foods to see bunches of colorful sunflowers and piles of fresh produce. On this day, we forgo the clover honey from Drange Apiary, Brockel's Chocolates caramel apples, eggrolls from Oriental Express and noodles and fresh-squeezed lemonade from Khanthaly's Eggrolls. We have spinach and feta black bean tamales from Montana Tamale Company in our freezer, but we do stop for a large head of broccoli and cauliflower at the Mountain View Colony booth.

The Yellowstone Valley Farmers Market provides a great opportunity for the Billings community to gather and taste, smell and see the food offerings from the area. Here, the opportunity abounds for meeting the producers, experiencing the raw products and savoring cooked creations.

Chapter 2

KATE'S GARDEN

GROWING FOOD FOR COMMUNITY

A few miles away from the busy thoroughfare of Main Street and around the corner from Lake Elmo is Kate Rosetto's sanctuary, fondly referred to as Kate's Garden. Rosetto operates a vital vegetable, fruit, herb and flower farm. Here she nurtures Mother Nature's bounty for Community Supported Agriculture (CSA), local food co-ops and restaurant sales. The herbs and flowers grown are incorporated into her aromatherapy and herbology products aptly marketed as Scents of Balance.

On Rosetto's website, scentsofbalance.com, she confesses, "We're not happy unless we have our feet in the dirt and green under our fingernails. Working with Mother Nature and all of her moods can prove challenging, but it is also very rewarding." Rosetto is reaping the rewards these days, after making great efforts in her garden. Her admitting, "I am kind of a control freak" demonstrates that she has embraced Mother Nature's positive forces, accepting some of nature's wrath and, yet, managing some of the natural provocations. In the full swing of summer, weeds are absent, and her plants are pruned and neatly trimmed, while her bounty ripens into abundance. The winter destroyed some of her fruit trees, but Rosetto looks forward to new possibilities.

Rosetto credits her family for developing the passion she has for food by sharing, "We canned, made raviolis. My grandpa would get seeds from Italy. I have this huge respect for using what we grow." Rosetto finds meditative benefits in cooking. Even after a long day of working in the garden, she looks forward to being in the kitchen to embrace the ritual of preparing food. Sometimes, she sips one of her infused vodkas while preparing her evening nourishment.

"I love the chefs in Billings," Rosetto says. "The chefs are making people aware of farmers and local produce." Executive Chef Tim Freeman of TEN, the fine dining restaurant in the Northern Hotel, secures flowers, herbs and produce from Kate's Garden. Freeman's sous chef, Tyler Ellis, comes out weekly to collect their product. To TEN's credit, the restaurant actually gives credence to the desire of chefs wanting to know the origin of the food they serve. In the near future, Freeman plans to further educate his kitchen staff by touring through Kate's Garden, sampling her wares and witnessing how food exists in its most organic form.

At seventy-one years young, Rosetto wants to continue expanding her business. Her passion fuels her desire to grow. She admits that if she could secure contracted clients for growing in her greenhouse, it would help bring in some income, especially during the colder months. At this time, she has about thirty varieties of herbs and vegetables on one and one-third acres. However, she has an aspiration that has not been fulfilled. "My worry is that I am going to die and not pass on my knowledge," she laments. "I am such an advocate for sustainability. My dream is to find an apprentice to help me." If only her German shepherd, Bodie, could talk as he keeps constant company. Rosetto wants to bring individuals and the community to a level of self-sufficiency. She emphasizes, "If we do not solidify our local food system, we will not be able to find it."

In the 1960s, Rosetto started Scents of Balance, a business where she makes lotions and creams from essential oils and herbs from her garden. She works with the herbs, flowers, vegetables and fruits she grows when creating her skincare and wellness products. She views these creations as food for the skin and soul.

So it is no wonder that she started a CSA program for subscribers, supplying people with food. Over sixteen weeks in the summer, she weekly provides five to seven of her freshest vegetables growing in the garden. Those in the program arrive once a week at an established time to pick up their goods. On her blog, she presents recipes on how to prepare the bounty. Rosetto wants to build community. Some of her clients take the time to talk to her, comment on the items and even tour the garden, learning where the produce actually comes from. Others, she says sadly, "don't really see the garden. They don't look at the herbs or the produce." These clients quickly collect their vegetables and herbs into their boxes and leave.

On this last day in July, purple, green and yellow beans are elongating on the bushes while yellow pear, orange and blue tomatoes continue to intensify in color. The last of the raspberries cling on. Japanese cucumbers dangle from the vine as patty pan squash expand under large, prickly leaves. In her medicine wheel garden, Rosetto wants to grow gooseberries and currants to harvest next year.

Rosetto carries the spirit of growing from Kate's Garden, not only to plants but, more importantly, to people, in countless ways.

Chapter 3

GOOD EARTH MARKET CO-OP

WHOLE FOOD FOR WHOLE LIVES

In 1994, the Good Earth Market (GEM) Co-op paved the path to food awareness for the people of Billings. As the only co-op grocery store in Billings, it continues to carry out its mission of "integrating local food systems, cooperative values and environmental stewardship in a lively community marketplace." According to Greg Jahn, retired longtime board member, the GEM started with "early foodies" as a buying club in 1987. For seven years, members ordered food every eight weeks. In 1994, the group established a permanent 1,800-square-foot storefront at 3115 Tenth Avenue North, in Billings' oldest grocery store, the Tenth Avenue Market. The GEM thrived there until early 2000, when the organization began to consider offering more products and possibilities.

The success of the cooperative philosophy at the GEM, where the grocery store is democratically run to benefit the members and the community, should be credited to the leadership and dedication of a handful of members. Ann Guthals founded and managed the market for years. Carol Beam has served on the board for a dozen years while providing leadership as president for nearly a decade. Greg Jahn's board stint included nine years, working many of those as vice-president with Beam. But mostly, the community stood behind the efforts to bring the membership to a current five thousand strong. Jahn credits Beam. As the GEM took the risk to expand, "Carol really shouldered the effort. She helped organize a strategic campaign to solicit the needed financial and community support."

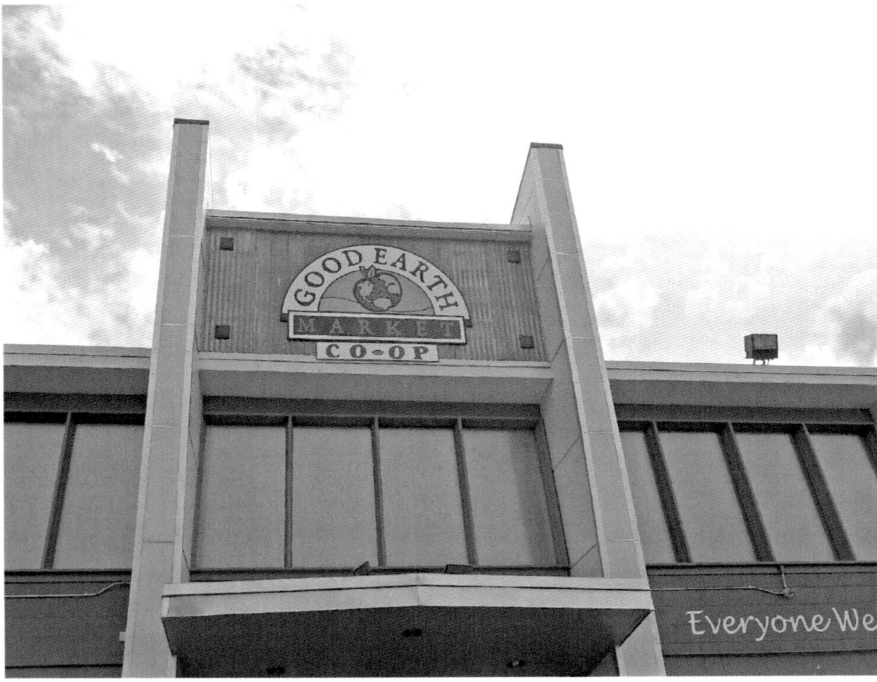

Good Earth Market is Billings' only co-op grocery store for healthy foods.

On February 19, 2006, the market relocated to the corner of Second Avenue North and North Thirty-first Street. Inside the old Gainan's Flowers and Garden Center Warehouse, which was once the Archie Cochrane Ford building, the Good Earth Market settled into its new home of nine thousand square feet. The Gainan family negotiated a long-term lease with the GEM, with rent increasing as sales rose. The renewal of the space came from the skills of Randy Hafer of High Plains Architects and Hardy Construction.

According to Dana Pulis in an article for the *Billings Gazette*, much of the architecture recycled materials from other places for the building and the grocery equipment. Ex–board member Nancy Halter recalled cleaning out grease from a cooking range secured from Smith's Food and Drug Center after it closed. Her attribution of the relocation success was: "We had great members that brought expertise to the table. We ended up with a great colorful building." In Pulis's article, Guthals described the building as "clean, funky with some character to it, but something anybody would feel comfortable in." The arts community led by Halter came together to paint murals and bring color to the space. On the ceiling of the café is painted a blue sky with billowing clouds, and on the walls above the entrance are

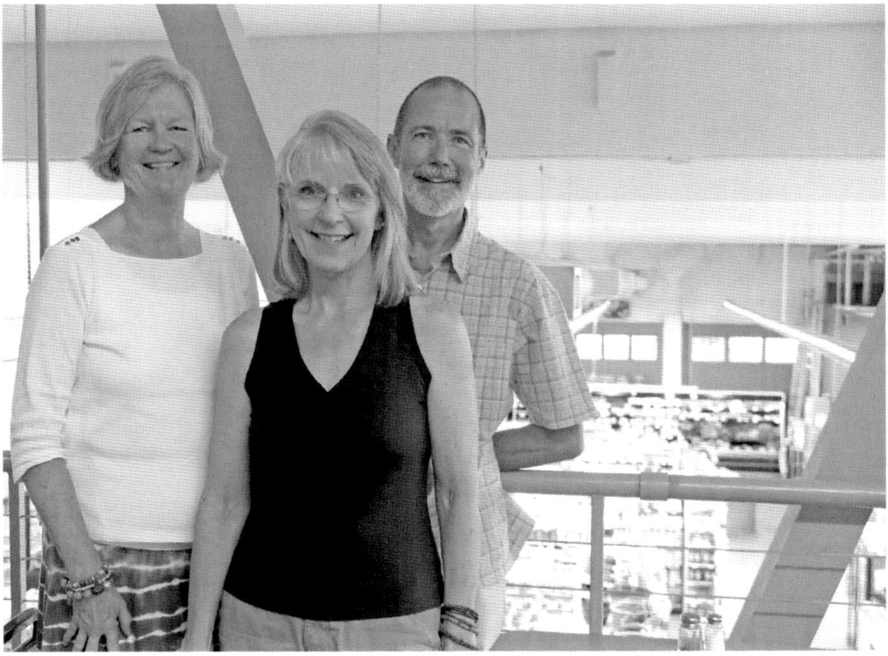

From left to right: Carol Beam, Nancy Halter and Greg Jahn, present and past board members of Good Earth Market.

paintings of food, fruits and vegetables. Offerings at the deli are written with colorful chalk on large blackboards.

When new stores such as Natural Grocers and Lucky's Market arrived in town, the GEM experienced a decrease in business, with the 2014 annual report indicating gross sales decreasing in the months these stores opened. However, the GEM should be proud that the market was one of the businesses that paved the way for these new enterprises to come into Billings. Many years ago, the culture of natural eating and the palate for varied foods were much more limited. In addition to the GEM, Mary's Health Foods, Bonanza Health Foods and Montana Harvest Natural Foods were some of the first wellness food stores in town. Bonanza Health Foods was the "original" health food store in Billings, founded by Jerry and Arthel Vincent in 1976. Mary's Health Foods came on the scene in 1994, while Montana Harvest Natural Foods arrived later and is currently owned by Mike Fagan.

Sunday Supper farm-to-table dinners were introduced by the GEM with the guidance of caterer Tom Nelson. Diners gathered in the GEM building during the summer months when fresh product was readily

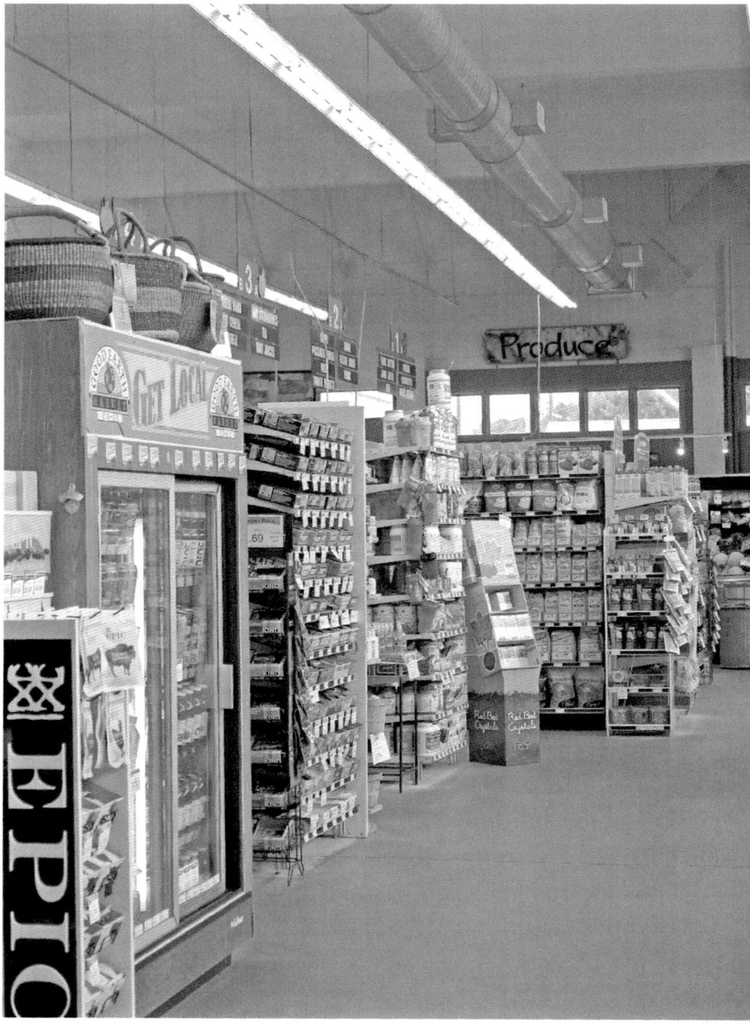

Members and nonmembers can shop at Good Earth Market.

available. Chefs—including Nelson and others such as Jason Corbridge, James Honaker, Dirk Frickel, Paul Reitz, Marcy Tatarka and Vicki Van Buskirk—were invited to cook family-style meals. Tables and chairs were set up in the aisles of the store, and employees volunteered with setup, waiting tables and cleanup. Live music provided entertainment. The "precursor" to the Sunday Suppers, according to Jahn, was block parties at the old location. Several dozen people would show up to "talk garden," Jahn says.

The old grocery store site is now occupied by Harper and Madison, a bakery and café owned by Joanie Swords since 2011. She, along with Lilac chef Jeremy Engebretson, recently retired chef Shane Weigel and, on occasion, Jason Corbridge, has continued the Sunday Supper tradition, naming their meal a "Farm to Table Dinner." In recent years, a long table has been set up with white tablecloths and flowers on Tenth Avenue North in front of the restaurant between Thirtieth and Thirty-first Avenues North on occasional Sunday nights in the warm months. After a multicourse meal, Marian Booth Green and even Joanie Swords have sung a jazzy tune or two for the crowd.

These days, the GEM is managed by Mike Howard, who has previous retail experience of twenty years. Beam believes, "We have come to understand that the experience of shopping needs to evolve. We need a lot more convenience items. Healthy alternatives with convenience." GEM will be turning its attention to improving the deli, fine-tuning and increasing the selections offered. Jahn says of the shopper, "You are shopping with your fork." Currently, the Deli Café offers soups, sandwiches, salads and entrées along with coffee drinks, smoothies and fresh squeezed juices.

Beam proudly says, "We are known to be very friendly to producers. We welcome local producers that meet our standards. They find us." The producers need to prove that they are growing sustainably. Rather than having to receive approval at a corporate level, as with big-name stores, a local producer can talk directly to a GEM staff member. Beam also discusses a local vendor, Danly Farms, which has received organic certification from the USDA as a result of the high standards it has set. He says about the owners, Mary Danly and Barbara Baresh, "They hold everyone accountable. They value the designation."

To be organically certified, requirements are stringent and include no treatments such as synthetic chemicals, irradiation or genetic modifications. The farmland has to be free of prohibited substances or management for at least three years. Organic products must be separated from non-certified products, and careful production and sales records must be kept. Periodic inspections ensure that these rules are followed.

Furthermore, Beam continues, "A big part of the co-op is in the producer fairs so the customer gets to know the producers. Producers also get to know each other…We need to get more education out there. If people will come here, it's a great place to shop. We have the friendliest people. People who want to work here have a commitment to the lifestyle. They have found a job that fits their passion." Jahn believes that the GEM has created an alternative culture that is "within the cultural creative dimension of good food, good community and good for the Earth."

The Good Earth Market will continue to be a steward of good food and good living for the community. Already, the work by people such as Ann Guthals, Carol Beam, Greg Jahn and Nancy Halter has redefined how some of us eat and shop here in Billings.

Chapter 4

DANLY FARMS

BEAUTIFUL BOUNTY IN MODERN PROGRESS

Up the street from the Laurel rail yards and Interstate 90 is Danly Farms. For ten years, Mary Danly and Barbara Baresh have proved how beautiful natural bounty can be created among modern progress. Below their three-acre farm, life and wares stream by as cars rumble along on the highway and trains grind and pound on the metal tracks.

This morning in early August, I wander into the fields with Baresh. At sixty-four years young, Baresh moves with precise intention and agility. Her steps and actions are quick as she tries to beat today's heat. At nine o'clock in the morning, temperatures are moving toward the mid-eighties, with a predicted high of one hundred degrees Fahrenheit later in the day. Right now, a partly cloudy patch shades the sun's rays. Tomorrow is the Yellowstone Valley Farmers Market, and she and Danly are preparing their vegetables and herbs for sale. They harvest, wash and package all their produce as though they are presenting a gift—encasing their passion and hard work to pass on to their customers.

Today, I am here briefly to help Baresh harvest the beets but more so to ask questions. She pulls the root vegetables from the ground, and my job is to remove the wilted leaves and those that have already bent over. I hold the beet in my hand to allow the leaves to project upward. Those stems that droop toward the earth are pulled off by hand. They are then stacked into a crate that has been placed on its side with the bottom against the sun. Any beets with blemishes are set aside.

Baresh admits, "I give each variety three tries," and if it is too difficult or impossible to grow, then it is not worth the effort to fight the natural

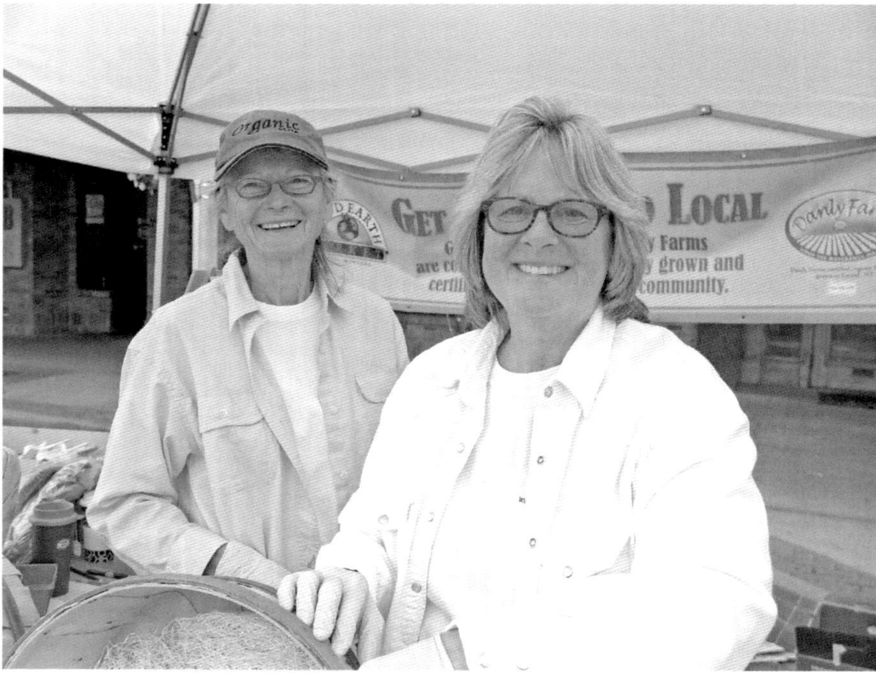

From left to right: Barbara Baresh and Mary Danly, founders of Danly Farms in Laurel, grow organic produce for the Yellowstone Valley Farmers Market and CSA.

elements. "Nature keeps you on your toes," she continues. Danly Farms does have different selections; for instance, growing eight or nine different types of kale and thirty varieties of tomatoes.

We process about one hundred orange and red beets, each around the size of a golf ball, some slightly larger and others much smaller. As we work, there are pockets of welcome calm when the anguish of motors and motion from afar seem to dim, letting in the sound of twittering birds and an occasional rusty-gate screech from a pheasant or two. Then the brush of a breeze brings a touch of coolness and hope that maybe this day will relent in its scorch. Finally, Chervil the Siamese cat comes over, brushing against us, providing another salutation.

Carrying the two crates of beets up from the farm rows requires attention. Divots in the ground, pipes for the irrigation and abundant growth form obstacles to navigate around and over. Baresh picks up the crate full of beets and bounds over the natural hurdles. She loads them onto a wagon and pulls it down a wood bridge crossing the irrigation ditch, up a narrow path along the chicken and turkey enclosure and

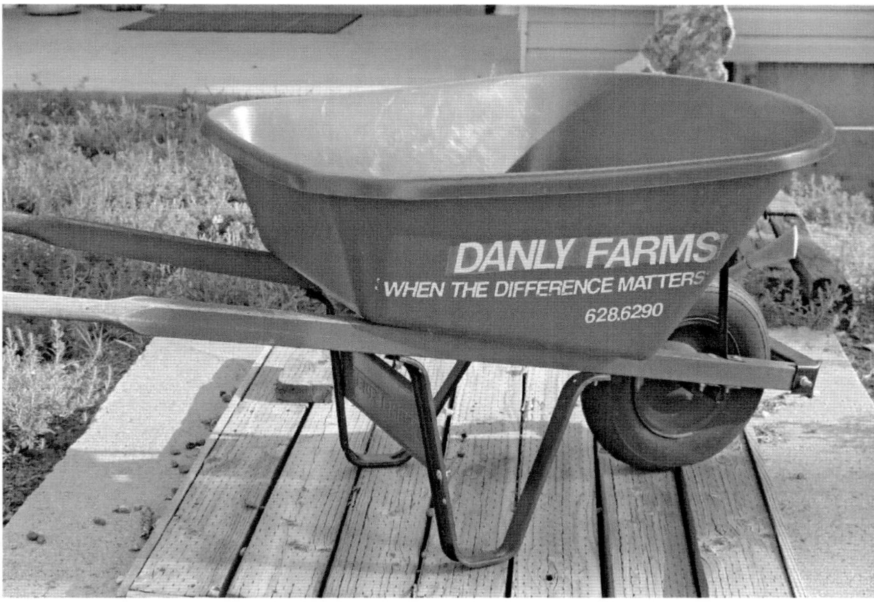

A wheelbarrow from Danly Farms in Laurel.

around a large pine branch blocking the lane. Along the way, she points out the dandelion greens, the cipollini onions, the artichokes, the red vein spinach and so much more. Then, beyond the herb and flower garden and before the grape arbor, we end up by the work shed. Before going in, Baresh hoses down the beets, removing any dirt.

Danly is inside the shed packaging yellow, green and purple beans. She slides them neatly into a plastic bag, all aligned with roughly an equal amount of each, weighed and then sealed. With humor, Baresh says of her yellow beans, "These are our favorite to roast, as they are our French fries. We cannot stop eating at one." Both Danly and Baresh are reflective. They demand a lot of themselves and set their standards high. As I continue to ask questions, Baresh dips bundles of beets she has assembled with root balls roughly the same size. Once they drain, she ties them off with a metal tie labeled with the words "Organic Grown." She trims the ties so they are short and even.

Danly and Baresh escaped the crazy Los Angeles lifestyle ten years ago. Baresh left behind her ceramic art career and Danly her film editing profession, after a dozen Emmys. Basically, they headed toward Canada and stumbled onto the property in Laurel. These days, they derive satisfaction in educating others in what they have learned in their farming journey. Danly says, "Why bother when you cannot educate the community?" Especially on market day, Danly tells of how when she is talking to one customer, another is usually listening. "Bystanders then want the item." She continues, "People are afraid of vegetables because people do not know what to do with them. We have interesting recipes to go along with the vegetables. Our simple recipes are the best. A simple technique, such as roasting instead of steaming, is a revelation." Danly says that many people cannot translate cooking techniques from one vegetable to another. For instance, a cook may roast asparagus, but he cannot apply the same method to squash.

We return to the field after Baresh harvests tomatoes from the new greenhouse they put in a couple years ago. They fondly call it "The Tunnel" as it is a half cylinder frame with plastic roll-down sides. Inside, peppers and tomatoes are ripening. I carefully try to follow Baresh to the tall green rows, trying not to trip over plants. Harvesting heirloom tomatoes can be challenging because they grow tight on the vine. Baresh goes in with some shears with care and finesse, as it is easy to nick a tomato when harvesting it. Heirlooms have more flavor, taste and texture, but what shows up at a market is truly survival of the fittest. They tend to damage more easily than supermarket tomatoes, so the yield is lower.

Aside from providing produce for the weekly Saturday market, Danly Farms also supplies forty CSA subscriptions for fifteen weeks during the season. The farm was the first one in the area in 2009 to provide this program as a way for consumers to buy local and seasonal food directly from a farmer. CSA customers can choose to pick up their bounty on two days in the middle of the week. This means they rush to harvest twice a week—once for the CSA and the other for market.

"People do not have a strong understanding of the seasons. The supermarket are the seasons," Baresh sadly says. Danly points out that vegetables are best enjoyed when they are in season—a summer squash should be eaten and enjoyed in the summer. Danly shares about what they grow, "We have varieties they cannot get in the market." Their selections are "horrible shippers. They cannot stay in a warehouse for a week. We concentrate on really tasty varieties."

In 2008, Danly Farms became Certified Organic for its vegetables, fruits and herbs, following a defined set of standards prescribed by the USDA that preserves the environment and avoids most synthetic materials, such as pesticides and antibiotics. The old dairy homestead is now a Certified Organic operation. Aside from the vegetables and herbs, the farm also produces fruit, laying chickens, heritage turkeys and organically formulated fertilizers. Their philosophy is best described through their motto: "When the Difference Matters."

Both Danly and Baresh are reflective and have come to accept the hardships as well as the rewards. After recently losing a dozen chickens to raccoons, full-grown trees to beavers and produce to grasshoppers, they continue to expand and refine their business. In the last couple years, they put in "The Tunnel," with drop-down curtains, which has allowed them to start production earlier and provides shelter for their tomatoes and peppers. They take one week off a year to travel to Arizona to see Baresh's aunt. During the cold months, they take inventory, organize their bookkeeping and strategize for the coming season.

The true reward comes during the Saturday farmers' market, as within an hour of opening, most of the several dozen heirloom tomatoes they brought for sale are almost gone. They have empty baskets where product used to be. Danly greets customers and is happy to explain how to best enjoy their produce. Baresh, with a warm smile, makes sure each customer leaves with good spirits.

Danly Farms has lived up to its slogan, for it has made a difference by introducing the first CSA in Billings and by showcasing and highlighting the bounty of nature. It demonstrates how beauty and taste can be created with attention and care.

Chapter 5

BENJAMIN HARMAN

THE FIELD HOUSE CAFE TREATS FOOD WELL

On the other side of the railroad tracks from downtown Billings is the Field House Cafe, located at 2601 Minnesota Avenue. In so many ways, it is not surprising that Executive Chef Ben Harman's restaurant, started three years ago, is located on the south side of town, away from the city's core. Harman is a renegade—fierce in his passion and belief in how food should be. The bottom of his menu, written in bold letters, encapsulates his spirit: "**We reserve the right to change anytime based on season, availability, boredom, or just because**."

The Field House Cafe is the first and only Certified Green Restaurant in Billings, receiving its status in 2012. In an article written by Jaci Webb for the *Billings Gazette* on June 1, 2012, the restaurant satisfied requirements in five categories. "Concerns such as energy consumption and reusing furniture and fixtures helped them earn the ranking. The tables and chairs were gleaned from the old Red Lodge Pizza, a spot Harman remembers fondly from his youth." In the center of the back dining room is a butcher block with a cleaver displayed in its middle under glass. The block came from Ringling, Montana, from the old Ringling Grocery Store. The rest of the eatery is decorated as though out of a catalogue page of West Elm meets Restoration Hardware, combining modern chic with antique and vintage.

Harman has come a long way. As he admits, "I was never a cooking prodigy. I was totally uninterested in cooking." In high school at West High, he took what he calls a "Foods" class as an easy elective. He learned to bake,

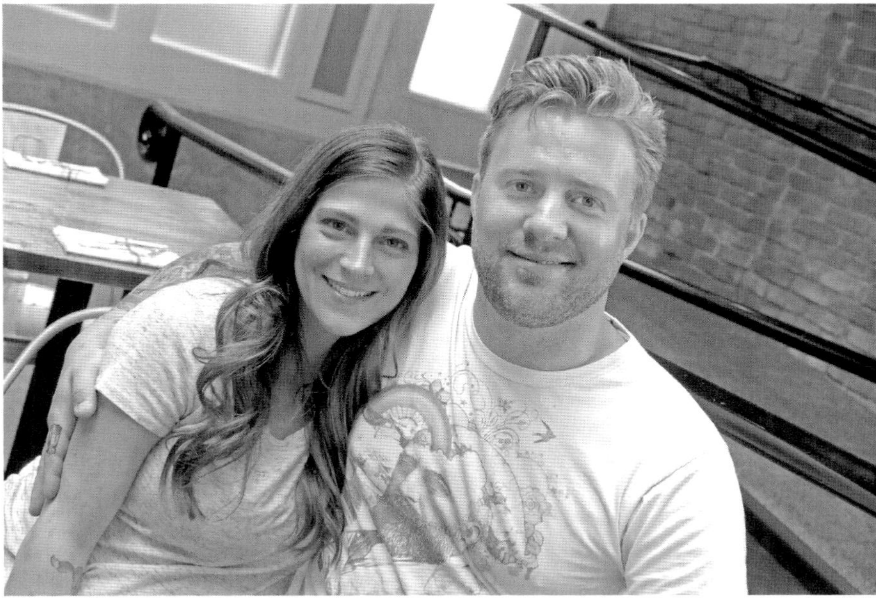

Krystal and Ben Harmon, owners of Field House Cafe.

but moreover, he says, "at the time, I was fond of the camaraderie. I liked the sharing. If I could cook myself, I would stay at home."

The Field House Cafe is a family affair, as father Steve has an office for his law practice here. On occasion, mother Joni is spotted. Next door, the Harman family renovated the 1916 meat distribution warehouse owned by Swift and Company Meats for loft-style apartment living. The innovative project received LEED Platinum certification and is on the National Register. Harman's wife, Krystal, works as the general manager at the café. After meeting in Orange County, California, when Harman was attending the Art Institute of Orange County, the pair returned to Billings after Harman completed his training.

They just gave birth to their daughter, Harlan. Krystal proudly says, "Ben is brave. He is ambitious about it [the restaurant]. He just created this." Harman had to create a business plan when he was in school, so when it came time to start the Field House Cafe, he had something in place to take to the banks. The Harmans confidently confess that they just knew the restaurant would be a reality.

On the restaurant's website, the Field House Cafe extolls that "everything is made from scratch with whole foods, right down to the ketchup. Join us in celebrating honest food, treated well." The menu is simple and concise with no flowery descriptions and lengthy explanations. The lunch menu offers a dozen selections, while the dinner menu has just a few more choices. Both have the "Brussels cashew-parmesan, sundried tomato aioli" as a choice. This popular item of fried Brussels sprouts showcases how Harman wants to present an unpopular vegetable in a more delicious way. He calls himself an "extremist" since he does not buy from major commercial food providers. His products are non-GMO (genetically modified organism), and he uses only oils such as organic sunflower.

At lunch today, PEI (Prince Edward Island) mussels are on the menu, cooked with preserved lemon, marjoram and honey. A baby kale salad is accompanied by hearts of palm, pecans and cotija cheese and tossed with a strawberry vinaigrette. A Vietnamese sandwich called a banh-mi consists of "hose chorizo. kimchi. cucumbers. carrot. Vietnamese mayo." Finally, even the burger is not ordinary, with "pickles. bacon. cheddar. onion confit. arugula. 1000 island. fries. house brioche." Dinner options follow in the same vein, with a meatloaf of "waygu beef. broccolini. potato. huckleberry bbq"; roasted chicken with "new potato. house bacon. rainbow chard. cumberland sauce"; and a steak selection, "responsibly sourced."

Harman continues to fine-tune his restaurant. A garden growing herbs and produce is found out back adjacent to the railroad tracks. This summer, new sails have been installed overhead to provide shade for those wishing to linger outside where chairs and tables have been placed. A large brick outdoor grill provides for smoking and barbecuing. The kitchen has been refashioned a couple of times to provide for more workspace and storage.

At the summer's end in 2015, Harmon made the decision to stop his lunch service and, according to the *Billings Gazette*, focus on dinners and create a new brand, dropping the "Cafe" from its name. But what Harman really wants is to "change people's relationship with food." He laments that in general, "people want value, a lot of food for not that much money." "People should feel no fear in eating here. We are not trying to be fancy," Harman shares. Then with some seriousness, he says, "Good food costs money." Slowly but surely, the Field House is succeeding in bringing diners south of the tracks to a place where "honest food is treated well."

Chapter 6

MONTANA AVENUE

FOOD FLAVORED WITH HISTORY

Montana Avenue holds the spirit of Buffalo Bill Cody and Calamity Jane. Located just north of the railroad tracks and the newly renovated Billings Depot, visions of success began here as passengers arrived to help build the railway, find gold, farm or ranch. This was where the taming of a wild country was conceptualized, but it took the brave and the tenacious to realize those dreams. Entrepreneurs such as the Yegens, the McCormicks and the Carlins provided feed and fuel for souls and spirits by opening hotels, bakeries, eateries and dry goods stores. Buffalo Bill helped H. Alfred Heimer build the Rex, and Calamity Jane sold high-octane libations and food along with a place to sleep. They brought a vibrant business spirit, which continues on today in Mike Schaer, Gene Burgad, Mark Hastings, Jeremy Engebretson, Michael Ulrich and so many others who have established commerce on Montana Avenue.

Mike Schaer's leadership made Montana Avenue what it is today. In 1983, he moved Computers Unlimited into an area that had fallen to the demise of pigeons, prostitutes and apathy as the city expanded westward. Wanting to re-create the safe and memorable Chicago neighborhood of his boyhood, he purchased buildings, only to resell some of them to people whom he believed had the same vision he possessed. In 1994, Schaer teamed up with Vicki Van Buskirk, owner of the Toucan Gallery at the time, and Judy McNally, president of the Billings Preservation Society, to clean up the avenue, removing abandoned vehicles from the street and installing streetlights in the alleys. Further beautification occurred in 2000 as new sidewalk landscaping with planters and metal work became established.

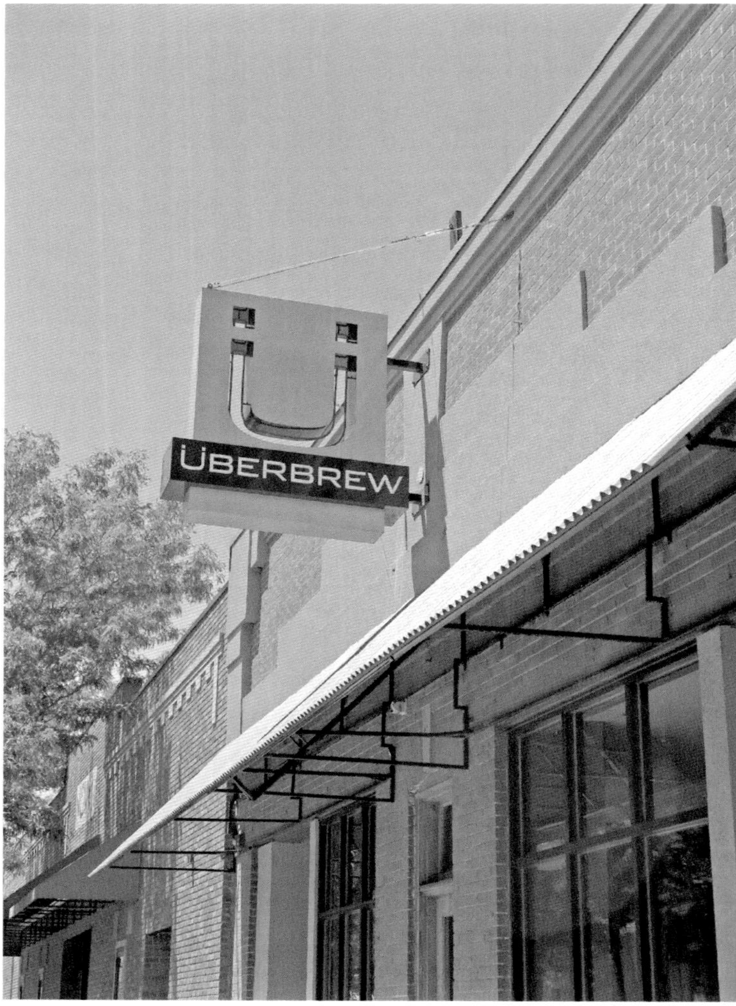

Überbrew, located on Montana Avenue, makes brews White Noise, Stand Down Brown and Alpha Force IPA.

The Rex Restaurant Bar and Grill has been a mainstay on modern Montana Avenue since 1976. The Rex Hotel Partnership bought the 1909 building from Senia Hart after she purchased it to save it from demolition a year earlier. The group remodeled the first floor to what the restaurant is today. Gene Burgad expanded the restaurant by adding the bar and outside patio onto North Twenty-fourth Street.

Though the Rex is best known for its Certified Angus Beef, it also features Billings' "Best Homemade Onion Rings," "Pan Seared Ahi Tuna," "Chicken

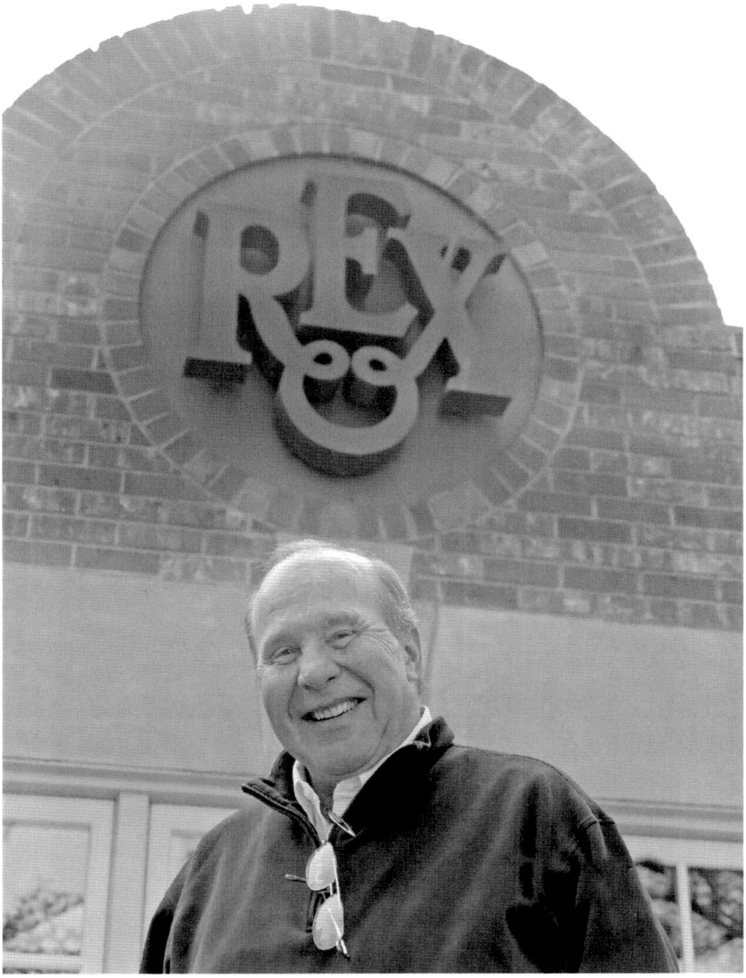

Gene Burgad, owner of the Rex Restaurant Bar and Grill since 1983.

and Andouille Sausage Gumbo" and "Beer Battered Shrimp" among the varied options.

Mike Schaer remodeled the McCormick Hotel building in 1998 as the McCormick Café. In 2002, across the street, he turned the Hotel Carlin into Q Cuisine, a fine dining restaurant, and a bar, Club Carlin. The later establishments have since become other venues. Cafe Zydeco, hailing from Louisiana, took over the Q Cuisine space in 2013. It features southern favorites including po' boys and "One Pot Cookin'" with selections such as shrimp and grits, jambalaya and crawfish étouffée. Its "Sandwiches and

Pita" include not only a "New Orleans Muffaletta" but also a sandwich named the "Gutbuster" with "grilled turkey, ham, pastrami, salami, roasted garlic, onion, peppers, banana peppers and provolone cheese served on a French roll with Aioli."

The McCormick Café was originally intended to be an Internet café when Schaer first conceived of the idea. But when he realized that most people had computers and global connection, he left the Internet part out to provide a place for breakfast and lunch and a cup of espresso. The café also has rooms in the back for meetings and conferences with audio-visual equipment available for use.

On large blackboards adjacent to the order counter, the menu spells out the food choices with some names in keeping with the Montana Avenue spirit, including "The Toucan," named after an art gallery across the street, with country white bread topped with scallion cream cheese, mushrooms, bacon, onions, tomato and mozzarella cheese; and the "Montana Avenue Omelet," made to order with choices of meat, cheese and other fillings. The building still retains the original brickwork and stamped metal ceilings. But McCormick's may be most famous for its crèpes. On Saturday mornings, Schaer and his wife, Cara, make fresh crèpes for the Yellowstone Valley Farmers Market.

Next door and sharing the same kitchen with McCormick Café is Cafe Italia, opened in 2008. Advertised as Billings' Italian pub, traditional Italian dishes and ones with a twist can be found here. There's "Vinnie Veal Piccata," "Spaghetti and Meatballs" and "Sausage Lasagna" for more familiar choices, with "Butternut Tiger Striped Ravioli" and "Pancetta Mac & Cheese" as offerings with a variation. Stone-fired pizzas consist of "Sausage, Pesto & Blue Cheese" and the old familiar "Margherita."

East on Montana Avenue is another Italian-themed restaurant. In 2009, brothers Matt and Jake Brosovich established Ciao Mambo for "immigrant-style Italian cuisine, prepared for you as you watch," as described on the restaurant's website. Two kitchens—one as the main preparation area and the other for pizza—open into the restaurant so the diner can be part of the cooking action. The Brosoviches bought the old Yellowstone Garage building and then invested $1.8 million in renovating the building to house the Montana-based chain, which also has branches in Whitefish and Missoula. With a motto of "Where Even Pasta Is Sexy," Ciao Mambo has an extensive menu featuring dishes named in Italian with descriptions underneath. "*Pollo con formaggio*," "two breaded chicken cutlets, ricotta, romano, mozzarella, parmesan and marinara baked in our brick oven"; and "*manicotti ripieni*," "pasta stuffed with ricotta, mozzarella and parmesan cheeses, baked in our brick oven with marinara," are two of the many hearty selections reminiscent of food cooked by an Italian grandmother or *nona*.

Aimee Brown, who has four children ranging in age from seven to fourteen years old, says, "My kids' favorite restaurant is Ciao Mambo. They love it because they are given a 'hunk of dough' when we first sit down. They can create something fun (flowers, snakes, happy face, kitty), and the staff will bake it and return it after dinner."

Located originally at 2519 Montana Avenue, Schaer opened the Log Cabin Bakery and started serving Starbucks Coffee. Here, cinnamon and caramel rolls, donuts and donut holes, cookies and bars were available to fuel the sweet tooth. At lunch, panini sandwiches were the popular offerings. In 2003, the Log Cabin Bakery storefront closed on Montana Avenue, and efforts were consolidated in its production facility located at 2401 Second Avenue North. After Q Cuisine closed in 2013, Executive Chef Daniel Roberts started Q Catering, sharing Log Cabin Bakery's kitchen space. The bakery has a small retail space in the front of the baking operation where fresh goods are sold.

Dickey's Barbecue Pit, owned by Ray Russell, occupies the former bakery space. He opened the franchise in the spring of 2013 to bring smoked flavors to Montana Avenue. Around the corner on North Twenty-sixth Street is Don Luis Restaurant, which has an extensive Mexican menu. With influence from Luis's heritage from a small town in Mexico and his life in America, dishes range from "Pork Chili Burrito with Beans" to "Mexican Cactus Salad" to "Patty Melt," satisfying any palate.

Back on Montana Avenue and then across four lanes of traffic is the Railyard Ale House and Casino, where live music acts bring rhythm to the avenue. Next door is Carter's Brewing, started by Michael Ulrich in 2007, with the taproom and brewing facility located spitting distance from the railroad tracks. There is a small deck out back for intimate train viewing. Appropriately, the brewery's logo contains the image of a train, and Carter is the name of the owner's firstborn son, who entered the world around the time the brewery opened. De-Railed India Pale Ale and Boxcar Brown Ale are popular beers.

Carter's Brewing was among the first microbreweries to come onto the modern beer making scene. Beer has been brewed in Billings since 1900, and original bottles with Billings Brewery labels were recently unearthed during the construction of Überbrew in the renovation of a Montana Avenue garage. As with all microbrew tap rooms, tastings are offered from 11:00 a.m. until 8:00 p.m., while food is served for another hour until nine o'clock.

The Billings Depot has become a popular wedding venue and event center. The building, constructed in 1909, was used by three railroads: Northern Pacific; Great Northern; and Chicago, Burlington and Quincy. Trailhead Spirits, owned by Casey and Steffanie McGowan, opened its distillery in the Beanery building. The McGowans make vodka, gin and whiskey with grain procured from their family's Highwood, Montana farm.

Finally, one establishment worth mentioning from a historical perspective is the Rainbow Bar at 2403 Montana Avenue. This bar opened in 1935 and to this day continues to attract many diverse souls.

Montana Avenue is the road that established the town of Billings, and to this day, it still holds hope for the future. This is where modern-day entrepreneurs established their businesses, as did those who founded and established the Magic City. The food and drink found on this street reflect the spirit and rugged individualism that make Montana unique.

Chapter 7
TOURING DOWNTOWN BILLINGS UNDER SKYPOINT

After relocating to Billings from California, where food trends are born, I can without hesitation recommend a food tour of Montana's Trailhead's downtown. The heart of the city has been enlivened with countless options—new restaurants, cafés, breweries, bars and bakeries. Now there is a martini bar (Doc Harper's), a wine bar (Bin 119) and an ice cream store (Big Dipper Ice Cream). There are two cupcake stores (Velvet Cravings and MAd Cupcakes) and a specialty cake store (Le Lustré Cakes, where offerings with beautiful and fun decorations and adornments range from mini to large cakes to satisfy the sweet tooth and for celebration). For the chocoholic, there is Brockel's Chocolates for truffles, and for the caffeine fiend, Rock Creek Coffee Roasters makes java from house-roasted beans.

Ethnic options include several Mexican restaurants: Guadalajara Family Mexican Restaurant, Sarah's Mexican Food, La Tinga and the 29th Street Cafe, which includes Latin plates and panini. The Athenian serves traditional Greek food, while Wild Ginger Japanese Steakhouse, opened in the summer of 2015 by Howard Shen and Tina Wu at the corner of First and North Twenty-seventh Streets, brings big-city Asian flavors with teppanyaki grills, a sushi and oyster bar and a lounge. Montana Brewing Company has anchored the dining and beer scene on Broadway Avenue in the old Montana Power Company building since 1994, with its microbrews, saloon and restaurant.

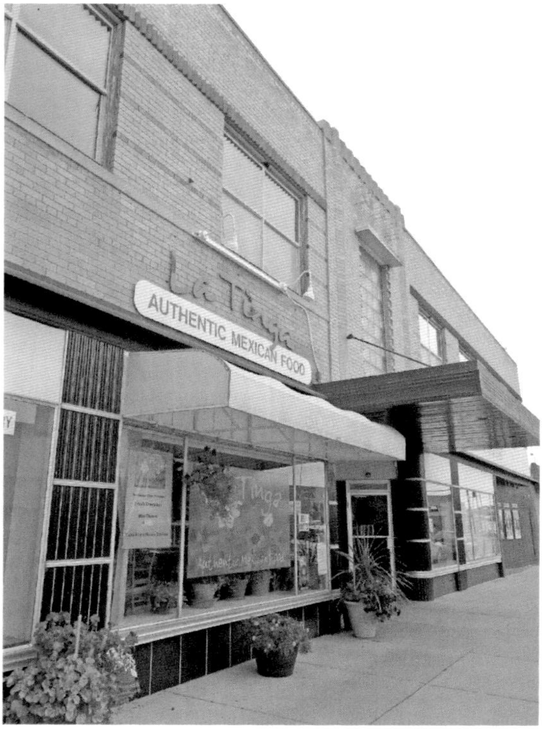

Left: La Tinga serves authentic Mexican food with options of tacos, burritos, tamales and tostadas.

Below: "Crispy Caprese Salad" with tomato, fresh mozzarella, basil and balsamic served at Stacked, A Montana Grill.

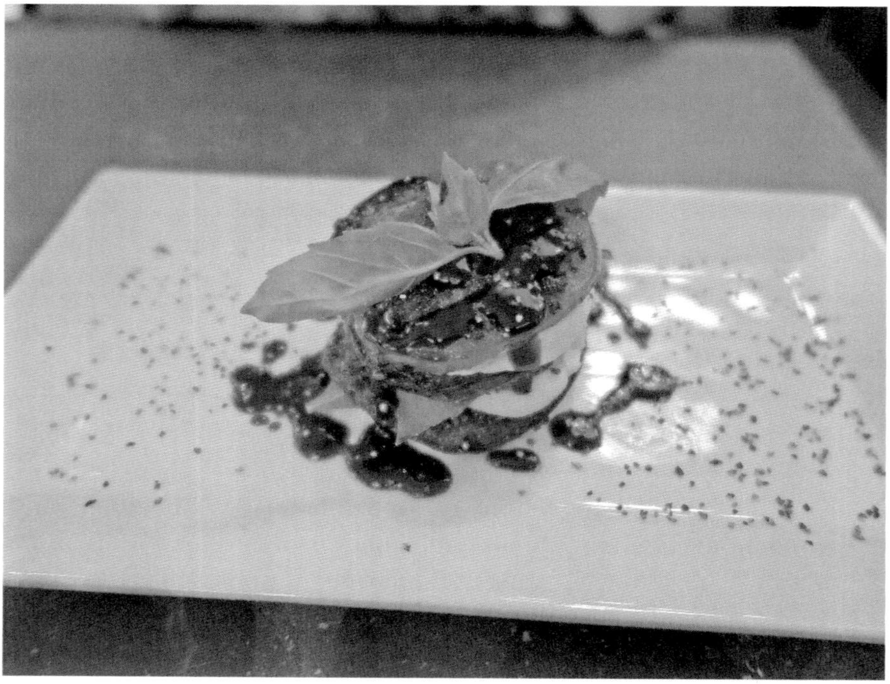

Directly across the street, Stacked, A Montana Grill, features burgers, sandwiches and much more. Rocket Wraps and Soda (wraps, salads and homemade sodas) and Soup and Such (soups, salad bar and bread sticks) make easy-to-carry-away food. For fine dining, Walkers American Grill and Tapas Bar, TEN at the Northern Hotel, Commons 1882 and Jake's Steakhouse are options, and in Billings, no jacket is required, so one can eat in comfort. For the best view, take the elevator to the Montana Sky restaurant at the Crowne Plaza Billings hotel for a bird's-eye view from the twentieth floor or the Billings Petroleum Club, which is located one floor above but is open to members only.

In one and a half days, a deliciously hearty walking tour can give a flavorful sampling of downtown Billings. Be forewarned that the suggested excursions require fortitude and an open-minded palate ready to

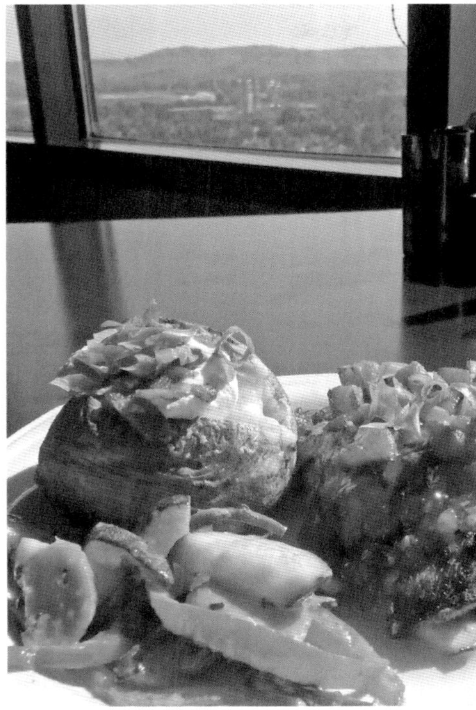

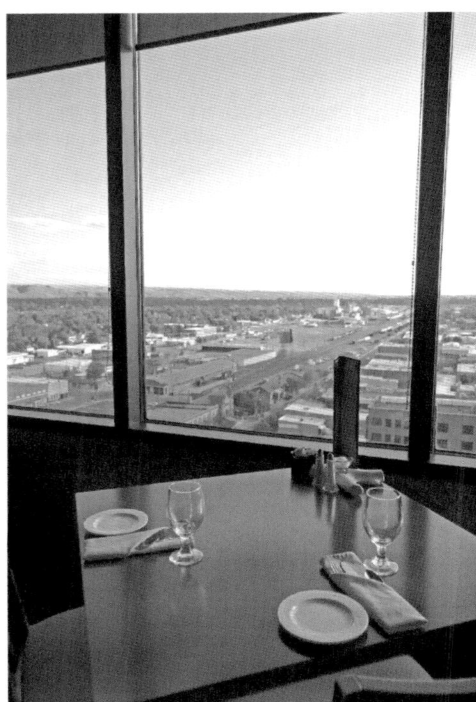

Top: "Apricot Pancetta Chicken" with baked potato and vegetables from Montana Sky Restaurant. *Courtesy of Montana Sky Restaurant, Jennifer Benfit.*

Right: The view of Billings and beyond from Montana Sky Restaurant on the twentieth floor of the Crowne Plaza.

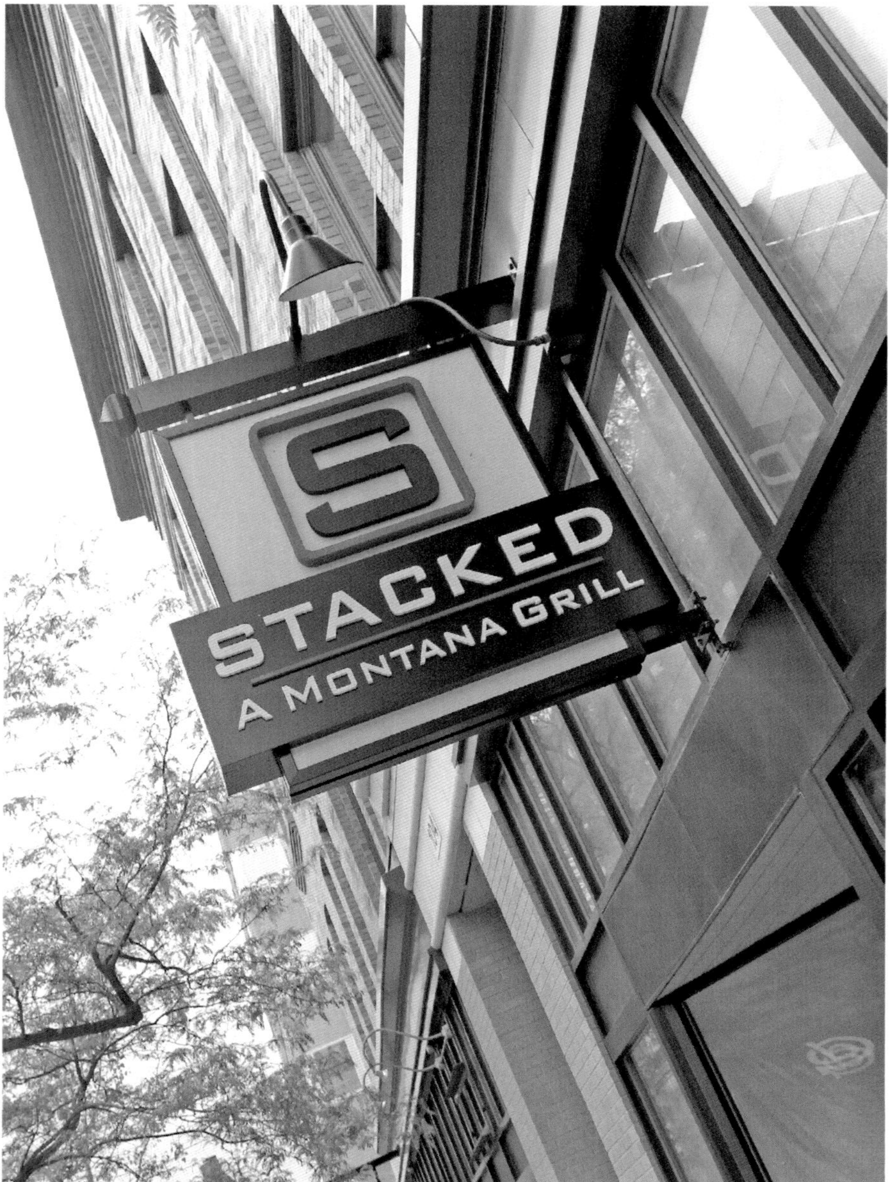

Stacked, A Montana Grill.

sample and taste. However, if you do have more time, I encourage you to linger a while or return several times to savor the food and drinks created by talented culinarians and entrepreneurs.

Stay at the Crowne Plaza Billings, Clocktower Inn or the Northern Hotel

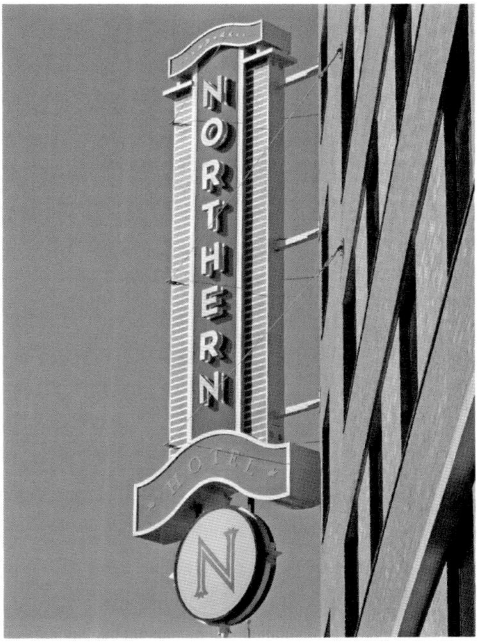

The modern sign for the historic Northern Hotel.

Accommodations in downtown Billings include the second-tallest building in town, the Crowne Plaza Billings hotel, affording the best views of the city across the Yellowstone River to the Beartooth and Pryor Mountains and north to the Rims. To the east of town is the Best Western Clocktower Inn, the downtown motel closest to Metra Park Arena and Cobb Baseball Field. The recently renovated Northern Hotel shines with new décor, combining cowboy chic and modern city elegance.

After checking in, head to SkyPoint, the seventy-three-foot sculpture suspended over the intersection of Broadway and Second Avenue North. Five "sails" come together in the structure that point toward the sky. While the sails provide shelter from the rain and snow, the spaces between filter in light.

Secure Sweets at Velvet Cravings and Broadway Deli and Café

Today's goal is to visit the Billings Public Library with a few decadent stops along the way. Heading north toward the Rims on Broadway, stop in at Velvet Cravings Cupcakes, where the pink and brown logo captivates with joy and whimsy. The glass display counter brings back childhood memories, with special treats including choices of a "Lemon Burst," "Root Beer," "Huck Finn" (a purple velvet cupcake with white chocolate) or "Pink Ballerina" ("a delicate dance of white wine, strawberries and white chocolate").

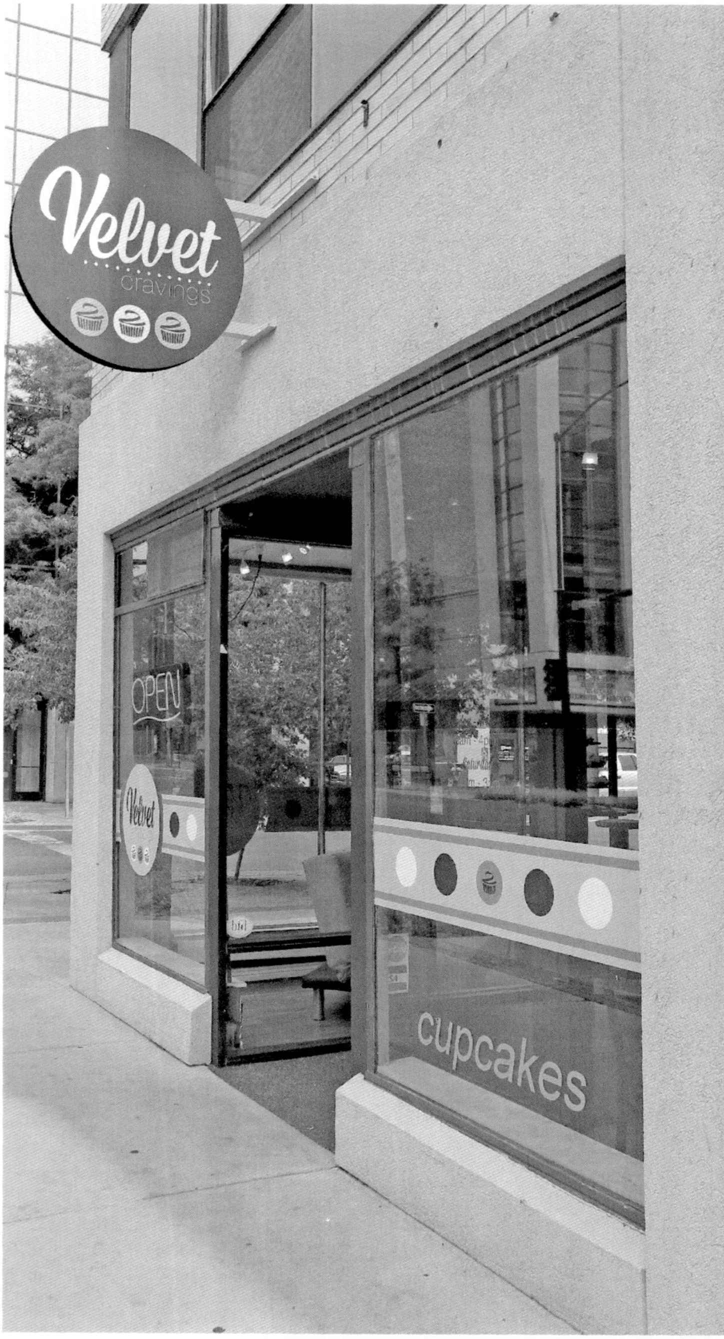

Velvet Cravings, located at 255 North Broadway, offers cupcakes named Huck Finn, Root Beer and Pink Ballerina.

In the next block continuing north is Broadway Deli and Café, housed inside the travel agency Travel Cafe. The black-and-white diagonally tiled floor shouts "café" reminiscent of an eatery or coffee shop found in France or Italy. On nice days, the west wall of the café slides open, bringing in the ambiance of Broadway Avenue. There is also a protected wood-decked patio out back. Here Rita Clippinger offers varied breakfast and lunch options such as "Mediterranean Chef Salad," "Turkey, Pear and Manchego Cheese Panini" and "Open Face Meatloaf Sandwich" topped with tomato, bacon, gravy and boiled egg slices. Her baked goods are irresistible, especially the oatmeal cookie with walnuts and chocolate-covered raisins. Clippinger was a personal chef and cooked at the McCormick Café before starting the Broadway Deli in 2011.

Billings Public Library and Sweet Cafe Learn and Linger

At the Billings Public Library, designed by architects Will Bruder and local O2 Architects, one can thumb through books for sale by the Friends of the Library in the Book Nook inside the Sweet Cafe, where an espresso drink or a cup of tea can be picked up along with a bagel or muffin. Tanya and Shane Weinreis opened this café at the request of local citizens.

The airy building space takes in the Rims and the bustle of Sixth Avenue North. The sixty-six-thousand-square-foot building, pending Gold LEED certification, encloses a Story Tower, a Reflecting Pool, TECH Lab and Montana Room. Abundant seating and work desks sit under high ceilings and natural light. Here, one can check out a book or download something to read or listen to.

Sips and Savors at Doc Harper's and Stacked

Back down Broadway, heading south, walk by the Alberta Bair Theater and pause to read the marquee and see what live entertainment is coming to town. Then stop at Doc Harper's for a "Spicy Pickle Martini," described as: "It's soo good! It sounds so bad, yet it's soo good! Smirnoff pickle brine, sweet vermouth & red chili flakes. Pickle garnish. Yumm!!!!" Many other spirited concoctions can be stirred, shaken and uncorked behind the

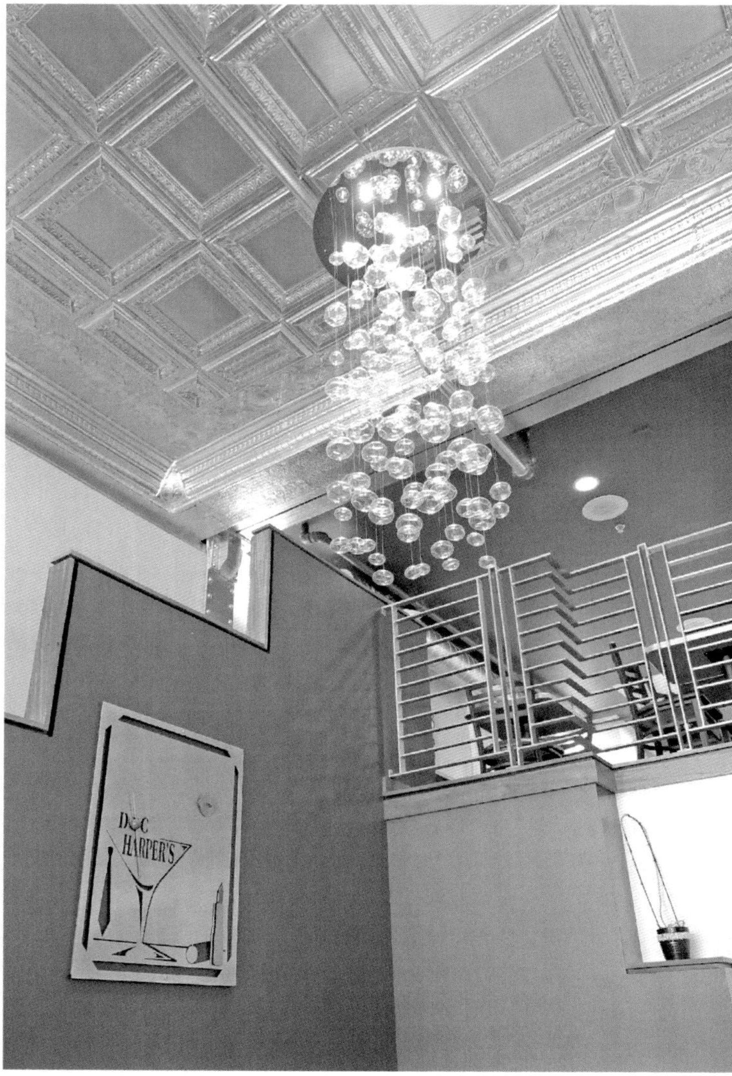

The round glass chandelier dangling from the metal stamped ceiling at Doc Harper's Martini Bar.

120-foot bar. Under "Doc's Light Foods" on the menu, designed by caterer Tom Nelson, Italian meatballs and shrimp cocktail make up some of the appetizer offerings. In early 2015, Bruce and Barb Harper remodeled the former zPizza space for the bar named after Bruce's father, Robert Dana Harper (Doc), who practiced in Sidney for forty-one years. With a chic geometric city style, grounded with a little heritage Montana, the bar brings

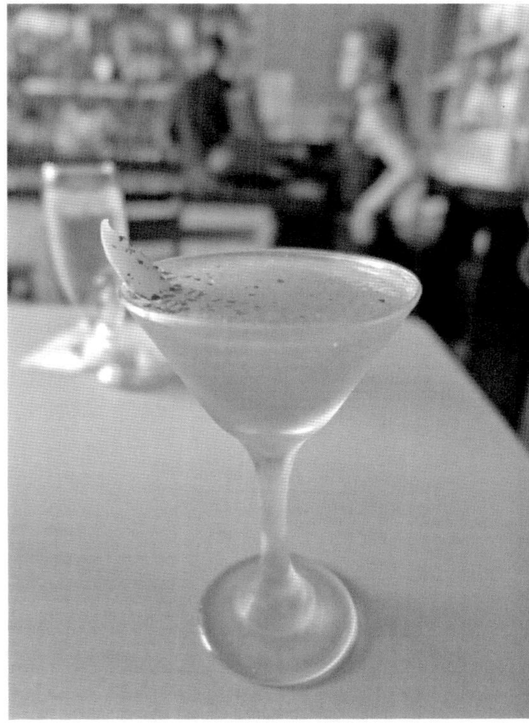

Right: "Spicy Pickle Martini" from Doc Harper's Martini Bar downtown.

Below: Angry Hank's Micro Brewery, maker of Anger Management Belgian Wheat, Street Fight and Massive Head Trauma Double IPA.

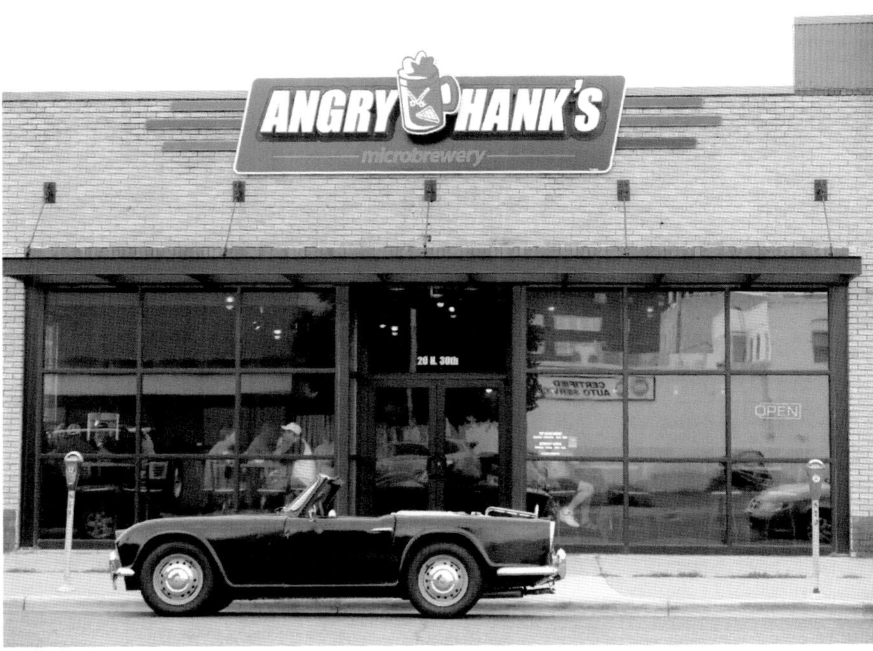

bling to Broadway. A bank of bench seating, with upholstered high backs lining the north wall, provides front-row viewing in the place to be seen. Tucked in the back under a modern glass ball chandelier is more room to gather, with additional space in an upstairs alcove.

Continuing down Broadway, slip into Stacked, A Montana Grill, and take a seat at the long concrete bar. Former food truckers Stephen and Stacy Hindman opened this brick-and-mortar eatery that alludes to layers of flavors in their featured burgers. Smoked meats, salmon and steak are also tasty choices. The walls feature local reclaimed barn wood and photographs of the Stordahl family ranch. A long high-top table made from wood planks from a Park City tree provides seating for a large crowd in the back. Order a pint of the Angry Hank's Street Fight Red and the "Crispy Caprese Salad" and "Wasabi Deviled Eggs." The salad is a stack of fresh basil leaves, slices of tomato and mozzarella topped with crispy bread crumbs.

Take in the View at Montana Sky Restaurant

To catch the sunset, the best viewing is at Montana Sky restaurant in the Crowne Plaza Billings hotel, one floor below the private Billings Petroleum Club. Take the elevator up to the twentieth floor for a perspective of Billings with railroad tracks below, the Rims to the north, the Yellowstone River to the south and the Beartooth Mountains off in the distance. Order the "Braised Short Ribs Poutine" ("bourbon braised short ribs, aged white cheddar cheese, green onion, chipotle sour cream and rosemary thyme gravy") or one of the other specials. As the sun sinks into the horizon, sneak into one of the restrooms and experience the view offered by the window that frames the landscape to the north. This restaurant seems to be forgotten by many who live in Billings, but the views and food are worth a visit.

A Movie and a Beer at Art House Cinema and Pub

By now, the Art House Cinema and Pub could be the next stop, with show times from Wednesday to Sunday. The theater, the remodeled Center Lanes bowling alley, was envisioned by Matt Blakeslee as a nonprofit independent movie theater where the belief is "Every ticket we sell, drink

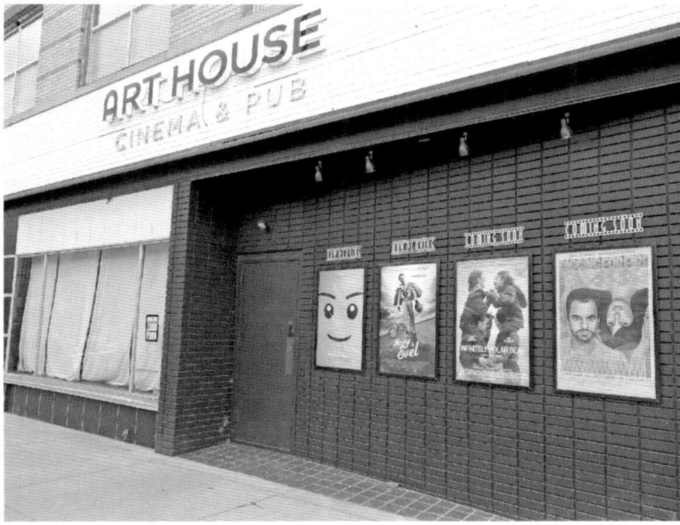

Art House Cinema and Pub is a nonprofit independent movie theater located at 109 North Thirtieth Street.

we serve, or popcorn we season has the sole purpose of seeing this city we love grow and thrive culturally." Order a glass of Yellowstone Brewing Company's Black Widow and a bucket of popcorn at the bar and settle in to watch the movie of the week.

Sip and Savor Wine at Bin 119

After emerging on the streets of downtown Billings, slip into Bin 119 on Broadway for a glass of wine. There are over thirty wines offered by glass or in flights. "Lobster Mac and Cheese" or "Crispy Skin Duck" are some of the menu choices. Owner Stephon Mentzer won a beer and wine license during a lottery and teamed up with Dan and Jen Konen to open Bin 119 in 2008. James Kordonowy designed the sleek interior of varnished wood and leather.

Hit the Trails, Rock Creek Coffee Roasters, Bernie's Diner, Stella's Kitchen and Bakery and Stirrup Cafe

The next morning, put on running shoes to run or hike the Swords Park Trail by the airport or the Jim Dutcher Trail near the Metra. Back in town,

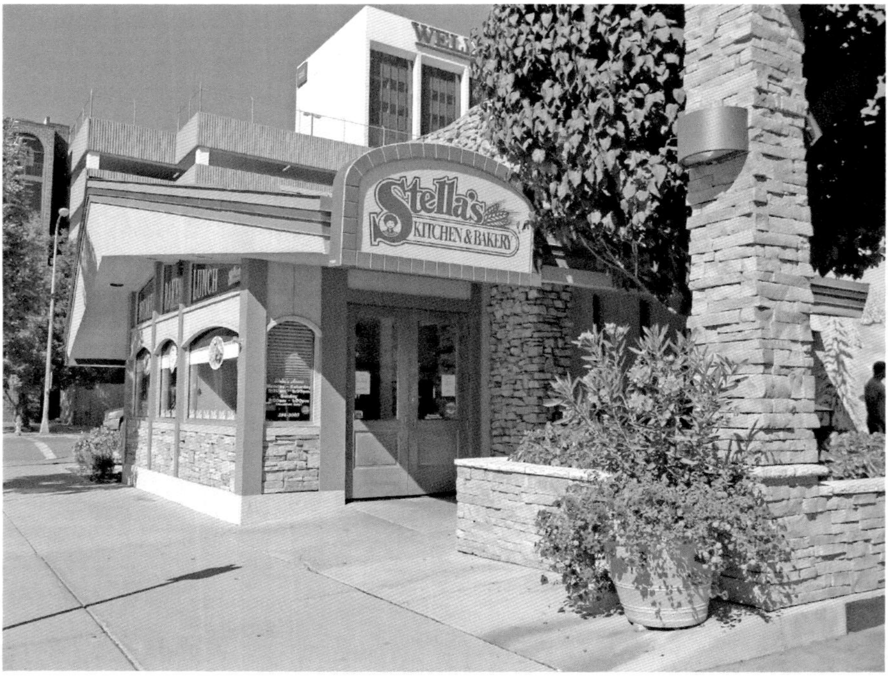

Owned by Ziggy and Stella Ziegler, Stella's Kitchen and Bakery is a popular breakfast and lunch spot.

pause at Rock Creek Coffee Roasters for a Chemex brew of house-roasted Sumatra, Guatemala or Jamaica beans after studying the big red Dietrich roaster flanked with burlap bags of raw beans in the back. The floor-to-ceiling windows are perfectly positioned for people-watching under SkyPoint.

For breakfast, Stella's Kitchen and Bakery, Stirrup Cafe in the Dude Rancher Lodge and Bernie's Diner are options for eggs, pancakes and waffles. Bernie's, named after the Northern Hotel's owner's mother, serves traditional breakfast favorites with a modern twist. Here it is difficult to choose between dishes such as "Biscuits and Gravy" with sausage gravy and poached eggs, "Chicken Fried Steak," "Elk Migas Skillet," "Captain Crunch French Toast" and the "Vacation Breakfast," consisting of a chocolate shake with chocolate cake. The restaurant is bright, shiny and red.

Stella's Kitchen and Bakery, opened in 1978 by Stella Ziegler and her husband, "Ziggy," started on Montana Avenue and later moved to its current place at 2525 First Avenue North. Lines form out the door during breakfast hours on the weekend. The bakery is famous for its cinnamon and caramel rolls but also offers healthy choices such as "7-Grain Hot Cereal" and oatmeal. Multiple home-baked bread selections arrive with the omelets and pancakes, along with a selection of ham, bacon or pork sausage. "Stella's Surprise," which combines hash browns, onions, peppers, ham and cheddar cheese with an egg on top, is one of the most popular dishes. Lunch serves up hearty salads, sandwiches and wraps.

The Stirrup Cafe anchors the iconic Dude Rancher Lodge. Dark wood and brick from the original St. Vincent Hospital house the western-themed dining room with a low-pitched roof, decorated in chic modern cowboy. Burnt orange mugs, arranged on the tables, pop color into the room, along with the rustic mica metal chandeliers hanging above. Windows banking two sides of the room shine light from the great outdoors. Here, options such as the "Dude Rancher Combo" and "Our FABULOUS caramel roll" can provide for a hearty beginning to the day.

Yellowstone Art Museum and Raven's Café d'Art, Tasty Art Pieces

After breakfast, the Yellowstone Art Museum is the final destination. From SkyPoint, head south on Broadway to the Catherine Louisa Gallery, with contemporary and twentieth-century fine art, and then back up Broadway into Lou Talbert Ranch Outfitters, where dudes and dudettes have been clothed for three generations. Around the corner on Second Avenue North, at MAd Cupcakes bakery and coffeehouse, "cupcakes with krazy flavors that are to die for, drool worthy, a devilish mess and with pretty designs" (as described on their Facebook page) are sold. Cupcake options include Choco Dough, Kool-Aid, Sunshine and Coke. The "A" in the shop's name refers to Anita Kantorowicz, the owner who took the reins in 2014.

After touring through the current exhibition at the Yellowstone Art Museum where a bright glass space encases the historic Yellowstone County Jail, visit the Visible Vault and the Artist in Residence across the street in another building. The museum's mission is to exhibit, interpret and preserve art with a focus on Montana and the surrounding regions. Located on site, the Raven's Café d'Art provides a quick refuel, including international choices such as "Spanish Grilled Polenta" ("green chili polenta grilled in garlic butter") or a "Roasted Vegetable Panini."

Western Heritage Center, 29th Street Cafe and Retail Therapy

The next stop is the Western Heritage Center, where the Romanesque sandstone structure once housed the Parmly Billings Library, but on your way there, be sure to peek into Le Lustré to view one of its sculpted cake creations. At the Western Heritage, learn about the history of the people and places of the Yellowstone River Valley and northern High Plains region. Bounce over to the recently opened 29th Street Cafe and order a "Latin Express Lunch Entrée" offered until 2:00 p.m. "One Grande Crispy Taco Lunch," with one corn taco filled with shredded pork, lettuce, tomato and cheese, or a "Carne Asada Panini" provides the energy for afternoon retail therapy at establishments such as Neecee's for comfy apparel, Montague's Jewelers, Gainan's Flowers and Garden Center and Barjon's Books, an independent seller of books.

Walkers, Jake's Steakhouse, TEN and Commons 1882

After a much-needed nap, head to Walkers American Grill and Tapas Bar, moseying up to the handmade mahogany and metal bar, facing a floor-to-ceiling glass two-hundred-bottle wine rack forged by local metalist Craig Whiteley. Guests are transported to an elegantly rustic place by the décor of leather, suede, hide and rope, graced with paintings by Gordon McConnell and photographs by Dennis Kern. Sip a "Neversweat Sour," made with Neversweat bourbon from Butte, or "27th & 1st Daquiri," with "Mount Gay Rum, fresh squeezed lime juice, simple syrup, and a dash of black walnut bitter." Sweet potato fries served with pecan-maple marshmallow cream, the bacon-wrapped dates stuffed with Spanish chorizo and Gorgonzola cheese, the "Blistered Shishito Peppers" or "Housemade Ricotta Bruschetta" with "prosciutto, arugula, pickled grapes & orange honey" make for delicious beginnings. Dinner ranges from "Grilled Atlantic Salmon" to "Grilled Angus Beef Flatiron Steak" and "Montana Natural Lamb Sirloin."

Jake's, Montana's premier steakhouse, is across the street from Walkers. Housed on the street-level floor of the historic General Custer Hotel, Jake's has been serving up steaks since 1979 in the downtown location, with a new branch opened in 2009 on the West End. At Jake's, think about starting with the "Coconut Crunchy Shrimp," "Onion Rings" or "Roadside Sliders"

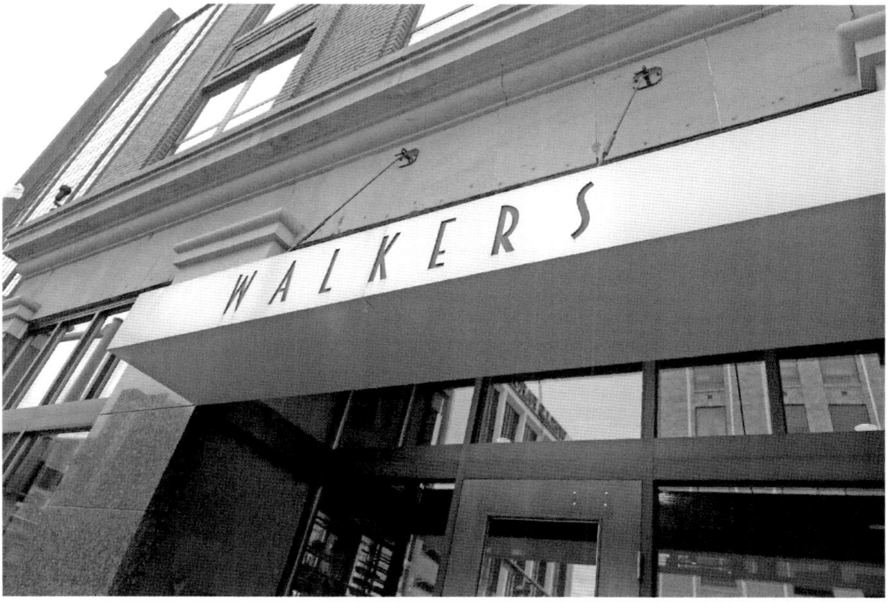

Above: Walkers American Grill and Tapas Bar at the corner of Twenty-seventh and First Avenues North.

Right: Jake's Steakhouse in the historic General Custer Hotel, built in the 1800s.

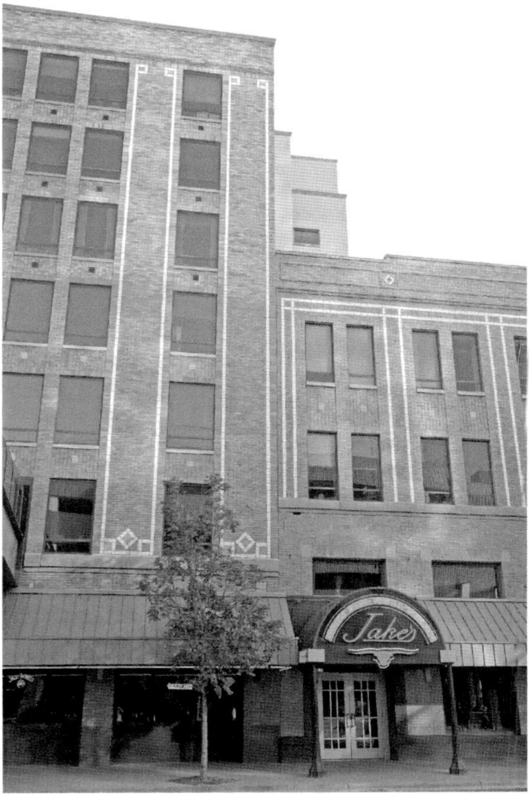

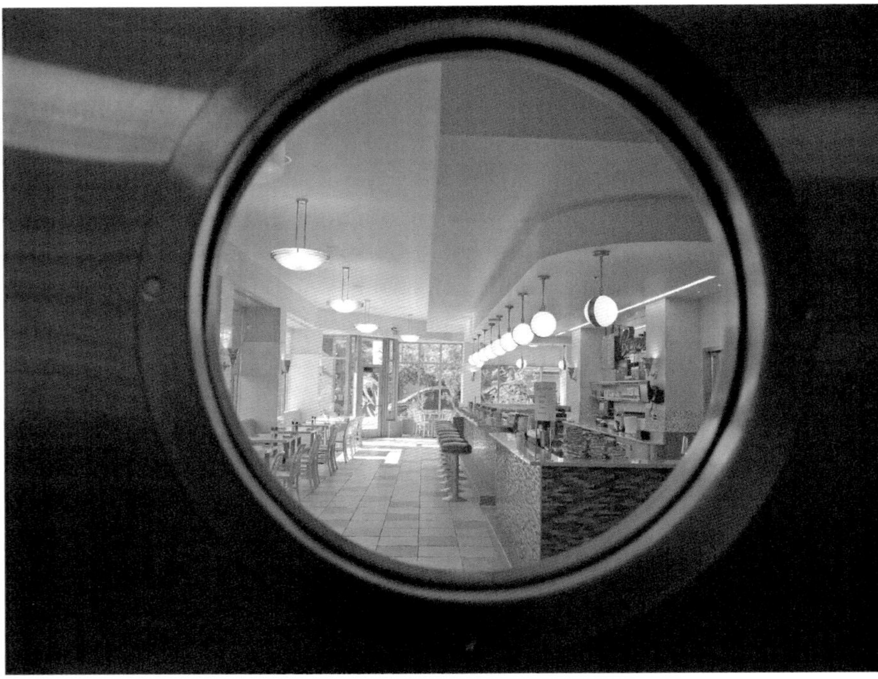

Bernie's Diner, a traditional diner with a modern twist at the Northern Hotel.

(bite-sized burgers with a "War-Horse-Tini" with jalapeños and strawberry purée) or a "Blackberry Six-Shooter" made with whiskey, blackberries and ginger ale.

Or wander to the Northern Hotel and enter TEN, the restaurant named after current owners Mike and Chris Nelson's father, Thomas Edgar Nelson. Here, whimsy meets western as red velvet envelops white leather in the banquettes. A large painting depicting a golden belle of the past pays homage to the restaurant that opened in the hotel in 1959. In line with the décor, order a "Spiced Cherry Mojito." Start with Chef Tim Freeman's signature appetizer, "A Walk in the Woods" (mushrooms and duck pâté), followed by "Lobster Cappuccino." Freeman's goal is to offer global flavors from local treasures. The main entrée could be the "Chicago Porterhouse" for those with a voracious appetite for beef or an "Elk Chop, Wild Mushrooms, Steak Fries, Pan Gravy" for those wanting wild meat. The menu is vast, elaborate and elegant, with many more delectable choices.

At the edge of the downtown corridor is the newly opened Commons 1882, situated in the former George Henry's restaurant building. On its website, the restaurant professes to stimulate "sensory nirvana" with its

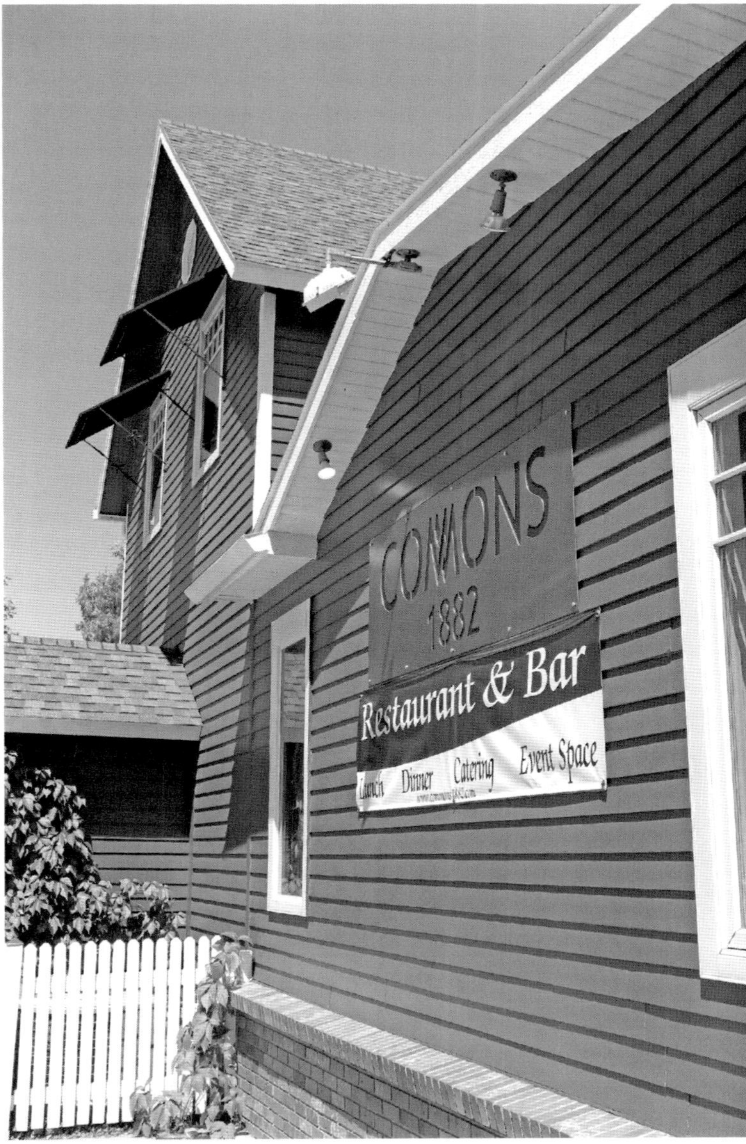

Commons 1882 serves traditional American fare in an elevated, extraordinary fashion.

culinary offerings termed "American New." From "Korean Tacos" to "Brown Shuga Baby Back Ribs" to "Cauliflower Steak," Commons takes an ordinary dish and amplifies it. Commons 1882 has two full bars, one downstairs and a more intimate one upstairs.

Juliano's Restaurant for Intimacy

Toward the hospital corridor away from downtown, Juliano's Restaurant, located at 2912 Seventh Avenue North, has been Executive Chef Carl Kurokawa's fine dining establishment since 1995. In the 1902-built Austin North House stable building, Kurokawa combines his Hawaiian roots with European-style food in his forty-seat intimate restaurant. Found in a residential neighborhood behind a row of hedges, this place provides a more intimate dining experience.

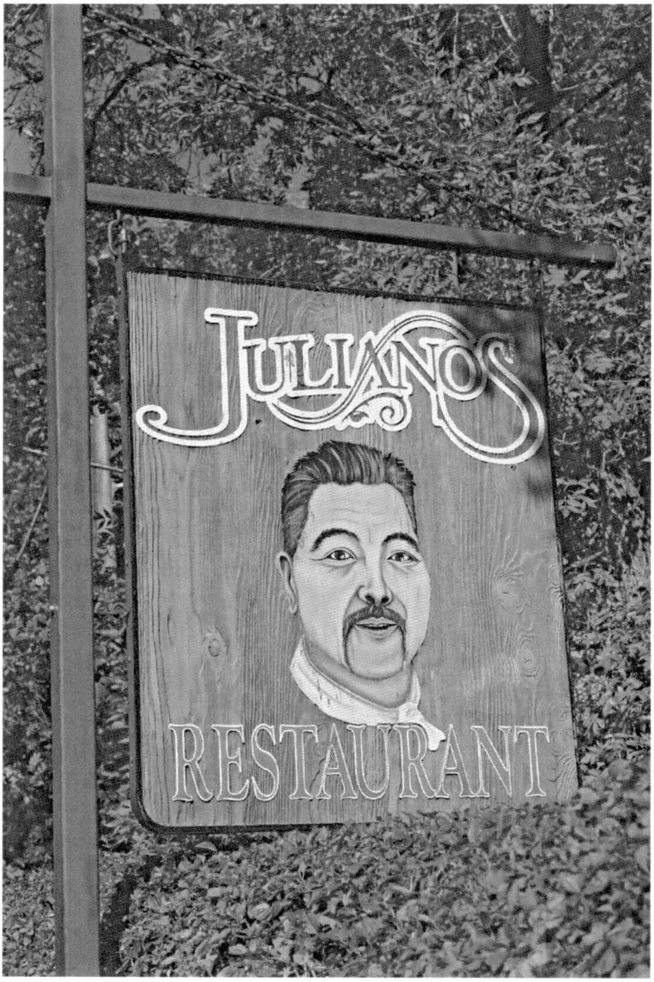

The image of Executive Chef Carl Kurokawa on the Juliano's Restaurant sign.

Screaming at Big Dipper Ice Cream

After dinner, appetite providing, wander over to Big Dipper Ice Cream. But anticipate a wait, as lines can curl out the door and around the corner. Billings has been screaming ice cream since this shop opened in 2015. Made from locally sourced Meadow Gold milk, the Dipper has introduced new flavors—including Cardamon, White Mint Oreo and Green Tea—to an eager populace. Stretching the adventurous palate even further, Big Dipper Ice Cream makes ice cream with local beer from Überbrew and Angry Hank's and cookie crumbs from Caramel Cookie Waffles. It's worth the wait.

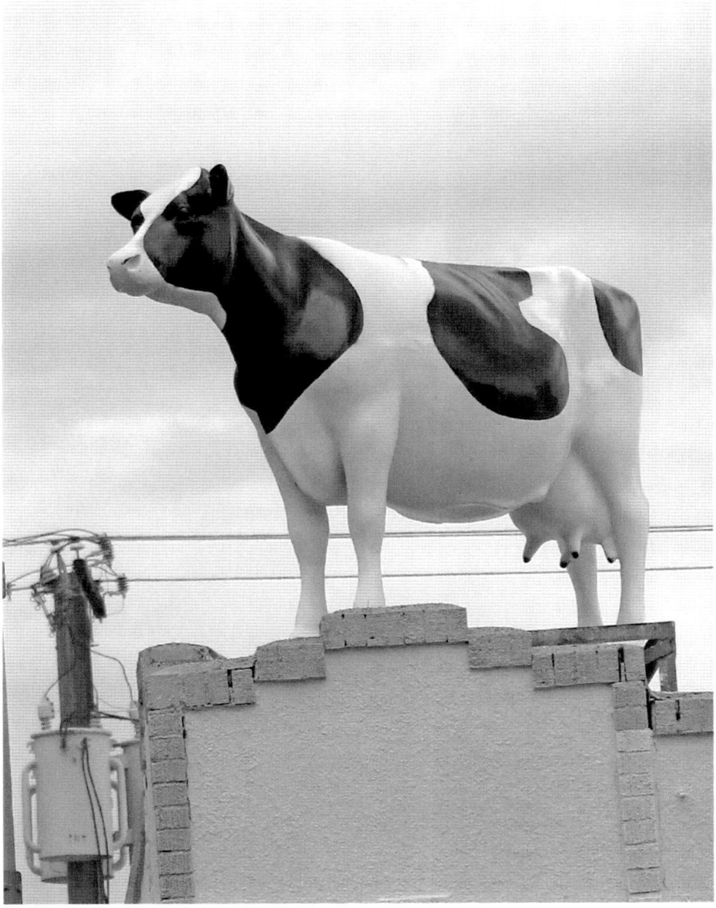

At 109 South Broadway, Meadow Gold continues to produce dairy products near downtown.

As Billings' palates evolve, the geographic world is contracting due to travel and technology, allowing access to new flavors and tastes. The influx of new chefs and retention of "seasoned" chefs provide the perfect backdrop for an expanding and vibrant culinary experience in Montana's Trailhead downtown.

Chapter 8

MARLO SPRENG

EXECUTIVE CHEF AT WALKERS AMERICAN GRILL AND TAPAS BAR

Marlo Spreng, executive chef at Walkers American Grill and Tapas Bar, is not afraid of hard labor. She fulfills the definition of a working chef as she tells of coming in on a Sunday morning when she is short staffed and then working into the night: "I worked the line, scrubbed dishes and mopped and did other things. It is so fun, so necessary. It makes me even more satisfied."

At forty-three years old, she has been in the culinary world for over twenty years. In Billings, she is one of a small handful of women leading a kitchen. She recalls pulling up a chair to the stovetop and cooking as a child. "I grew up in the '70s when there was not a lot of fancy food." Spreng said her mother worried about her because she struggled in high school. Then her mom found a book on cooking schools, and this led Spreng to consider a culinary education. "My school counselor did not even know about cooking school. I told her about it." Spreng applied to the College of Culinary Arts at Johnson and Wales University in Providence, Rhode Island.

The school not only accepted her but also granted her a scholarship. Spreng's mother was concerned that since she did not have restaurant experience, she might not like the discipline. "I got to college and was on the dean's list. I was happy to stay late, write reports and even help out." Spreng attributes her success by pointing out, "It is easier to learn something that you enjoy." Spreng thrived on the East Coast. Being from Denver, Colorado, she joked that after seven hours of driving she would still be in the state.

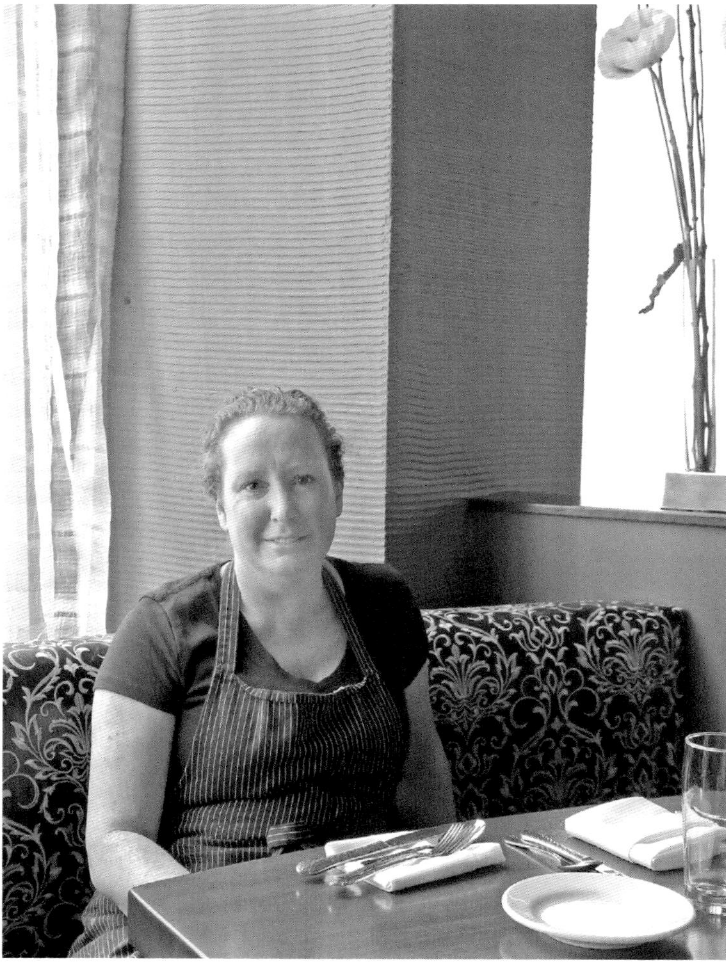

Executive Chef Marlo Spreng of Walkers American Grill and Tapas Bar.

From Providence, she could go to New York for the weekend or take the train to Pennsylvania.

When Spreng returned to Denver for the summer, she applied for a job at Tante Louise because it was near her mother's house and she could walk to work. She confesses, "I was not smart enough to know I was not qualified for the job." This fine dining French restaurant made everything from scratch. "I could make anything I wanted. Even though I was a grunt pantry cook, I was happy. I got to make duck pâté and salmon gravlax. I learned more there than I learned my first year in school." Her experience that summer brought more value to what she was being taught in school.

Spreng credits her mother with instilling a good work ethic, stating, "My mom was a single mom. She divorced when I was eight years old." Spreng continued her hard work ethic during her last summer in culinary school. She spent the summer in Islamorada, Florida, completing an internship at the Cheeca Lodge and Spa. "I worked nonstop. I would wake up before the sun," she says, "and then work until dark."

After college, Spreng worked as a sous chef at Tante Louise. Then she moved to Vail, Colorado, where she became chef de cuisine under Executive Chef Rick Kangas at the Grouse Mountain Grill in Beaver Creek. Together, they took a team to cook at the James Beard House in New York. Then in 1999, Spreng came with Kangas to cook a dinner at Walkers for the first Montana State University–Billings Foundation Wine and Food Festival. Eventually, Spreng went back to Denver to become the executive chef at Tante Louise until it closed. Then she worked briefly as a private chef.

Around this time, Bill Honaker, the owner of Walkers Grill, was looking for an executive chef. Because he had been impressed with Spreng's talents, witnessing her skills during the Wine Festival, he contacted Kangas to see if she would consider taking the job. In 2005, she moved to Billings with her then boyfriend (now husband), Jeff. Three years later, motherhood led Spreng to leave Walkers after she gave birth to her son Greyden. They relocated to St. Louis, Missouri, to be closer to her husband's family.

But as fate would have it, three years later Walkers lured Spreng, her husband and their son back to Montana's Trailhead, and she was back at the helm of the kitchen in 2012. Currently, Spreng is concentrating on the restaurant's offerings. She says lightheartedly of her diverse clientele, "We have to make a lot of customers happy. We have to make the son who is a hipster happy, as well as the mother and the grandfather." Spreng views the tapas portion of the menu, as well as daily specials, as an opportunity to be more creative. She has come to accept that she cannot make major changes in the core menu, such as eliminating the James Beard's Famous Meatloaf, for fear of the backlash from loyal customers.

"We have such a broad menu. We are trying to hone our skills in what we are doing," she realizes. Spreng works with Sous Chef Dylan Fletcher and a staff of ten but knows she needs more help. With unemployment low, her selection pool is small. In building a team, she says, "We really concentrate on character and the willingness to work hard."

Spreng derives her inspiration from the Internet and from eating out. The latter option is more difficult because of the hours she works and the time she needs to spend with her family. Spreng does excitedly share of a recent experience when Honaker took her to Portland, where they experienced fifteen restaurants in two and a half days. Before that, she confesses, "I was at a creative standstill."

So what is Spreng's favorite skill in the kitchen? She confesses, "I love fish, not just eating it, but dealing with it." For the restaurant, "I have fish flown in from Hawaii and Seattle." Who knows? With Spreng's hard work and determination, she may become a fishmonger somewhere, someplace. Hopefully for Billings, not anytime soon.

Chapter 9

TIM FREEMAN

EXECUTIVE CHEF AT THE NORTHERN HOTEL

Executive Chef Tim Freeman of the Northern Hotel is bringing global flavors to local bounty in Montana's Trailhead. These days, Freeman leads the kitchen for TEN and Bernie's Diner as executive chef and director of food and beverage. After living in six different countries, including Russia, Portugal and Nairobi, and traveling to countless others, Freeman wanted to "raise his daughter and son in God's country." "Why not look into living in Montana? I started looking for a job here in Montana, Oregon and Wyoming," Freeman shares. After leaving his job in Kenya, he went on holiday to visit his sister in Denmark, where he saw the posting for the chef's position at the Northern Hotel. "I have no connections here at all. Just the fact that Montana is a really cool place to live, close to Yellowstone Park." With his wife, Aileen, from the Philippines, he talked of how tiring it was to live in a country with 100 million people. He was yearning to return to the United States.

Freeman believed, "I thought I had a leg up having worked overseas. It is one thing to go as a tourist. It is a whole other thing to live in a place for a couple of years." Freeman shares the benefits of having the experience of immersing in a culture. While living in Southeast Asia, he talks of a popular noodle dish: "You can just order pad Thai. But unless you live and immerse and understand every dish, you do not really know the dish. Why are the peanuts crushed? They are whole for a reason." Then with curry, for instance, he believes there is a reason to the methods and sequential addition of ingredients. He asks questions of himself: "Why work in steps? Why cut galangal? Why use dried shrimp?"

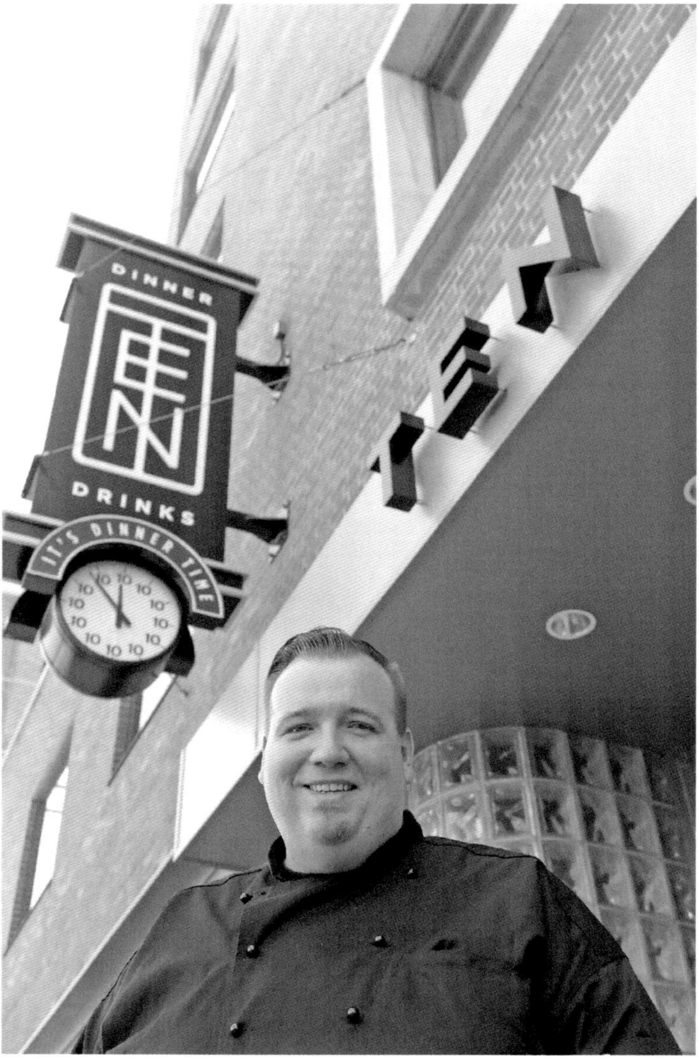

Executive Chef Tim Freeman of TEN at the Northern Hotel.

Early in 2015, Freeman participated in the World Gourmet Society Festival with his sous chef, Tyler Ellis. The purpose of the society that includes gourmets and Michelin-starred chefs is stated: "A global club for food enthusiasts to discover new culinary landscapes." Freeman's five-course menu included his signature dish, "Walk in the Woods"—mushroom soil, foraged mushrooms, pheasant terrine, black truffle, trout roe—and featured other Montana products such as flathead cherry syrup, venison and huckleberry spread. The theme continued with a Montana-sourced cheese course made up of "beer mountina, brie de bitterroot, and black truffle goat cheese."

In addition to his international experiences, Freeman worked with Wolfgang Puck at Spagos in Beverly Hills, as a chef de partie in Washington, D.C., for the Clinton administration and as the chef for the governor of Ohio, George Voinovich. Now Freeman can add the restaurant TEN and Bernie's Diner to his resume. Although Bernie's serves up comfort food from yesteryear, there is a "modern twist." "Captain Crunch French Toast" and the "Elk Migas Skillet" are unique to this "lighthearted and fun diner."

"The separation between a good chef and a great chef is technique," he states. Freeman credits a chef he worked for early on as a dishwasher who told him, "'If you are going to make it as a chef, you have to try everything.' He really hammered home that you have to eat." The practice led Freeman to Sullivan College in Louisville, Kentucky, for a culinary education. These days, he carries this belief to his own staff. He is adamant: "They eat everything unless there is a dietary reason."

Freeman has a tough job at TEN at the Northern Hotel, with an intention that "embodies elegance and brings back memories of the previous Northern Hotel as a place to meet, greet, and enjoy good food and drinks." It is advertised as "serving traditional cuisine, with unique international flavors." Freeman wants to be "using more local products," which encourages customers to "step out of one's comfort zone" with further prodding of "Let's not get set in our ways. We must keep progressing, moving forward."

At press time for *Billings Food*, Freeman had won the competition against Bobby Flay on the cooking show *Beat Bobby Flay* with his pad Thai noodles. Freeman says, "I went to New York confident that I had the skills to beat him. I am hoping the win opens up opportunities for me to go back to the Food Network and for opportunities for Billings."

With the new remodeled hotel by the Nelson brothers and Tim Freeman leading the food revolution and education, TEN and the Northern Hotel will soon establish a place of their own in the culinary landscape.

Chapter 10

JEREMY ENGEBRETSON

EXECUTIVE CHEF AT LILAC

"Local from scratch, responsible cooking. Modern American food with a fistful of approachability" is Jeremy Engebretson's mantra for his restaurant, Lilac. Stated boldly on his website, Engebretson has put his passion and his pocketbook into his business. "Everything I had ever saved is on the line," the executive chef shares.

Though Engebretson spent summers helping at his aunt Carol Carpenter's restaurant, CC's Family Restaurant in Miles City, when he was younger, he earned a degree in business information systems from the University of Montana in Missoula. While he was working as a coder at the university after graduation, he quickly found out that programming was not something he enjoyed doing. So at night and on weekends, he worked for free at Scotty's Table, a restaurant that highlights "the best of the region and the season." Then he became a sous chef at a private ranch club and later pursued some catering work with Riversong Gourmet.

In 2009, Engebretson and his wife, Donielle, moved back to Billings to be near her family. At first, he wanted to take over the restaurant space at Seventeenth and Poly Drive that housed the old 17th Street Station Restaurant. Unfortunately, the building was torn down and replaced with law offices. The realtor he was working with then brought him to 2515 Montana Avenue when Lin Lin and C.W. Lo were in the process of closing their Sweet Ginger Asian Bistro and Sushi. After signing a lease with Mike Schaer and receiving approval from the Montana Avenue sign review committee, Engebretson opened the doors of Lilac in the summer of 2012.

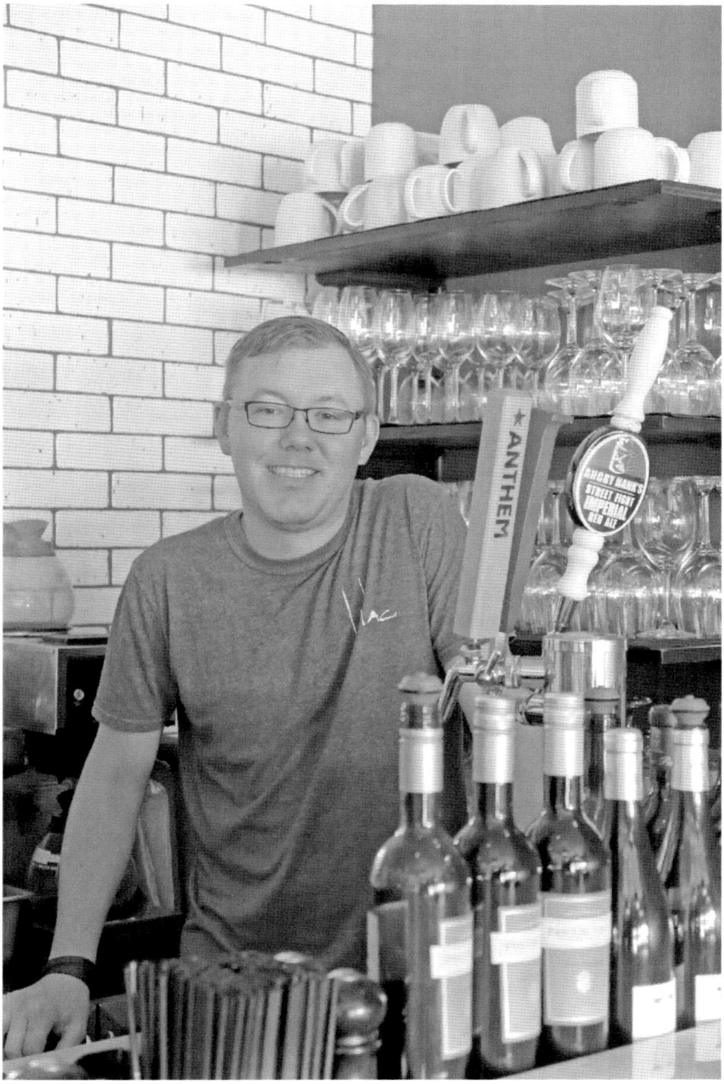

Executive Chef Jeremy Engebretson creates modern American cooking from scratch at Lilac.

The first challenge was building a customer base, and Engebretson tells of how hard he worked to bring in diners. "We do focus on making people happier. We think about our clients all the time," he says. From the ratings on popular dining sites such as yelp.com and opentable.com, Engebretson should have less worries these days as, overall, he rates four and a half stars with hundreds of reviews.

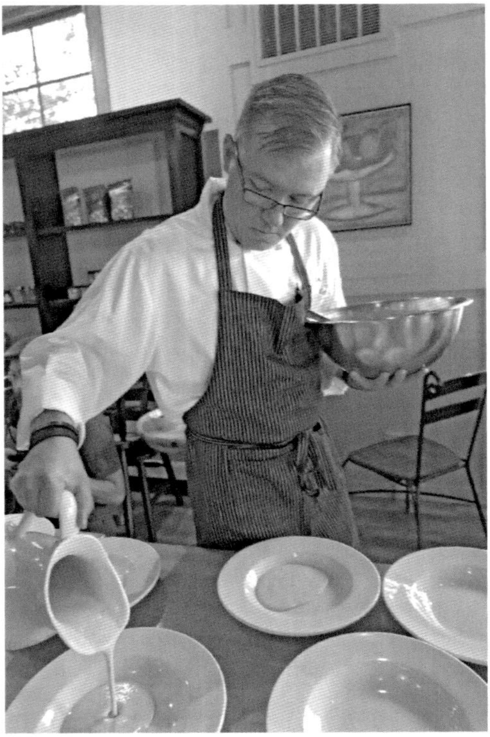

Left: Executive Chef Jeremy Engebretson of Lilac preparing for the farm-to-table dinner "An Evening Under the Stars."

Below: "An Evening Under the Stars," a farm-to-table dinner for 150 guests on Tenth Avenue North.

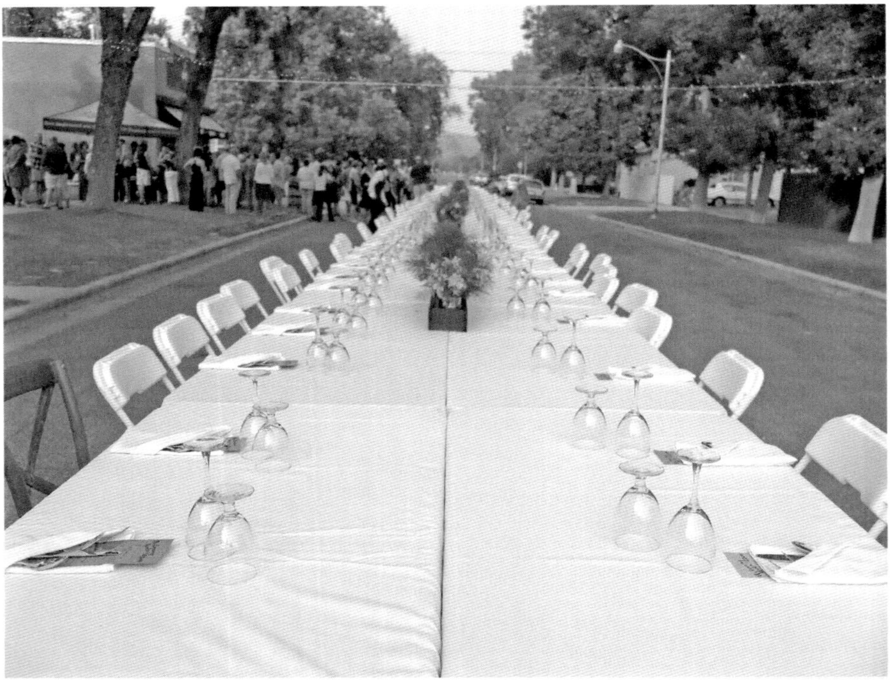

Engebretson says of his food, "It is with the times. Modern, not the sixteen-ounce steak." He continues, "Our menu is mostly driven by product or we have a method or idea. We may put a new steak on the menu because Rainer cherries are available and in season" as a good accompaniment. So currently, he is offering a "Flat Iron Steak—brie, almond, cherries, brandy, onions soubise." For many diners, a term such as "soubise"—describing an onion sauce based on a béchamel sauce or one with flour, butter and milk—is new. Subtly, Engebretson is educating diners with terms and flavors. But to please different palates, one can choose a cheeseburger with bacon, cheddar and house fries or braised short rib with potato gnocchi and caramelized onion, as well as "Cedar Plank Zucchini" served with cucumber raita, gruyère crumble and purple barley. Then, to challenge a more adventurous palate, "Beef Tongue Tacos" and "Blue Cheese Cured Lamb Ribs" may be available.

Engebretson changes his menu of around a dozen savory choices three times a week. A dessert menu offers a small handful of in-season sweets. On the occasional Sunday night in the summer, he has teamed up with Harper and Madison and with now retired Chef Shane Weigel and Jason Corbridge, along with proprietor Joanie Swords, for "An Evening Under the Stars, a Farm to Table Dinner." Long tables lined with white tablecloths are set up in front of Harper and Madison on Tenth Avenue North between North Thirty-first and Thirty-second Street. A small farmers' and crafts market precedes appetizers and drinks. Then, about 150 people sit down to a three-course meal highlighting the season's wares. Afterward, Marian Booth Green has provided jazzy entertainment with a few tunes from Harper and Madison proprietor Joanie Swords.

"Honestly, I go to bed at night knowing I am doing what I want to be doing," Engebretson proudly says. For those of us eating in Billings, we want him to get a good night's rest every night so we can continue to appreciate his approachable American food.

Chapter 11

DAVID MAPLETHORPE

EXECUTIVE CHEF AT THE REX RESTAURANT BAR AND GRILL

Executive Chef David Maplethorpe has been a stronghold at the iconic Rex Restaurant Bar and Grill, as well as in the culinary community of Billings. For over forty years, Maplethorpe has worked in a kitchen. Here in Billings, he has anchored the Montana Avenue establishment for over twenty years. In between, he has utilized his skills to help better the community, often pairing up with Juliano's executive chef Carl Kurokawa. Together they cook multicourse fundraising dinners for organizations such as the Montana State University (MSU) Billings Foundation and the March of Dimes. As a longtime member of the Cooks and Chefs of Montana, Maplethorpe has teamed up with others in the group for such events as the Annual Strawberry Festival to prepare a sixty-five-foot shortcake and Daring Pairing: Sip and Savor with Montana's Best Chefs, combining local culinary talent with wines from past MSU Billings Wine and Food Festival winemasters.

Maplethorpe taught at San Jose State University after earning a master's degree in political science from the University of the Pacific in Stockton, California. After less than a year, he quickly realized that he had chosen the wrong career path. For a handful of years, he owned a cabinet shop before embarking into the restaurant business. His culinary career began when he ended up in Denver working at the Westin Hotel, first as a busboy and then offering to do any job because "I told my boss I just wanted to cook. I did menial jobs for three years." Coincidence brought him to Montana and finally to the Rex in 1994.

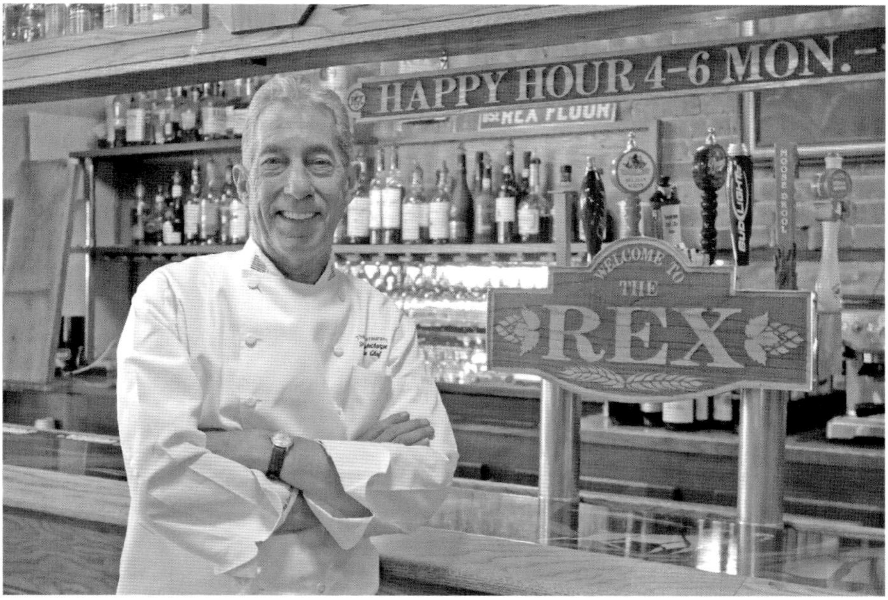

Executive Chef David Maplethorpe of the Rex Restaurant Bar and Grill.

Then after a five-year interlude in Texas, where he helped open the Dakota Chop House and served as executive chef, Gene Burgad, owner of the Rex, called for Maplethorpe's return to Montana. During his absence, he had maintained his relationships in Billings. He says, "Carl Kurokawa and I would still do our dinners. I would stop in. We never strayed far. I consider this home."

The Rex was recognized by the National Cattlemen's Beef Association with the 2007 National Foodservice Beef Backer Award for being the Innovator of the Year. The Rex won the coveted title "by preserving a 25-year tradition of serving the 'best steak in town' while managing to integrate new cuts like the Flat Iron and Ranch Steak into menu applications." Burgad says about beef: "It is such a huge part of the Montana economy, and we are passionate about bringing quality beef to our Montana community." Maplethorpe's grill mastery has shaped a long-standing tradition of excellence in beef preparation.

Then in 2012, Maplethorpe worked with Chef Tyler Ellis to fire up a bison steak for the Travel Channel cameras. Filming for *Steak Paradise*, Maplethorpe was not nervous, according to a *Billings Gazette* article reporting that he chopped parsley at warp speed with his French knife. Perhaps the spirits of Buffalo Bill Cody and Calamity Jane, who have been known to frequent the Rex in years past, were watching over the chef's performance.

Comfortable in his own skin, Maplethorpe fits the image of a master chef, with a shining smile and a full head of silver hair crowning his cowboy good looks. To unwind, he reads the *Billings Gazette*, the *New Yorker*, *Newsweek* and *Time* magazine and watches the Fox Channel. After work, "I go home all wired up. I shower and enjoy reading." Maplethorpe adds, "My retirement goal is to leave the day I turn seventy." That is only sixteen months and counting. His legacy will be the impact he had on building the preeminent steakhouse in Billings.

Chapter 12

WHERE IS THE MEAT?

One does not have to go far to find beef in Billings. Prime cuts can be found on almost every menu in town, but there are restaurants that feature this protein-rich food. Several have been staples for the carnivores in town.

The Rex Restaurant Bar and Grill has been serving up steaks since 1909, and to this day at Gene Burgad's establishment, a juicy slab of beef can be savored. Jake's Steakhouse, housed in the General Custer Hotel building downtown, and now in a second facility on the West End, also fires up choice cuts of meat. In the old Granary building, Bistecca continues the beef tradition, combining Italian and American flavors served in an elegant dining room or al fresco on the sheltered patio, along with an extensive drink menu, featuring twenty-two beers on tap.

TEN at the Northern Hotel has a menu infused with flavors from around the world, but one of its standout items is the "Chicago Style 42oz Porterhouse." Served with creamed spinach, steak fries and garlic mushrooms, it will satisfy any meat craving. Down the street, Walkers American Grill and Tapas Bar offers up a variety of choice cuts in a cosmopolitan setting and features a very lively bar scene in the evening.

On the West End, CJ's Bar and Grill is known for its fried potato skins, called "skins on fries," and its smoked meats from the applewood-fired grill. With a drive-through window, the wood-fired steaks and seafood along with house-made barbecue sauce and "skins on fries" or sweet potato fries can be enjoyed on the go. According to General Manager Matt Burton, CJ's was originally founded in 1976 by Dick Nelson, who named the restaurant after his son Charlie James, but it is currently owned by Tom Pelatt and Dave Holland. The restaurant has the comfortable ambiance of a mountain home accommodating an L-shaped wood bar seating up to a dozen people and a fireplace for warmth in the winter.

Even farther west, Montana Rib and Chop House began in Livingston in 2001 and opened in Billings a half dozen years later on the West End near Highway 90. Founded by Burke and Melissa Moran, the chain now has ten locations nationwide. Aside from the Certified Angus sirloins and rib-eyes they serve, they also have chicken fried steak, pot roast, seafood and chicken. Their house sides include carrot soufflé and squash casserole, as well as an "Awesome Baked Potato" with all the fixings. This place brings in the crowds, especially on a weekend night.

Then, on the casual side—think Carharts and baseball caps—at the Muzzleloader Cafe and Powderhorn Lounge, steak along with "Liver & Onions," "Breaded Veal" and "16 oz Sizzling T-Bones" can be secured at reasonable prices.

One of the most popular hamburger joints in Billings is the Burger Dive on North Twenty-seventh Street. In 2014, Chef Brad Halsten brought home the honor of winning the Best of the Bash Award at the Food Network South Beach Wine and Food Festival hosted by Rachael Ray. Halsten won with his "Blackened Sabbath Burger" featuring "blackened seasoning, bleu cheese, bacon, onion ring & garlic mayonnaise." The grand prize included $10,000, and the burger is offered on Red Robin's premium burger menu.

Red and white floor tiles, cola signs, a huge round neon clock and vintage salt and pepper shakers set a nostalgic stage at the Burger Dive. Each table is wisely supplied with a full roll of paper towels to mop up the juices that ooze from the delectable burgers served here. Everything comes in plastic baskets lined with wax paper. Aside from the one-third-pound Angus beef patty such as the "Outlaw Burger" or the "Juicy Lucy Burger," there is the "Spicy Tuna Burger" and the vegetarian "Geezer Butler Burger." The burgers and fresh-cut fries pair nicely with the milkshakes made with Wilcoxson's ice cream.

For good old-fashioned goodness, King's Hat Drive-in near the Western Sugar Co-Op is the place to go. This is the "Home of the Flying Burger," a burger sandwiched between two pieces of white bread sans crust. Come here for a chocolate malt and a burger, and you will step back in time.

Aside from the locally owned establishments, Main Street, Grand Avenue and King Avenue brim with national franchises that offer a quick burger. On

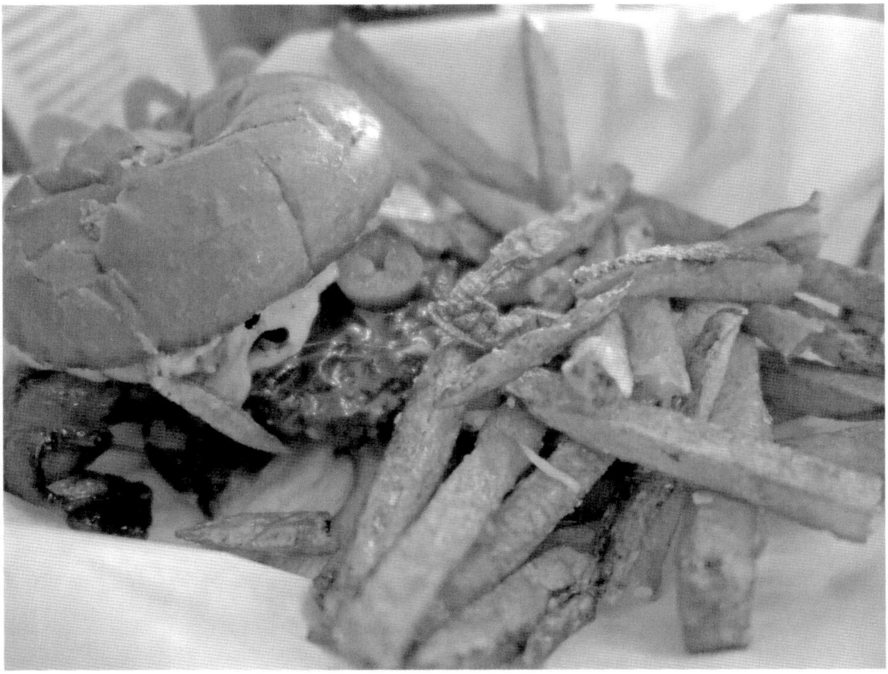

Above: "The Bandit Burger" with jalapeños, bacon, pepperjack cheese, barbecue sauce, spicy mayonnaise, tomato and lettuce from the Burger Dive.

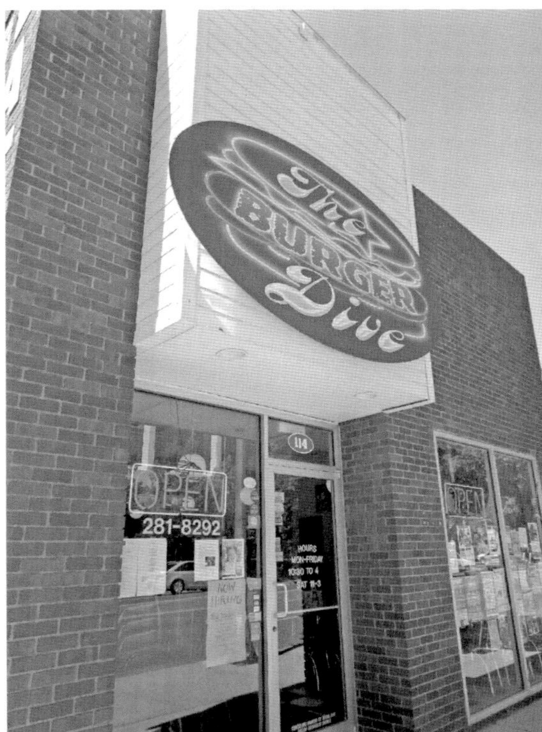

Right: The Burger Dive has been serving Billings since 2010 with premium Angus beef burgers.

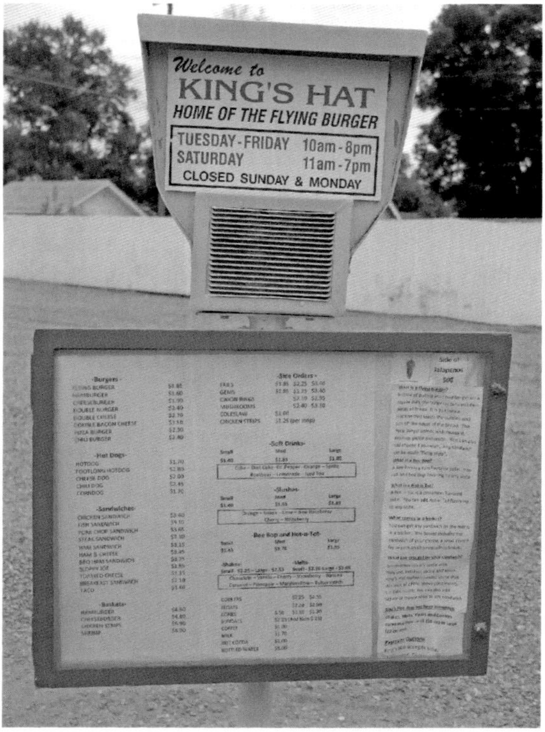

Left: At King's Hat, drive through for a good old-fashioned burger and the famous flying burger.

Below: King's Hat on South Thirty-seventh Street across the street from the railroad tracks.

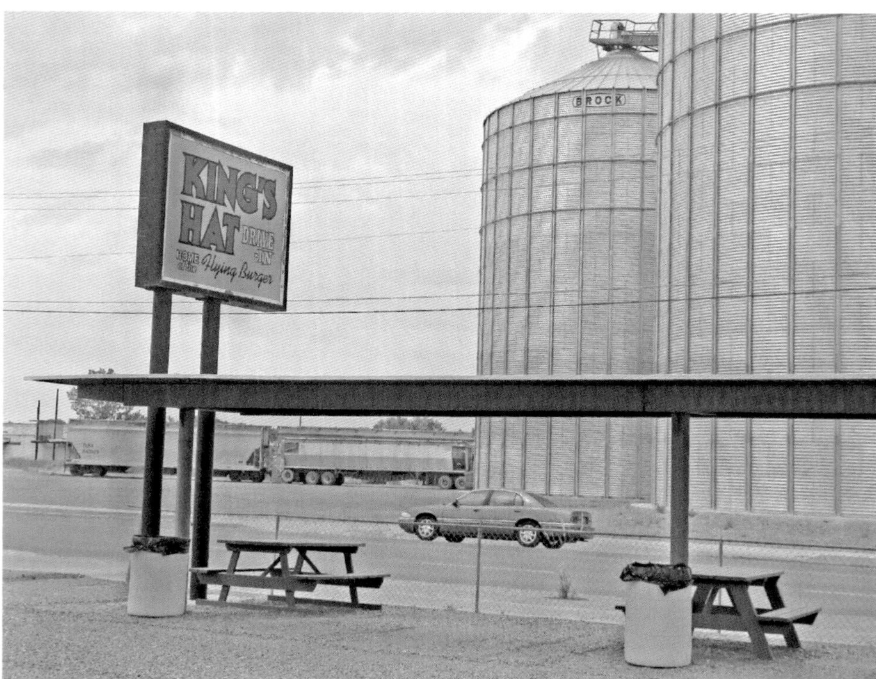

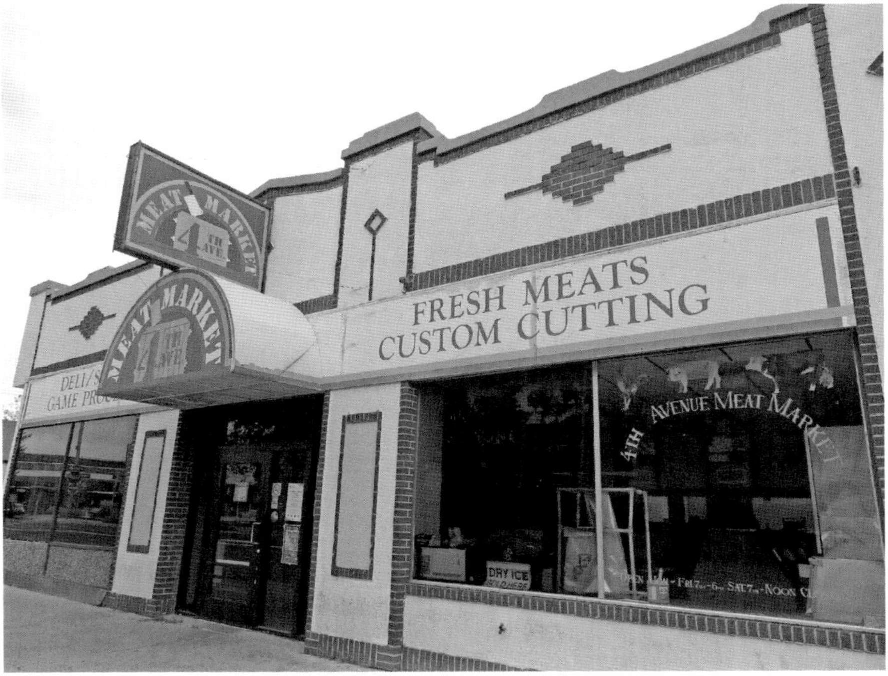

4th Avenue Meat Market retains its old name but is now located at 117 North Twenty-fifth Street. This is the place for that special cut of meat.

the West End, name-brand restaurants such as MOOYAH Burgers Fries and Shakes and Steak 'n Shake also offer up meat slabs to the hordes.

For those do-it-yourselfers, several notable specialty meat markets have fresh-cut beef to grill, roast, smoke, stir-fry or braise. Ranch House Sausage Company, 4th Avenue Meat Market, Meat and Poultry Palace and Poly Food Basket can supply a hunk of beef, as well as other cuts of meat and seafood, for everyday eating or for those special occasions.

Under the Big Sky, where antelope and black Angus roam, Billings is the home where no discouraging words will be heard for finding a good burger or steak.

Chapter 13

RESTAURANTS, BAKERY AND SPECIALTY MARKET TAKING BILLINGS TO THE HEIGHTS

Several locally owned eateries in the Heights make diners stop, chew and swallow in the hustle and bustle of daily routine. More than fifty thousand motorists travel up and down Main Street each day, moving within Billings or transiting toward Lockwood, Shepherd or Huntley or even in the other direction to Roundup. At speeds of forty-five miles per hour or faster, drivers move quickly by. It is no wonder that fast-food chains such as Sonic Drive-In, McDonald's, Wendy's and KFC have a presence in this frenetic area of Billings. However, restaurants such as the Vig Alehouse and Casino, Blues Barbecue, Bull Mountain Grille and Okinawa Sushi and Asian Bistro, as well as Rae Rae's Bakery and Amaya Oriental Market, provide food worth stopping for.

Sean Graves, owner of the Vig Alehouse and Casino, offers a fun place for "Very Important Guests." The name of the sports bar and casino plays on the Yiddish slang from the Russian word *vigorish* for winnings and, in the southern parts of the United States, a term for being cool and hip. The establishment's warm, dark wood room has ample seating with more intimate booths and high tabletops branded with the initials "VIG." Over a dozen big-screen televisions line the walls. In good weather, there is a large patio in the back to sip "Vignature Cocktails" such as the "Liquid Frickle" with huckleberry vodka mixed with an energy drink or "The Cleanse" with cucumber vodka and soda water.

On the menu are creative categories named "Temptations" for appetizers, "Vings" for Chicken Wings and "Vignature Burgers"

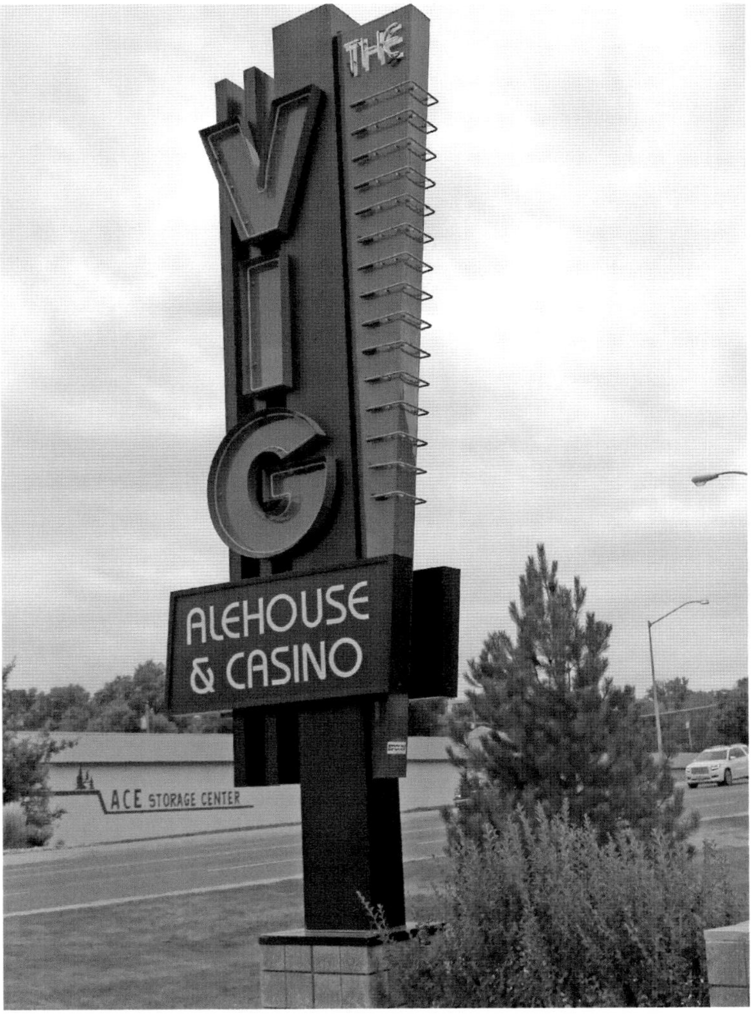

The Vig Alehouse and Casino in the Heights is a place for very important guests to get a beer and watch a game or just to gather.

playing on the word signature. "The House Favorites" include the "Mac & Cheesy Speakeasy," described as "So good it should be illegal! Smoked gouda & extra sharp white cheddar cheese sauce tossed with macaroni noodles & bacon. Served with a slice of cheese bread." If this offering is against the law, then the Vig's popular burger would guarantee a jail sentence. "The Big Smack Burger," made with a "Certified Angus Beef Burger topped with mac n' cheese & bacon. Served on a brioche bun," is quite sinful.

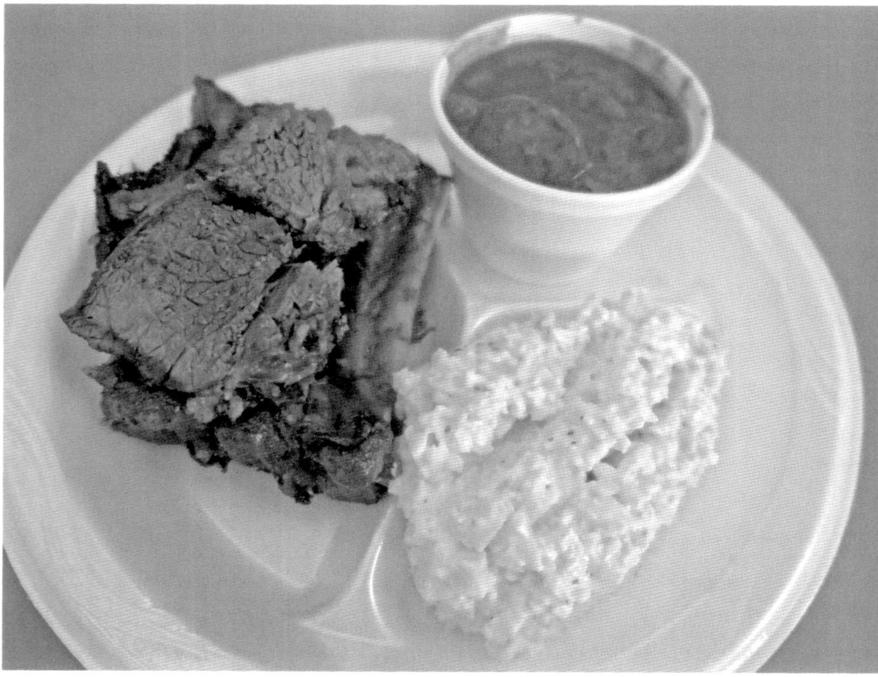

Blues Barbecue brisket with two ribs, potato salad and spicy beans.

Across the street from the Vig, inside the Cenex Town and Country Supply Convenience Store, is Blues Barbecue. Here, Ken and Kim Hager ask in their advertising, "Are you blue?" Of course, the ad continues on with a cure: "Try some BBQ." On their website, the first line of their post is: "There's nothing better than seeing a smile on our customers' faces. We believe our barbecue food is something you'll tell your family and friends about." For a dozen years, word around town has been that Blues Barbecue is the place to go for smoked meats. The Hagers start everything from scratch. Their ribs can be secured at two dollars apiece, or a small rib plate comes with four ribs and a choice of two sides and a fountain drink. Sides include "Potato Salad, Coleslaw, Pit Baked Beans, Ranch Pasta Salad, Garden Salad, Baked Potato or Baked Yam." On this day, spicy baked beans were also available, with a kick from jalapeños and rich flavoring from pork sausage. A takeout window allows for easy pickup. Blues Barbecue also sells portions for a large crowd, such as the "Crew Pack," with "2 racks of ribs, 2 pounds of turkey or ham, sausage or shredded pork, 3 large sides and 6 buns" to feed approximately ten people.

Bull Mountain Grille is one of the last restaurants on Main Street before the turnoff to Roundup, tucked in the corner of the former Kmart complex now anchored by All American Pharmaceutical. Billings developer Ernie Dutton teamed up with Chef Duane Haugen in 2009 to open a family restaurant that touts itself as "A Real Montana Steakhouse." The décor is Montana barn, with hay bales wrapped in plastic stacked on a high shelf above the restaurant and booth dividers simulating fencing on a farm, with brand-themed blankets neatly draped over the sides. Red metal siding, a barn door and rustic wood floors complete the ambiance for this restaurant. In the foyer, customers are dared to a "Steak Challenge." A framed sign explains: "The epic challenge consists of a 78-ounce Ribeye: two ounces shy of five pounds. Challengers must finish the entire steak (yep, that means all the marbling too!) along with a heaping side of loaded mashed potatoes, garden salad, & a Bull Mountain dinner roll. The Ribeye cannot be prepared above a medium due to its massive size." The challenge must be completed within sixty minutes, with the prize of getting a mug shot on the "Wall of Fame" and the meal at a cost of $109.99 compensated.

At Bull Mountain Grille, a large variety of turf and surf options are offered. Fresh green salad comes with dressing choices on the side, including a rich house-made bleu cheese dressing. Appetizers include "Bull Skins" ("Potato skins topped with queso cheese, bacon bits, and diced green onions") and "Chicharrones" ("Our spin on popcorn chicken. Lightly breaded and served with delicious queso ranch"). Other options include crab cakes and sautéed mushrooms, but to "remind you of branding on the ranch," "Rocky Mountain Oysters" or bull testicles are also offered. Rib-eye, filet mignon and sirloin steaks come cooked to desired doneness with creative sauces such as merlot and peppercorn and tomato vodka. The fish options, titled "Fin," include salmon, dover sole, tuna and shrimp. Pasta choices include "Smoked Buffalo Ravioli" and burgers "Bunkhouse" and "Campfire BBQ." If a diner has room, "The Bull's Cow Pie" and "Lemon Drop Cheesecake" are dessert possibilities.

On the drag at 1414 Main Street is Okinawa Sushi and Asian Bistro. A small parking lot sits in front of the restaurant next to the busy thoroughfare. Every day from 2:30 to 5:30 p.m., Okinawa Sushi presents happy hour with a two-for-one sale. A sushi bar accommodating seven people forms the backdrop at the rear of this small restaurant with walls painted red—the color of power, courage and energy—and decorated with round paper lanterns. A selection of Asian food includes traditional sushi rolls and stir-fried noodles—yakisoba and ramen. Though "Agedashi Tofu" and "Edamame" are more common options, "Monkey Brain" with deep-fried crabmeat, spicy tuna and avocado is a more unique selection. Specialty items such as "Tempura & Spicy Rolls" include "Hot Night Roll," described as "In: Red Snapper Tempura & Cucumber, Out: Spicy Tuna." "In" refers to the ingredient inside the roll and "Out" to what is on top. The "Sapporo Roll" encases shrimp tempura, crabmeat, spicy tuna, jalapeño tempura and spicy scallop draped with red snapper tempura on the top. Other categories include "Deep Fried Rolls" with a seaweed wrap and "Tempura Rolls," fried with a bread coating. Both are served with the house special sauce with mayonnaise and sriracha and eel sauce. No alcohol is served, but diners are welcome to bring a spirited beverage.

Nearby is Rae Rae's Bakery, which, since 2012, has attempted to bring a healthy baked alternative to Montana. Tina and Christa Stetson bought the White Fish branch of Rae Rae's, and when Krista moved to Billings a couple years later, she opened a bakery in the Billings Heights. The store sells a variety of gluten-free baked goods such as bread, muffins, scones, cupcakes and frozen pizza dough. Other choices include cinnamon rolls and cream pie. Stetson focuses on wheat-free products, using 100 percent organic products with no soy and gluten with dairy- and egg-free options.

In a small strip mall diagonally across from Walmart is Amaya Oriental Market. This small, clean market has a good selection of Filipino, Thai, Vietnamese, Japanese and Chinese food products that are neatly stocked on shelves. Several freezers hold frozen dumplings such as siu mai and potstickers. Also, wonton wrappers, Chinese sausage and fishballs can be secured. A refrigerator stores milks, tofu and drinks. Dry goods include a variety of Asian cookies and candies, along with a variety of rice and noodles. Oyster sauce, soy sauce and hot sauce can also be found. For being located far away from an Asian population, this store provides more than enough flavors to satisfy any yearnings for food from the other side of the world.

Let Main Street take you to new Heights. Instead of just traversing town, you should slow down, take a slight detour and stop to smell and taste the food offered at the Vig, Bull Mountain Grille, Blues Barbecue and Okinawa Sushi and Asian Bistro or take home some baked goodies from Rae Rae's and Asian treasures from Amaya Oriental Market.

Chapter 14

MARCY TATARKA

CHEF AND OWNER OF BEYOND BASIL CATERING

Marcy Tatarka brings life to celebrations and new beginnings. As a neonatal intensive care nurse at St. Vincent Healthcare by day and caterer for her business, Beyond Basil Catering, located in the Heights, by night, she is constantly nurturing and nourishing. Her work as a nurse started in 1989, and she began catering in 1993. But with both professions, she has learned to handle unexpected situations that come up with efficiency and humor. Tatarka gets the job done with little fuss and fanfare.

Unlucky and lucky thirteen plus ten years ago, Marcy Tatarka impressed a wedding planner when she was planning her own wedding. Luckily, Tatarka's catering business has blossomed, while unfortunately she has parted ways with her ex-husband, Dan. The special treats of lemonade with a sprig of fresh mint and cheesecake and cookies on a pretty plate showed Tatarka's creativity and her love of sharing food.

Tatarka's journey has been filled with adventure. In her bio for the 2015 Montana State University–Billings (MSUB) Foundation Wine and Food Festival program catalogue, she shares, "Marcy has been fortunate enough to work with some great people in the industry. She has taken classes from Masaharu Morimoto, Feran Adrià, Jose Garces, and Rick Bayless. She has had the great pleasure of food styling for Jamie Oliver and has catered for many celebrities and concerts, from Alice Cooper to Elton John." Additionally, she cooked for the Eagles and Blake Shelton. Of Shelton, she tells, "He was just a sweetheart. He was so amazed with the food." He encouraged others to eat her food. "Cookie, he called me cookie," as she served him sweet potato pie.

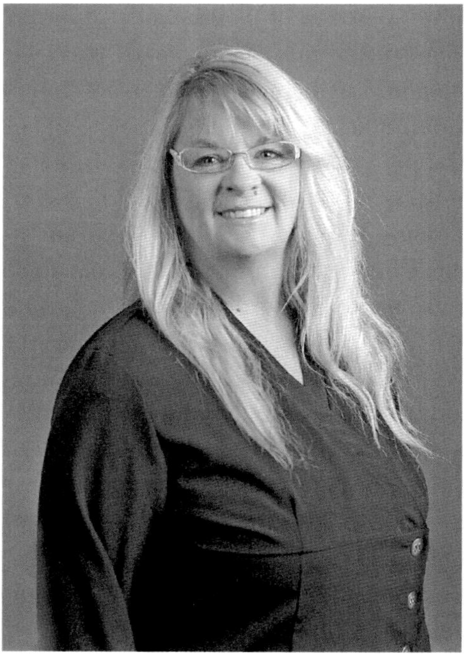

Chef Marcella Tatarka of Beyond Basil Catering. *Courtesy of MSU-Billings Foundation.*

On *Jamie's American Road Trip* blog site, Jamie Oliver endears Tatarka as an "absolutely lovely cook" after they met in Wyoming, where she worked for him on a television production. He posted her recipe for Cornish pasties.

For thirteen years, Tatarka has hauled her one-ton kitchen box truck with a barbecue, a motor home and another truck with a golf cart down to Sturgis, Wyoming. Here she provides the breakfast concession for the city workers who service the infrastructure for the annual Sturgis Motorcycle Rally. After opening at 7:00 a.m., by 7:15 a.m. she has fed at least eighty-five people. "I want them to be fat, sassy and happy," she says with a smile. She wants to serve them good homemade food that satisfies and continues by saying, "I go through at least two cases of bacon a day." After her first year, Tatarka quickly learned that handing out premade burritos from atop a food stand window would not be satisfactory for her. Quickly she advocated for real food, such as South Dakota pork, and then established a better work setup. She transported her trucks and trailers down to Wyoming, which provided a better work environment. Then, on a more personal level, Tatarka further expresses, "I wanted to see people face to face," so she placed tables on the ground to pass out food and provide better service.

Every year for over a decade, Tatarka has contributed her talents to the MSUB Wine and Food Festival. Her behind-the-scenes help has been invaluable, supporting cooking classes taught by Raghavan Iyer, Christy Rost, Lars Kronmark and Lin Lin and C.W. Lo. She, along with Mike Callahan and Jim Carlson, led teenagers from the Café Protégé Culinary Arts Program to the National ProStart Invitational cooking contest in San Diego in 2008. These days, she continues to teach for the Passages (CAP), Culinary Arts Program, for food service training and employment from referrals from the Montana Women's Prison. The participants receive instruction, in-house food service experience, work release in the community and job placement assistance.

As Tatarka gets busier and busier, she continues to have the want to teach classes to share her knowledge. With her get-it-done attitude and her culinary experience, she might have a trick or two to teach, but in the meantime, she will continue to nourish and nurture many.

Note: At press time for *Billings Food*, Tatarka had made the decision to close down Beyond Basil Catering to restructure.

Chapter 15

ASIAN FLAVORS QUICKLY SPICING UP MONTANA'S TRAILHEAD

Not so long ago, there were only a handful of Asian restaurants in the Magic City. When the city was founded in 1882, Chinese workers arrived to work on the railroad, and then in later years, the Japanese arrived to support work in the beet fields. In 1901, the number of Chinese restaurants listed in the Polk City Directory was half of the total number of establishments found under the "Restaurant" category. Men such as Henry Young, Lew Quock, Sam Young, Yee Ching and Yee Sam Lee owned restaurants located on Minnesota Avenue, while Sam Young operated on Twenty-seventh Street.

In the last five years, there has been an explosion of Asian restaurants in Billings. Aside from the long-standing places that have been around for almost a decade, such as NaRa Restaurant, Siam Thai Restaurant, Golden Phoenix, Shanghai Village and Cham Thai Cuisine, new restaurants such as Wild Ginger Japanese Steakhouse, Sushi Bar, Oyster Bar & Lounge; Umi Japanese Steakhouse; and Fancy Sushi Asian Fusion have recently come onto the scene. Tao New Asian, Asian Sea Grill and Sushi Bar and the Board Wok have also flavored Billings with tastes from the Orient. The latest addition is JP Kitchen Asian Bistro, opened at 805 Twenty-fourth Street West.

JP Kitchen Asian Bistro opened its doors in September 2015. Owners Kalvin and Ken Tang are carrying on the family legacy of Asian restaurants in Billings. Though a tribute to their parents Stephen and Selina, who owned the now closed Palace off King Avenue for over twenty-six years, this restaurant is decorated in sleek modern design in colors of black and red.

The compact menu includes contemporary Asian cuisine such as "Smoked Trout Fried Rice" and "Tofu and Romaine" but still includes crispy spring rolls and potstickers. The kitchen is open to the dining room, bringing sizzle and clang to conversation. Long community tables provide for large groups, as well as the opportunity to share a meal with new dining companions.

NaRa Restaurant, a family-run business since 1998, is famous for its Montana-sized sushi rolls and homemade Korean and Japanese food. Korean native Mia Settergren, along with her mother and two sisters-in-law, originally started the business. "My mother was an incredible cook," Settergren shares of her family's matriarch doing the cooking in the beginning. They all shared in the waitressing while her sister-in-law Young Ran Shin pitched in with some of the kitchen work and continues to fire up good food to this day. At first, her brother Young Soo Shin helped with the cleanup and washed dishes when they started their business. But Settergren jokingly admits, "We know Asian brothers are opinionated," so she initially allowed him only limited visits. "They can come in and eat, but they cannot tell us what to do." Very soon, her brother could not stop providing advice. "We got so irritated we sent him to sushi school in L.A. for six months," and he eventually became the head sushi chef.

About a year later, Settergren's brother and sister-in-law bought her out so she could focus on raising her three children. Over the years, her brother established a loyal following, and affectionately these customers in the know fondly named NaRa a "sushi steakhouse" for the generous-sized rolls he made. In the 2000s, the Shins' daughter So Hyun waited tables while her brother Dae started making sushi. Settergren says that when Dae went off to college in Bozeman, the deal his parents made with him was that if he "did not get straight As, then he would have to come back to work" at the restaurant. Not quite fulfilling the challenge, according to Settergren, the family then sent him to the best sushi school in Korea.

For the last couple years, Dae and his wife, Tanya, have taken over the reins of running the restaurant. They updated the interior, enhanced the sushi bar and removed the fish tank by the door. Tanya's mother-in-law, "Mom," makes each dish coming out of the kitchen with care. The Korean pancake *chun*, made with just vegetables or with seafood, is so popular that it is not offered on Friday and Saturday nights, as there are not enough pans and burners to handle the demand. Young Soo cooks each dish to order, so food always arrives on the table fresh and hot. Settergren says of the spirit of NaRa, "The restaurant really has family feel. This restaurant treats diners like friends and family."

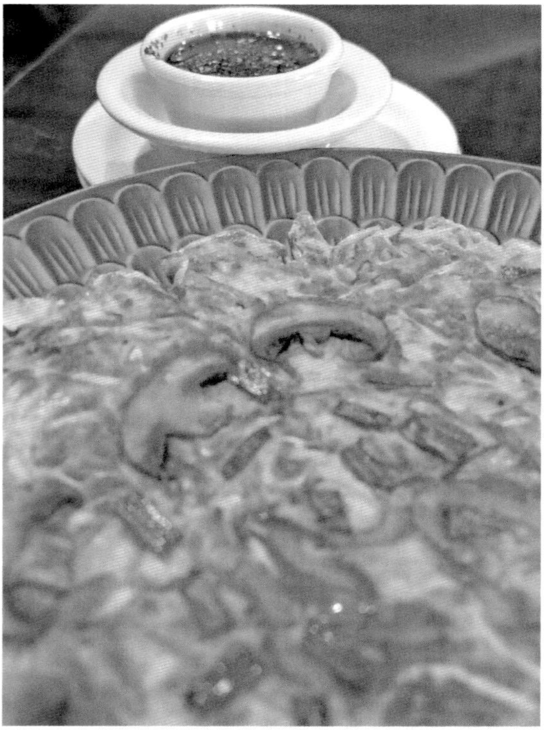

Left: From Nara Sushi Restaurant, "Vegetable Chun," a Korean-style pancake made with fresh vegetables served with house special spicy soy sauce.

Below: Eli Van Hook gives a thumbs up for the Nara's "Nacho Roll" he is enjoying with his mom, Jeni Fruichantie.

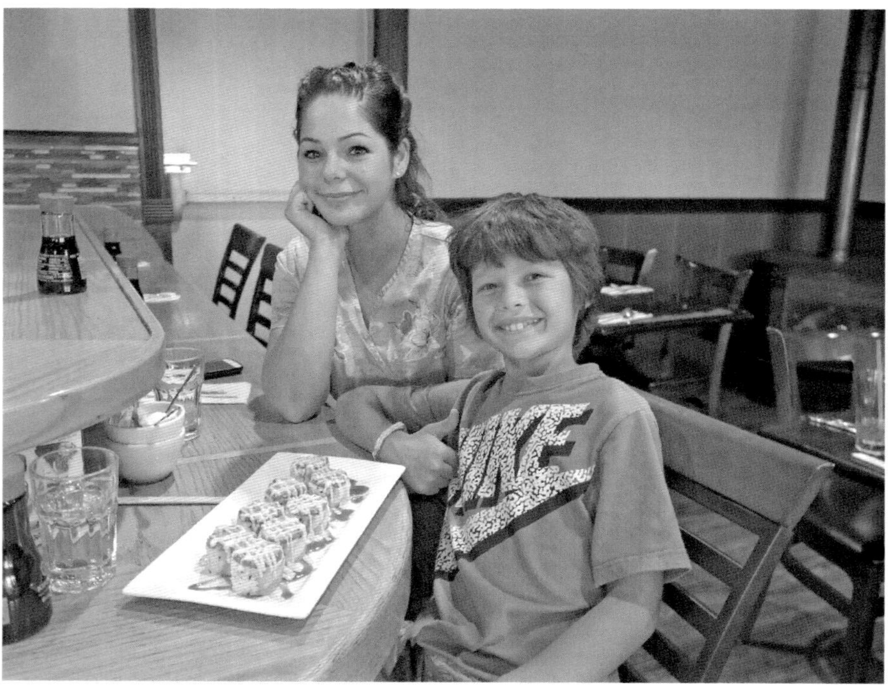

Siam Thai Restaurant has been located in the West End in a strip mall just off King Avenue since 2001. Owner Thawee "Nit" Williams learned to cook as a child growing up in Udon Thani in the northeastern corner of Thailand. These days her son, Preecha Thaseethong, plays the role of chef, creating the fresh and spicy flavors for Billings' diners. Over the years, Nit has played all roles in the restaurant along with her husband and partner, Ray. Mostly she provides a wonderful and warm welcome to patrons. To stock the small grocery store selling Southeast Asian, Japanese and Chinese products next to the restaurant, the couple would often drive monthly down to Denver.

This light-filled restaurant, with white tablecloths and always a fresh flower in a small long-stemmed blue and white vase, holds the spirit of the statue with hands pressed together in prayer welcoming every guest. Wait staff, uniformed in traditional Thai silk dress, take orders from the menu, including traditional pad Thai noodles, satays and curries. But selections also include "Ped Krapao (Basil Duck)—Boneless batter fried duck topped with spicy basil sauce and garnished with steamed vegetables," "Papaya Salad—Julienne green papaya, roasted peanuts, green beans, tomatoes and lime juice" and "Goong Kaew—Seasoned shrimp wrapped with rice paper deep fried and served with a sweet chili sauce."

In the summer of 2014, Nit helped Doug and Betsy Madler open a mobile restaurant also called Siam Thai in the Bakken oil patch in North Dakota. For workers in the middle of nowhere, the restaurant provides a spicy respite in a region where food is strongly swayed by German and Norwegian influences.

One of the first food trucks to hit the roads of Billings was Khanthaly's Eggrolls. After closing their Laotian restaurant on the corner of Thirteenth and Grand Avenues in 2002, owner Khanthaly Keutla and her husband, Sisavath, served up their famous pad Thai noodles, egg rolls and fried rice out of a truck. At the weekly summer Yellowstone Valley Farmers Market, they anchor the northwest corner under SkyPoint. The popularity of the Asian flavors has also brought Oriental Express and Board Wok to serve up egg rolls and noodles along with other Asian dishes. During the week, Khanthaly's Eggrolls are served in the Transwestern parking lot at the lunch hour. The food truck concept is still in its infancy in Montana's Trailhead, and Billings Food Truck Tracker (billingsfoodtrucktracker.com) reports where and when diners can find street food in Billings. Aside from Khanthaly's mobile restaurant, other trucks on the scene reported by this site include Fat Taco, Mexican Flavor and Noah's BBQ. Blog site Food Trucks IN (www.foodtrucksin.com/city/billings_mt) also has a short list of the food trucks found around Billings.

Tao New Asian features two hundred menu options. Located in the commercial retail zone in the West End, it is conveniently across the street from Costco. After owning restaurants in Columbus and Big Timber, John and Christine Chen opened Tao in 2012. Not only are Chinese, Japanese and Thai dishes offered, but there are also Korean options. Signature dishes include "Crispy Sea Scallops," "Pineapple Curry Duck," "Lobster in Thai Ginger Sauce" and "Korean Style BBQ Ribs." Teriyaki, sushi rolls and noodles round out the menu. Tamra Millikin takes her eight- and nine-year-old boys here because, she says, "the rice and chicken satay are great for little hands. The soups are a big hit as well." The kids' menu contains children-friendly choices such as "Corndog & Fries" and "Grilled Cheese & Fries."

Other restaurants serving Southeast Asian flavors are Cham Thai Cuisine and LemonGrass Thai Restaurant. LemonGrass Thai Restaurant, located in the middle of box store central on King Avenue, extends delicious karma. The family-run restaurant finds owner Natthiyada Alford in the kitchen and her daughter Thimaporn Kwanboochan working the front of the house. Gold statues of Buddha with a pointed headdress sit on dedicated alcoves on the saffron-colored walls. The popular pineapple fried rice comes in a cored-out pineapple, while the fresh spring rolls come with rice paper wrapping fresh lettuce, cucumber, carrots, shrimp and rice noodles with a spicy dipping sauce.

Cham Thai Cuisine, located downtown, offers "Authentic Thai Cuisine, Siamese and Chinese Food." The menu includes sweet and sour "Tom Yum Shrimp Soup" served in a stamped metal pot; "Puffed Crab Curry—Deep fried imitation crab with curry powder, carrot, potato, cream cheese in wonton skin served with sweet and sour sauce"; "Larb Chicken, Beef or Pork Salad"; green, red or yellow curries with different meats and vegetables; and "Chili Mint Leaves Squid" and "Garlic Trout." Woven tapestries and woodcarvings provide the Asian décor that sets the ambiance for the restaurant.

In midtown, located on Grand Avenue near Thirteenth Street, is Fancy Sushi Asian Fusion Restaurant, owned by Jimmy Li. Li arrived from Fuijian, China, to settle in New York about fourteen years ago. He worked in the family restaurant business, but feeling that the Big Apple was too crowded, he relocated to Billings. His connection was with his cousins Howard Shen and Tina Wu, who now own Asian Sea Grill and Sushi Bar and the new Wild Ginger Japanese Steakhouse Restaurant. Li's family is large, with a grandmother who had eight children. "I have forty cousins, and half of them are in New York," Li shares. This resource provides for skills at the sushi bar and in the kitchen. While his

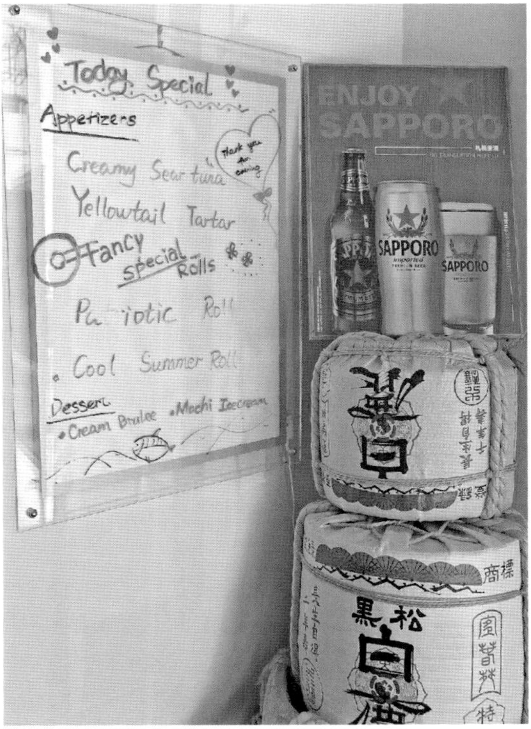

Right: Fancy Sushi Asian Fusion entrance at 1313 Grand Avenue.

Below: Fancy Sushi Asian Fusion chef Yu Guan Wang (left) and owner Jimmy Li.

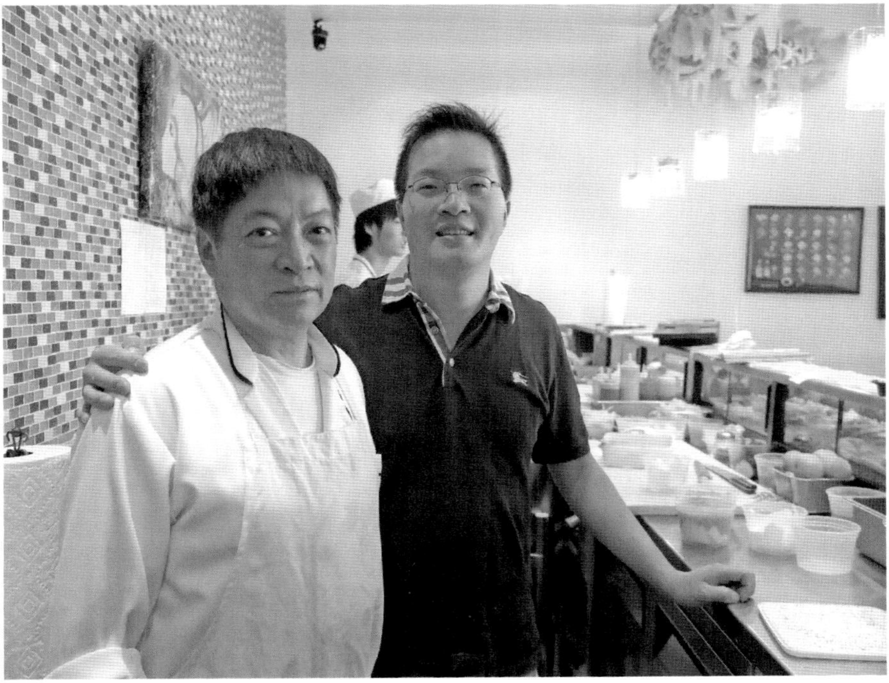

brother-in-law Jack Wang provides talents at the sushi bar, his father-in-law, Yu Guan Wang, cooks in the kitchen.

Fancy Sushi Asian Fusion Restaurant flashes a touch of glitz with a wall of crystal strands dangling from the ceiling with the restaurant's name spelled out. Purple and blue neon lights edge the top walls, providing a festive glow. While a sushi bar dominates a back corner wall, providing a bright area, the tables and chairs and the intimate booth seating along the front windows and the back wall are black, giving a chic feel. For birthday celebrations, a recorded birthday song is played overhead, with the singing in a playful Asian accent.

The menu is huge, with almost twenty selections under the "Fancy Special Roll" category alone. More than a dozen options are found in the "Special Roll" heading, and "Sushi and Sashimi à la Carte" choices number almost two dozen. Dumplings and tempura can be ordered for appetizers, while main courses include Chinese dishes such as "Kung Pao Combination" with scallops, shrimp, beef and chicken and Japanese "Salmon Teriyaki" to "Diner Box" choices with teriyaki or tempura accompanied with "Soup, Salad, Shumai, Rice, Yaki-Tori and a California Roll." Fancy Sushi Asian Fusion's interpretation of certain dishes such as *chirashi*, which is normally a large bowl of rice topped with slices of raw fish and vegetables, have arrived at my table on a mound of shaved ice lit with a colorful tea light. The rice, fish and vegetables were creatively presented with wisps of dry ice spilling from the platter.

Howard Shen and Tina Wu are bringing Asian food to Billings with gusto and establishing a dynasty. Along with their Golden Phoenix Chinese Cuisine, Wild Ginger Japanese Steakhouse has brought a chic Asian urban vibe to the city with Asian fusion cooking. Shen and Wu started Asian Sea Grill and Sushi Bar on King Avenue in 2011. Two years after they opened, they added a room of teppanyaki grills for an entertaining cooking and dining experience. The concept replicates the Benihana culinary adventure where chefs provide fast knife work and furious cooking at a tableside grill. Asian Sea Grill also houses a bar, a lounge and a dining room. This concept is duplicated downtown under taller ceilings and among artful elegance in a seven-thousand-square-foot space.

At Wild Ginger, there is also a fresh oyster bar and sushi bar. A mural of Tina Wu painted by Vincent Sanchez graces the back wall, while a mirrored bar with flat-screen televisions forms the backdrop in the bar and lounge area. The restaurant sits near the North Twenty-seventh Street corner, while the hibachi restaurant is on the other end of the long space. A large fish tank separates the restaurant from the bar and lounge area.

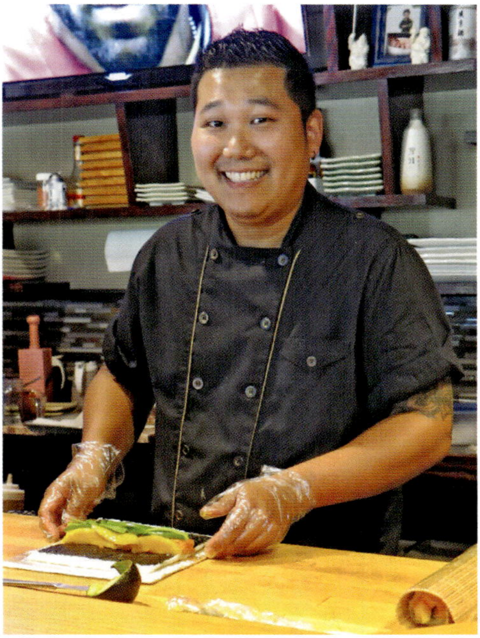

Nara Restaurant's sushi chef, Dae Shin.

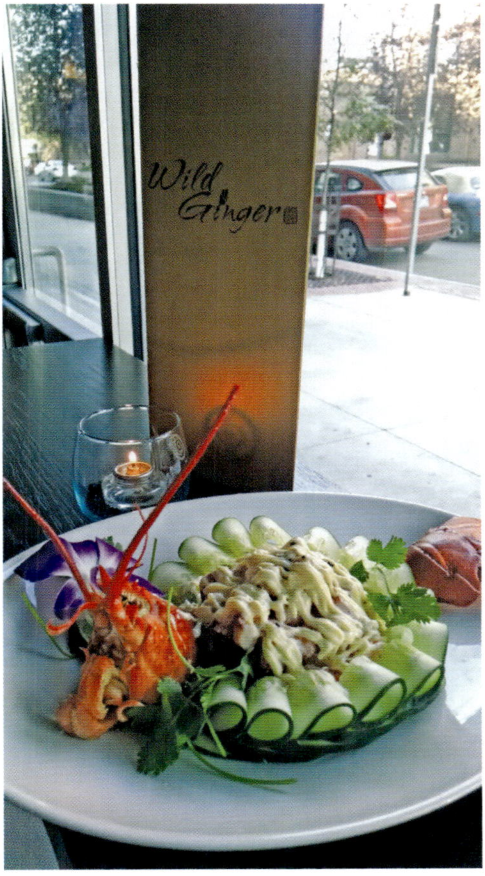

Lobster salad from Wild Ginger Japanese Steakhouse, located at the corner of North Twenty-seventh Street and Montana Avenue.

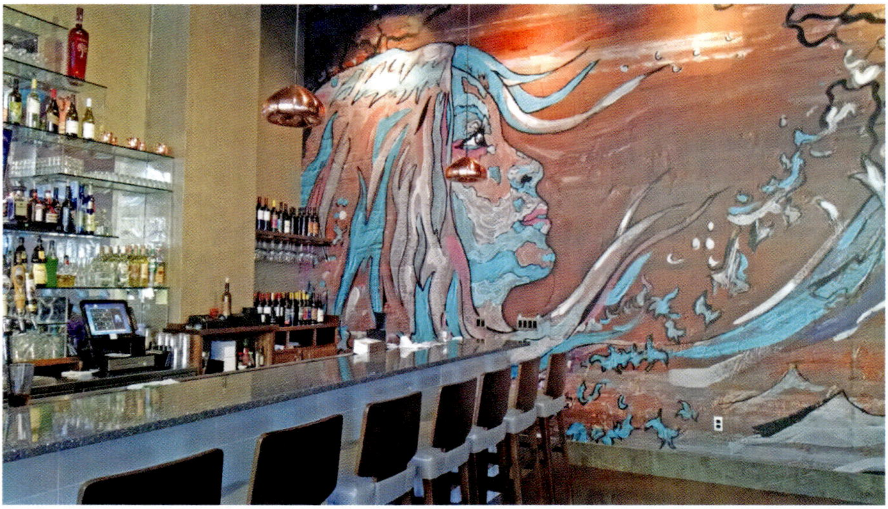

A mural of Tina Wu painted by Vincent Sanchez by the bar at Wild Ginger Japanese Steakhouse.

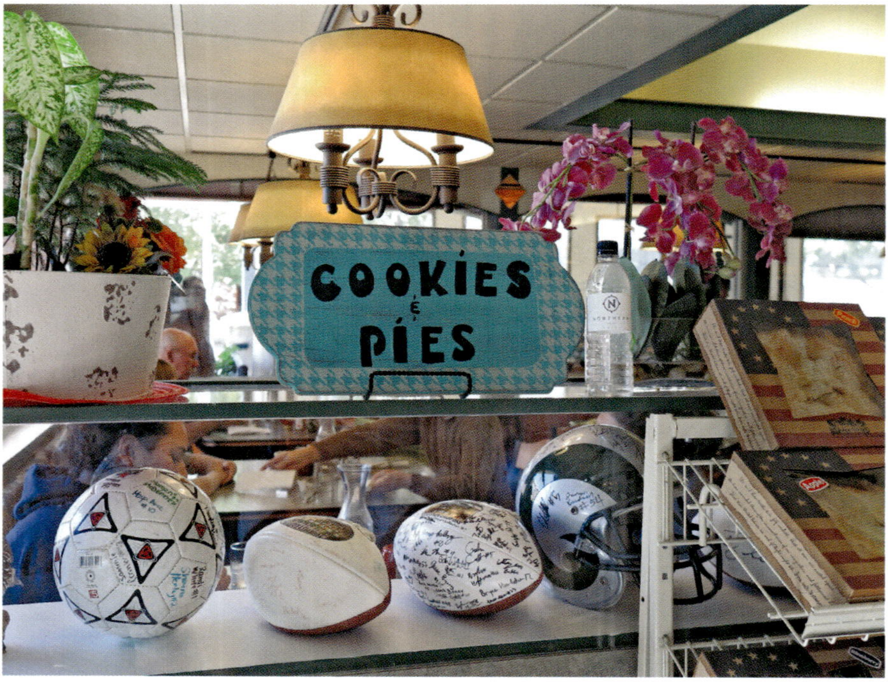

Stella's Kitchen and Bakery has been serving up baked and community goodness since 1978.

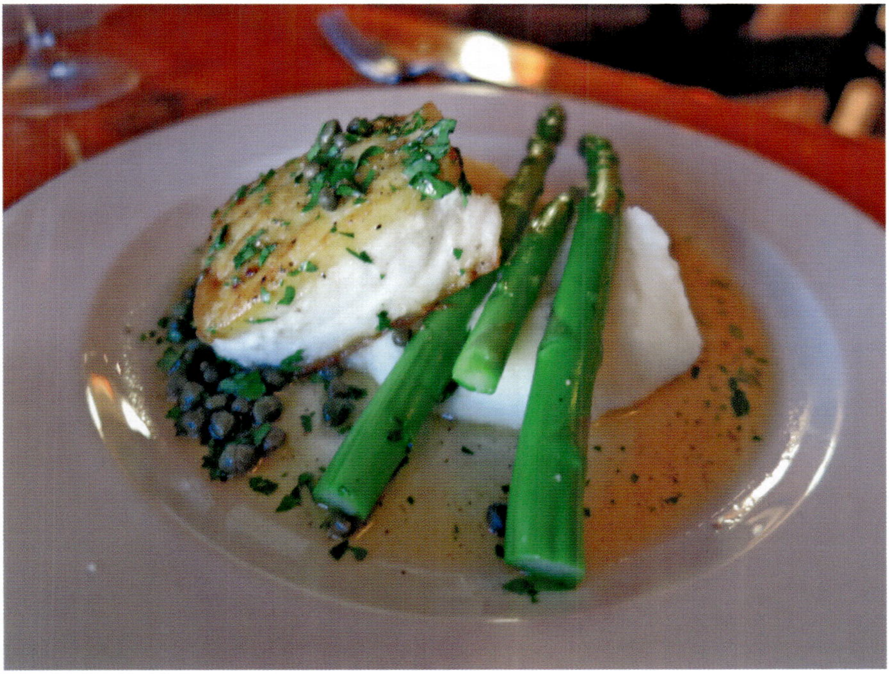

Above: Halibut with a caper beurre blanc, mashed potatoes and asparagus from Bistro Enzo.

Right: Bistro Enzo, owned by James Honaker, serves American, French, Asian and Italian cuisine in a European ambiance.

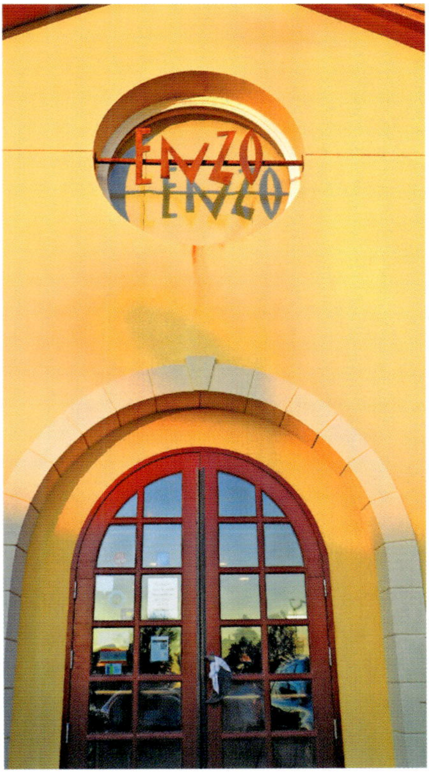

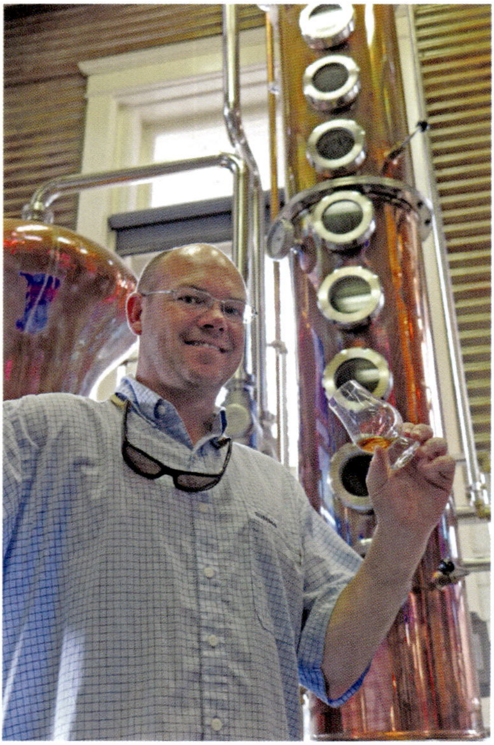

Left: Casey McGowan, owner of Trailhead Spirits, makes vodka and gin from grains secured from his family farm in Highwood, Montana.

Below: Mary Johnson, owner of Crazy Mary's Fish and Chips, serves generous portions spiced with her flavorful personality.

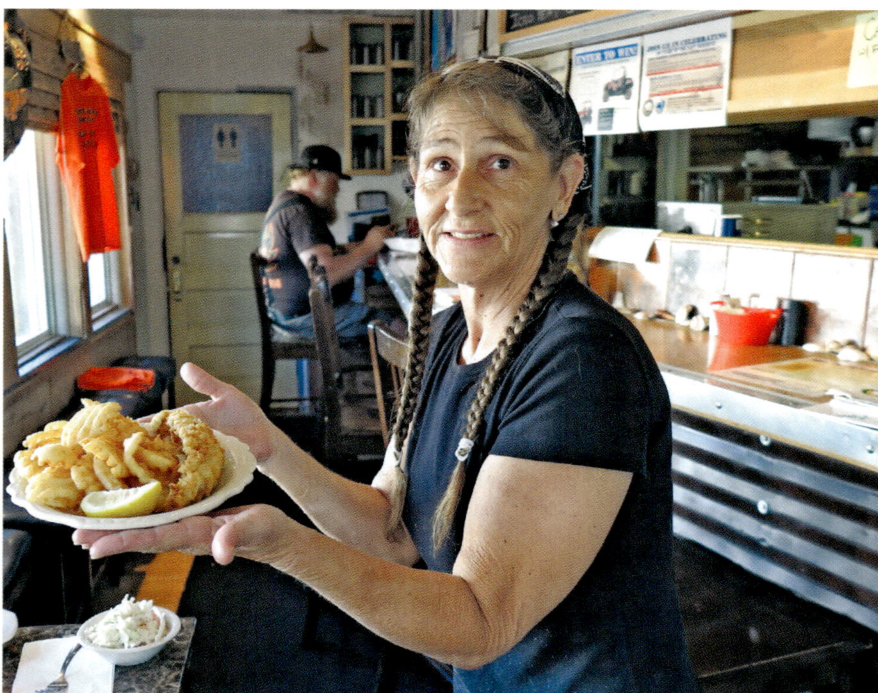

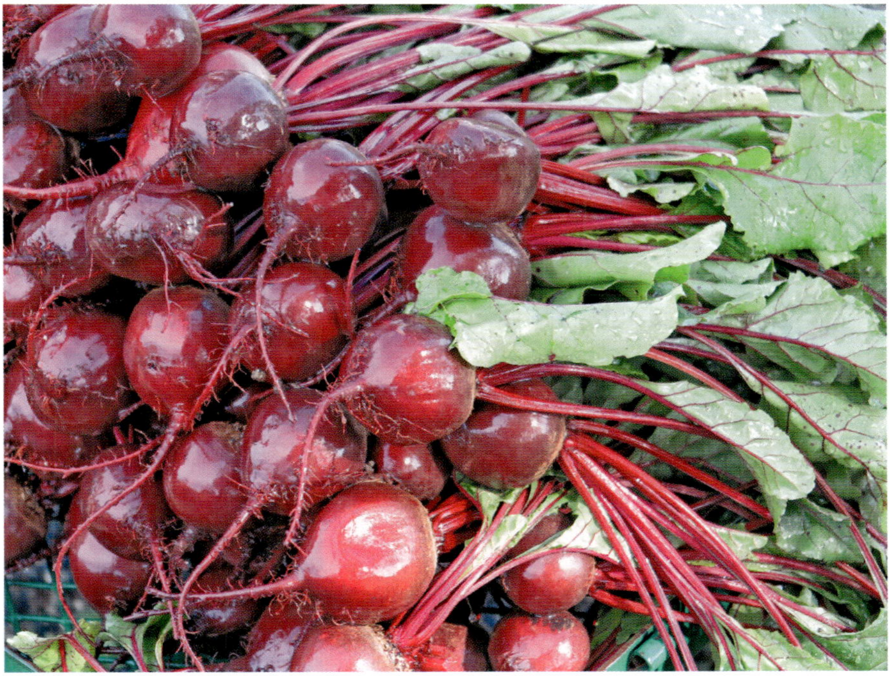

Above: Freshly picked beets grown by Danly Farms after a good rinse with water.

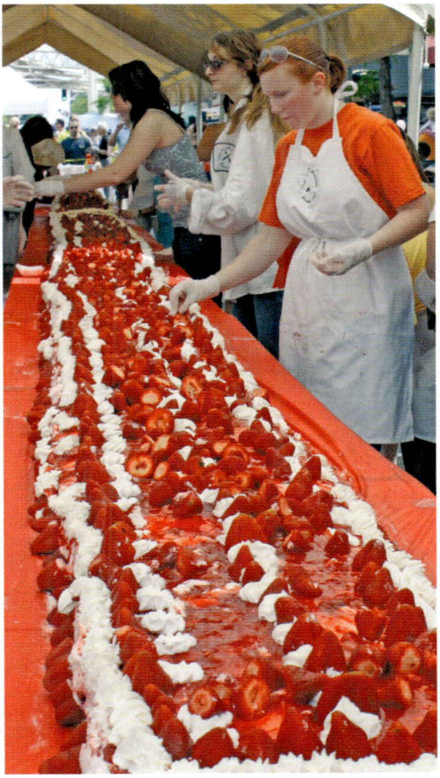

Right: Strawberry Festival is a celebration of all that is spring into summer with an over sixty-foot-long strawberry shortcake. *Courtesy of Downtown Billings Alliance.*

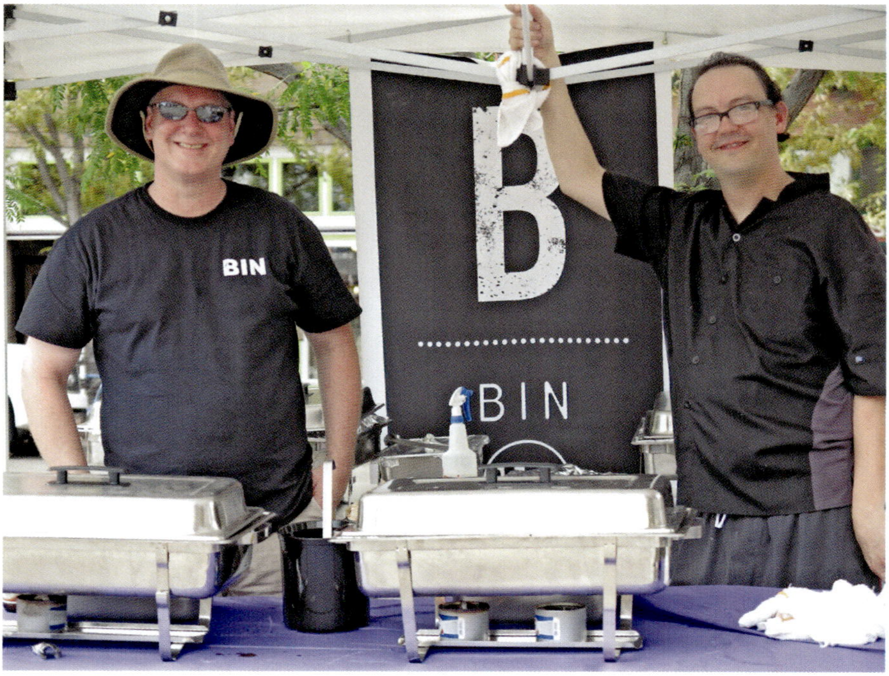

Bin 119, American Bistro and Wine Bar, with Stephon Mentzer (owner, left) and Derik Jeanotte at Taste of Summer.

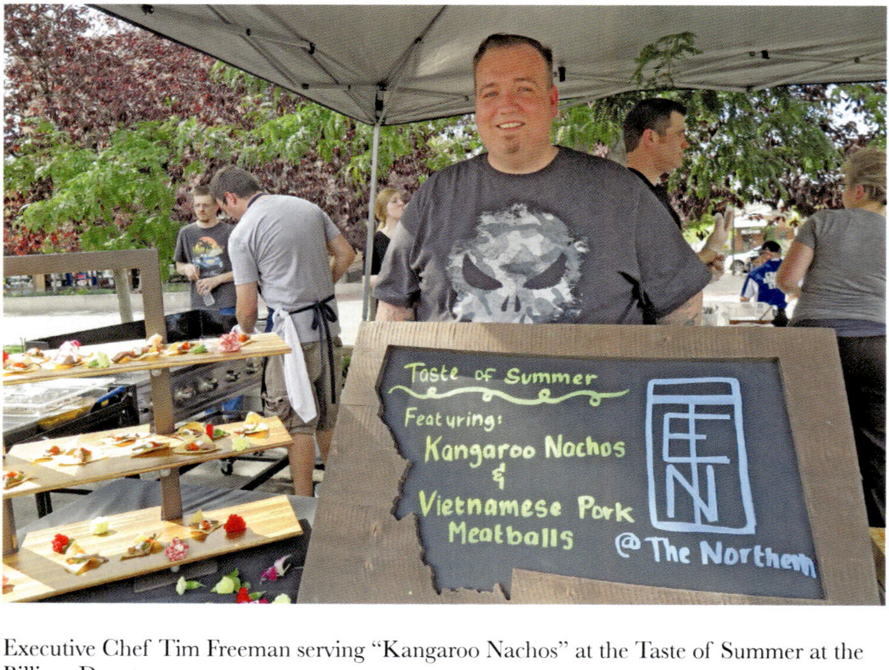

Executive Chef Tim Freeman serving "Kangaroo Nachos" at the Taste of Summer at the Billings Depot.

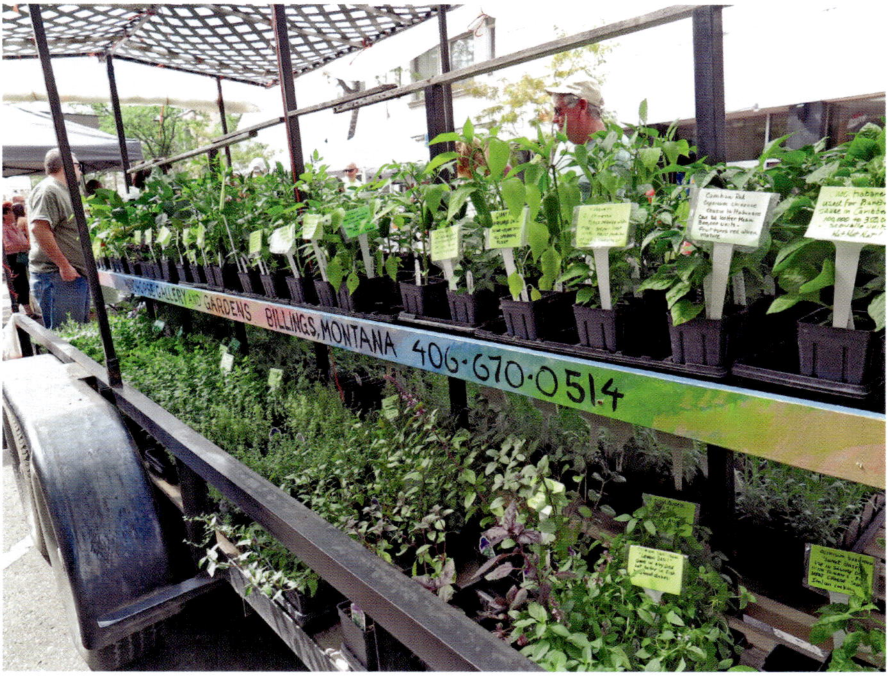

Above: Windhorse Gallery and Gardens, owned by Cena Anderson, provides a variety of herbs and plants.

Right: Khanthaly Keutia serves up her egg noodles with bean sprouts, carrots and peanuts from her food truck.

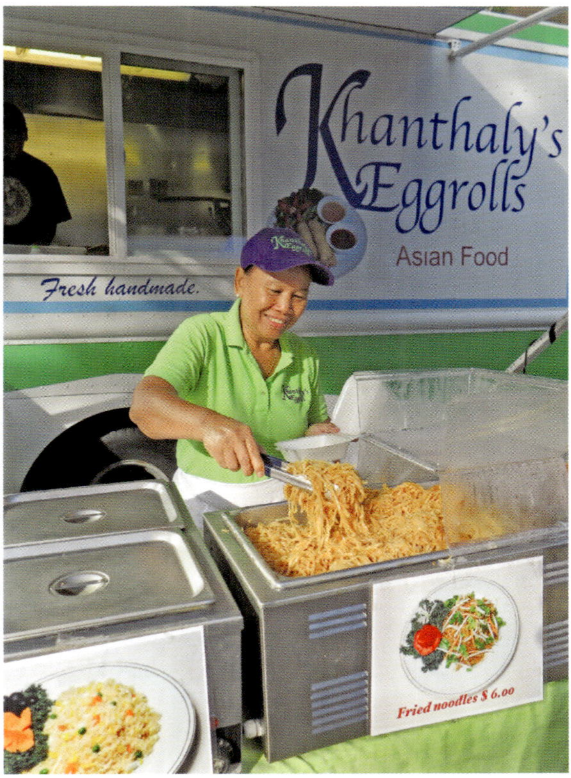

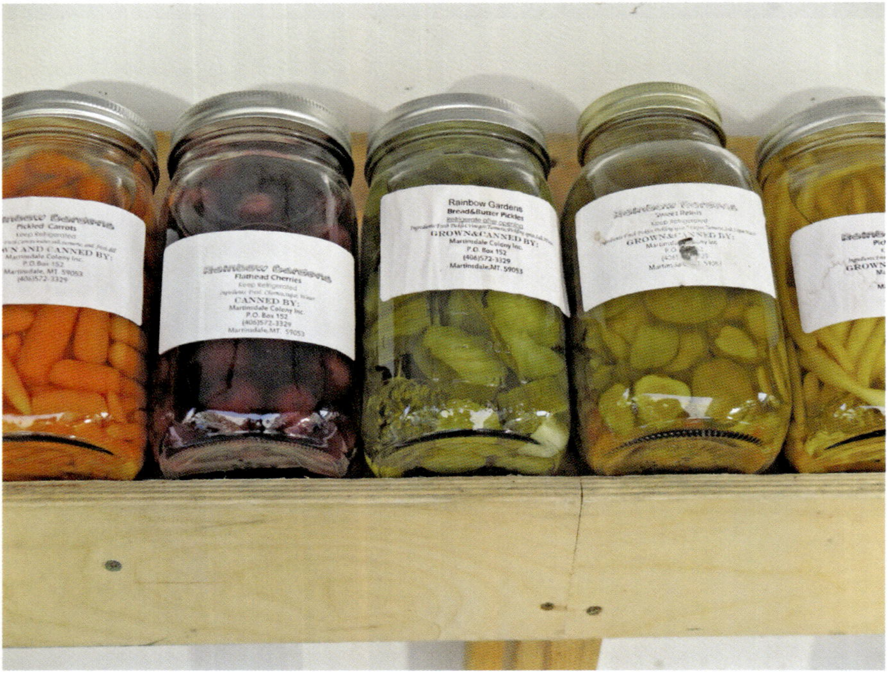

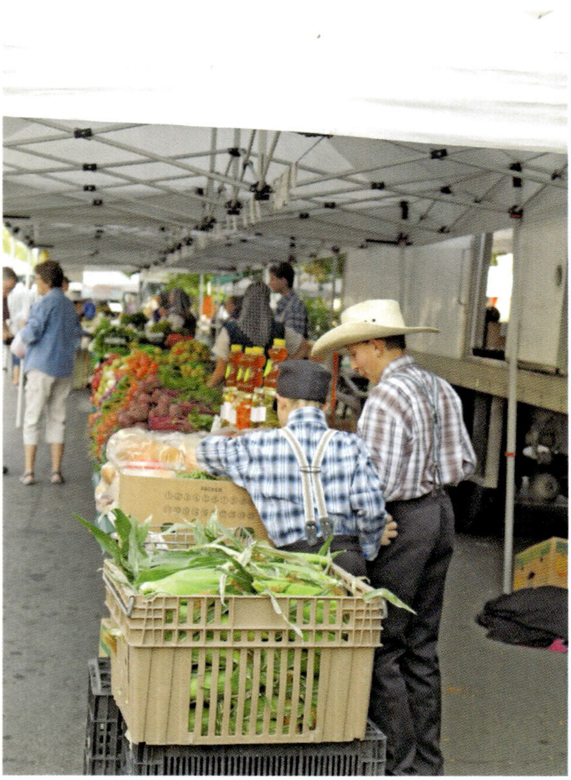

Above: Pickles from the Martinsdale Colony.

Left: Fresh produce comes from Hutterite colonies such as the Mountain View Colony.

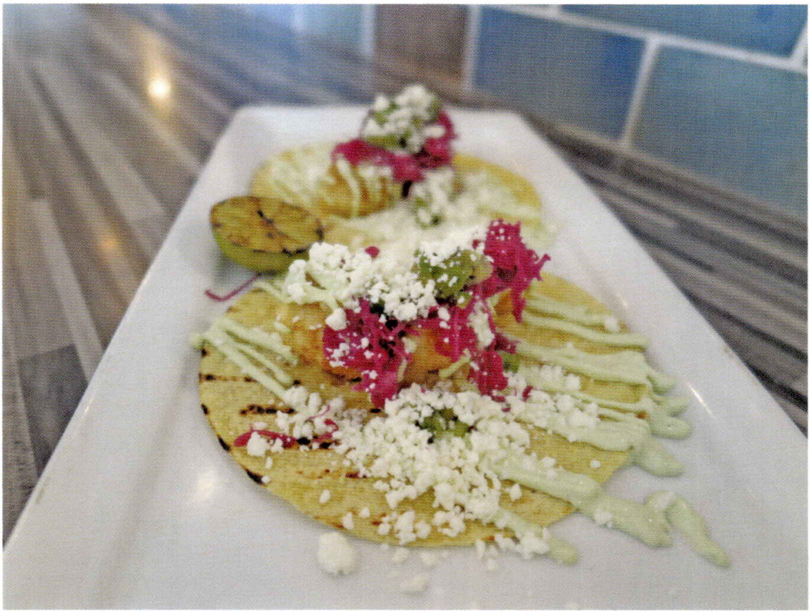

Fish tacos from Field House Cafe made with wild halibut, cabbage, kiwi salsa, cotija cheese, ginger and crema.

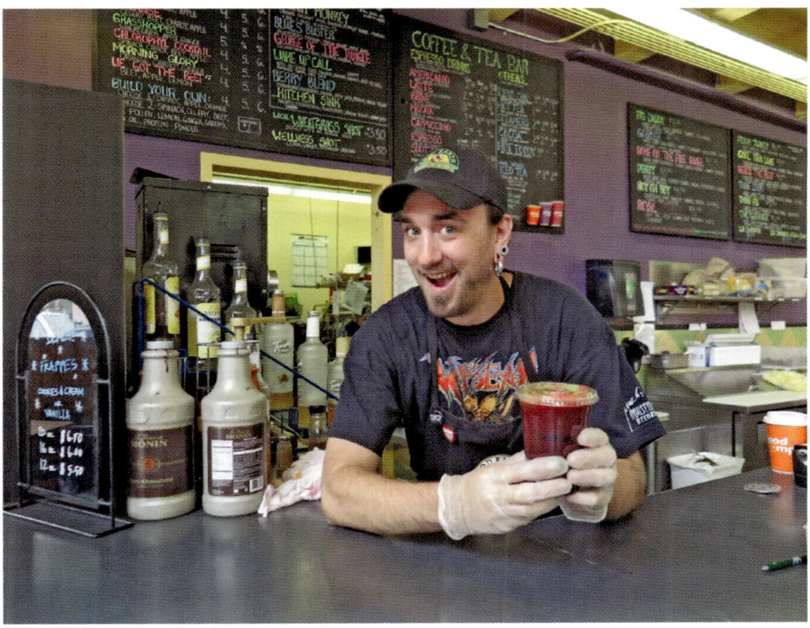

Benjamin Meyer at Good Earth sells a "Chlorophyll Cocktail" made with spinach, carrots, beets and apple.

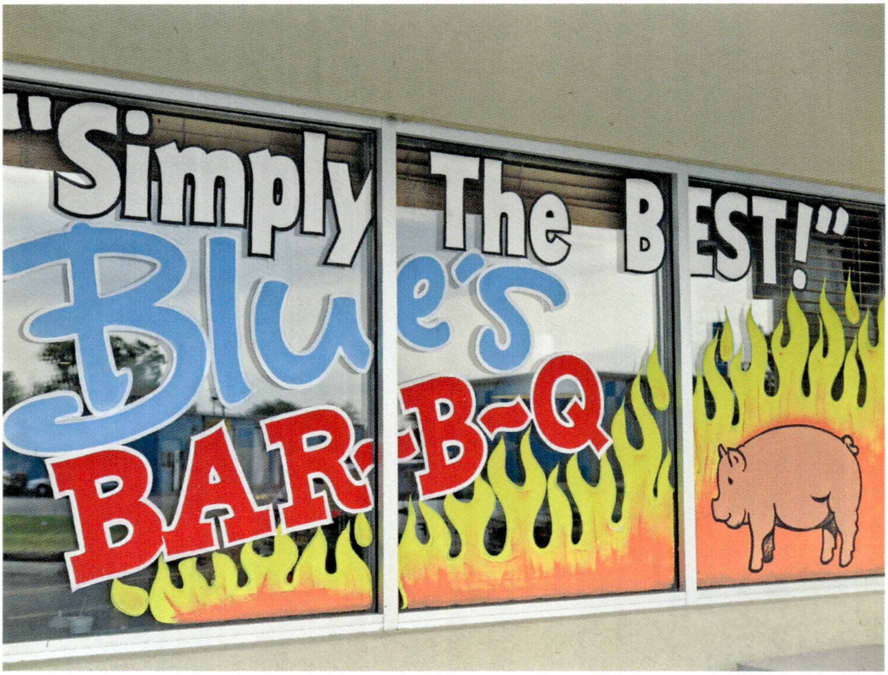

Blues Barbecue, located at 523 Hilltop Road in the Heights, will take your blues away with barbecue.

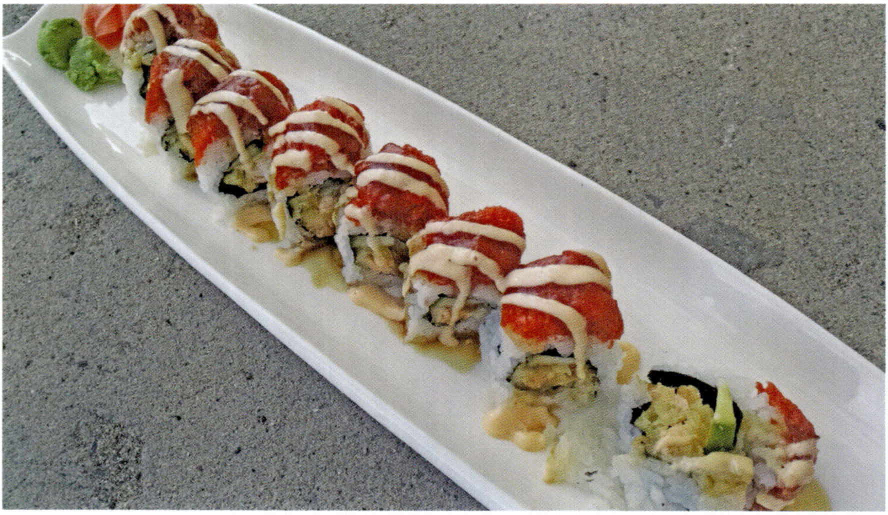

Okinawa Sushi Asian Bistro's "Hot Night Roll" with red snapper tempura and cucumber topped with spicy tuna.

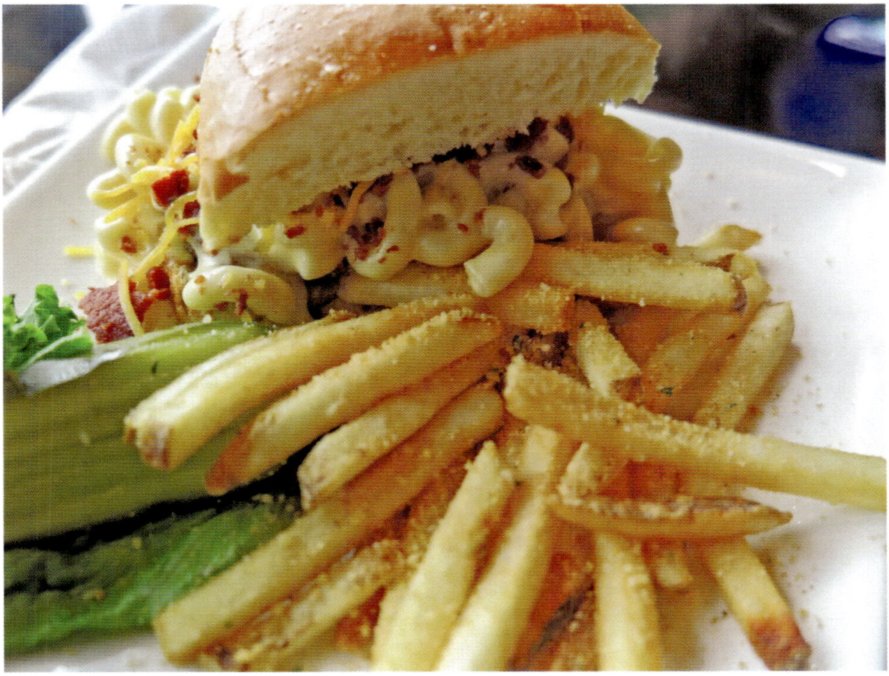

The Big Smack Burger is made with Angus beef and topped with mac 'n' cheese and bacon served on a brioche bun with garlic fries.

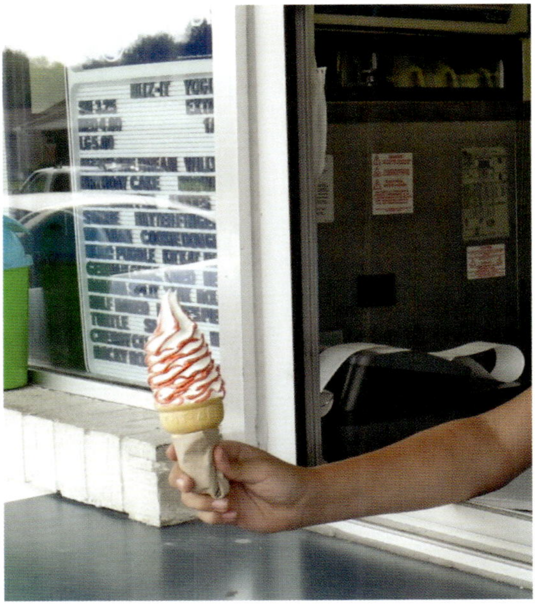

A swirling summer delight served up at Softie's. *Photo by Deborah Goffena.*

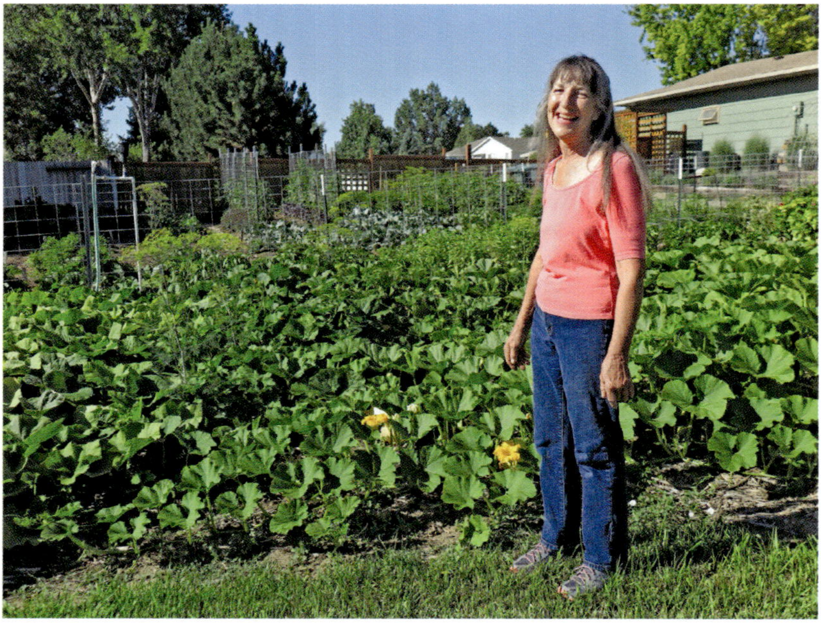

Kate Rosetto standing in Kate's Garden, where she is happiest with dirt and green under her fingernails.

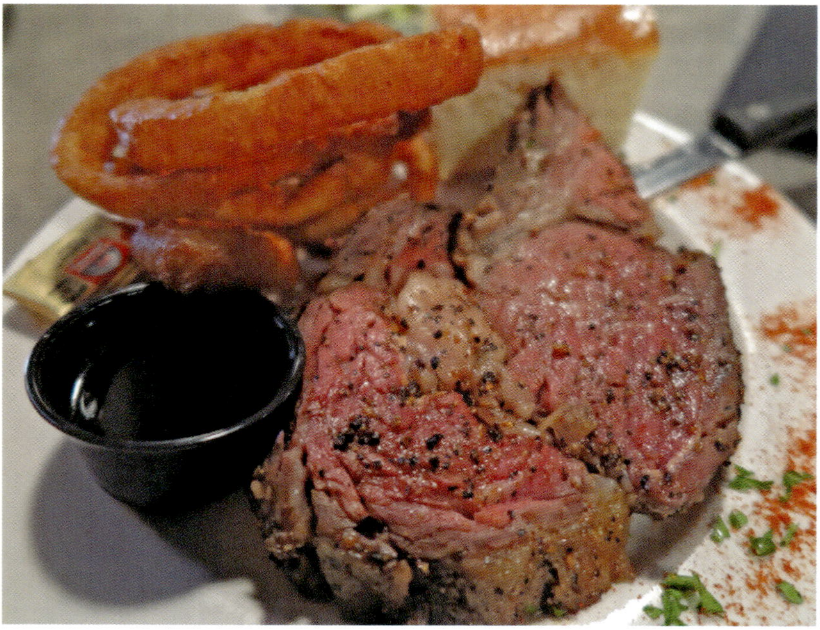

"Trailhead Ribeye" and onion rings from Bull Mountain Grille.

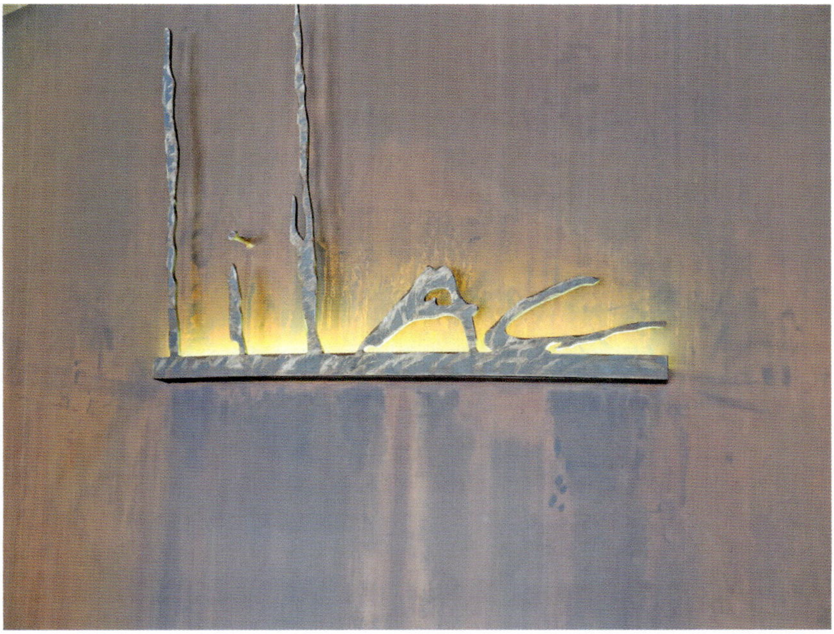

Lilac brings "Modern American Food with a Fistful of Approachability" to historic Montana Avenue.

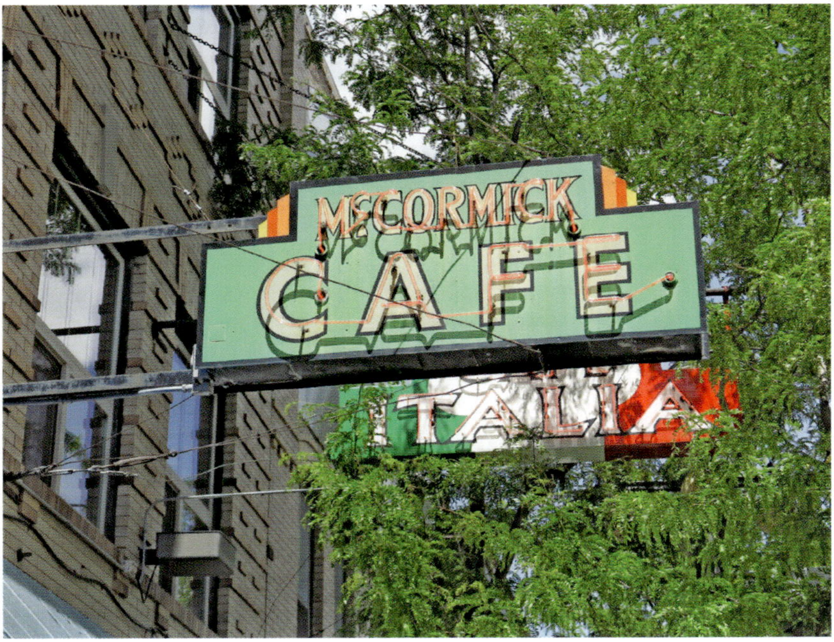

McCormick Café and Cafe Italia, restaurants established and owned by Mike Schaer on Montana Avenue.

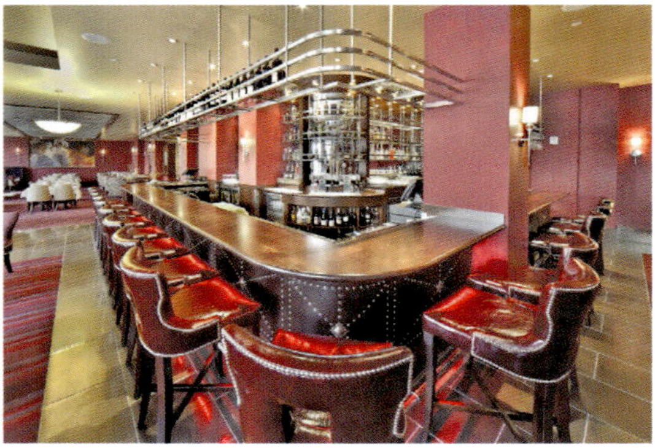

The bar and fine dining restaurant at TEN in the Northern Hotel.

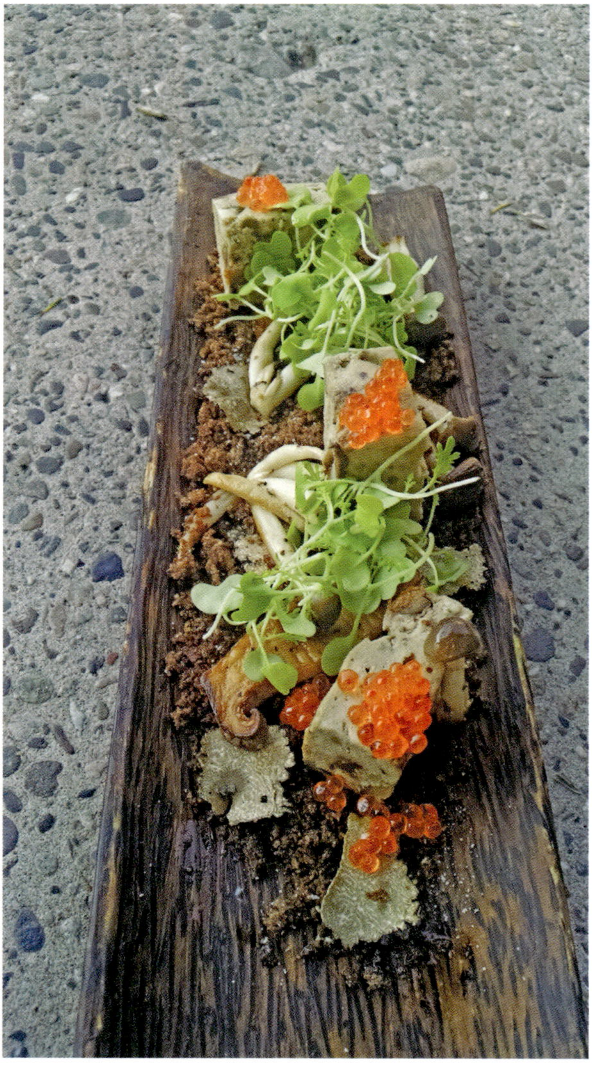

"A Walk in the Woods" with "Mushroom Soil, Foraged Mushrooms, Fine Salt, Trout Roe, Duck Terrine, Fresh Burgundy Truffles" from TEN in the Northern Hotel.

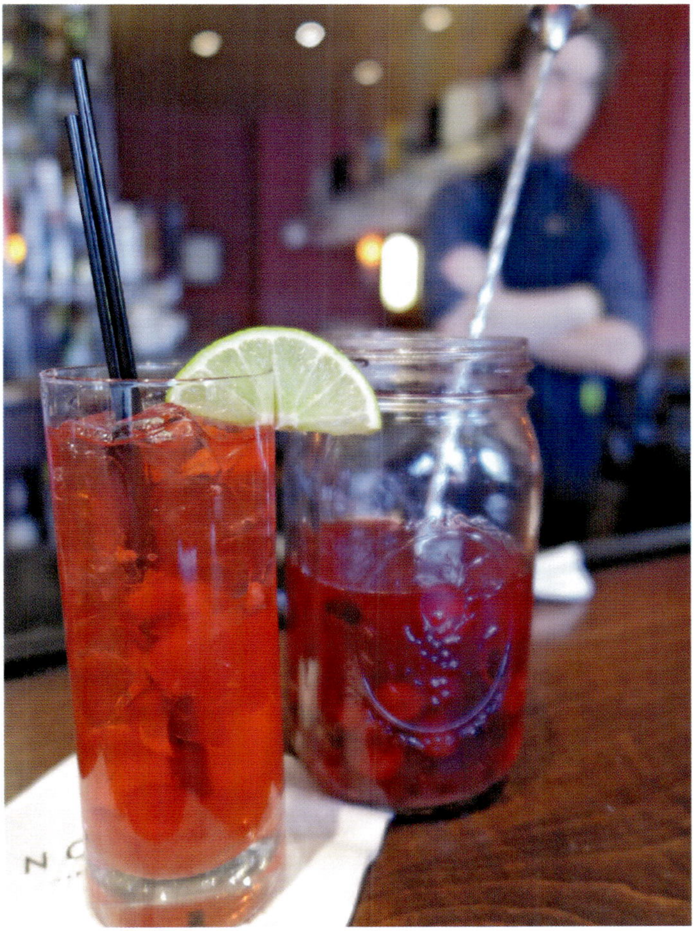

Right: TEN's "Spiced Cherry Mojito."

Below: The Italian-built sixteen-bottle WineEmotion Dispenser at Simpy Wine.

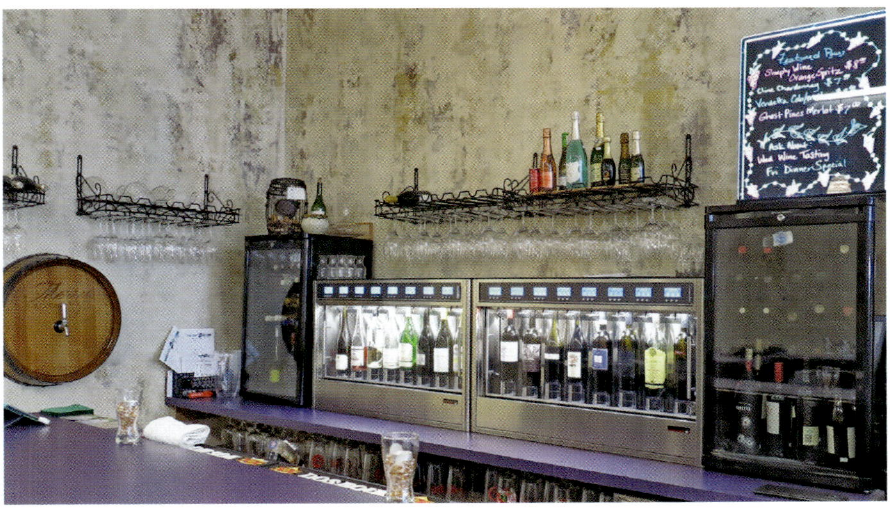

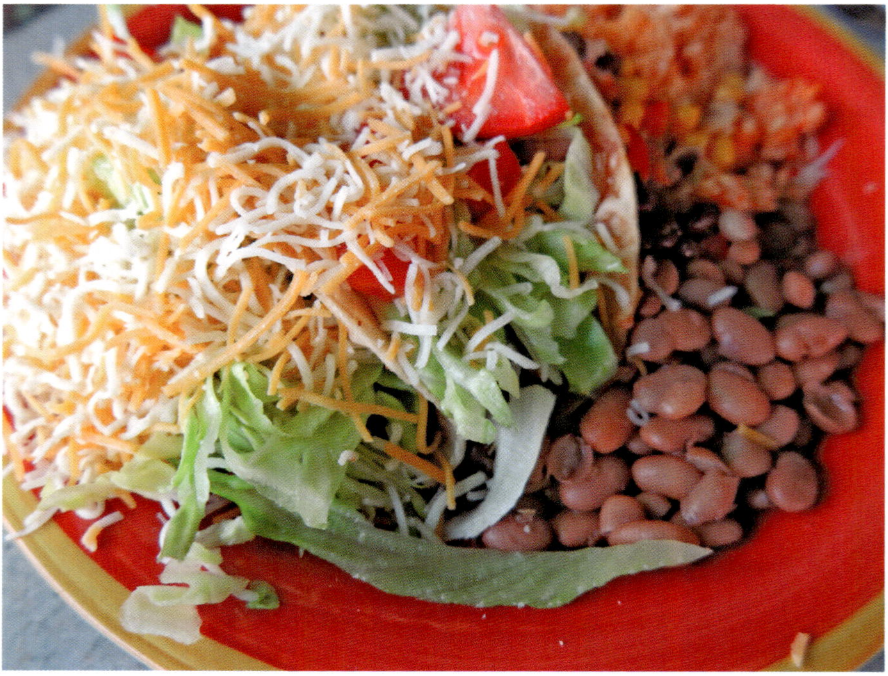

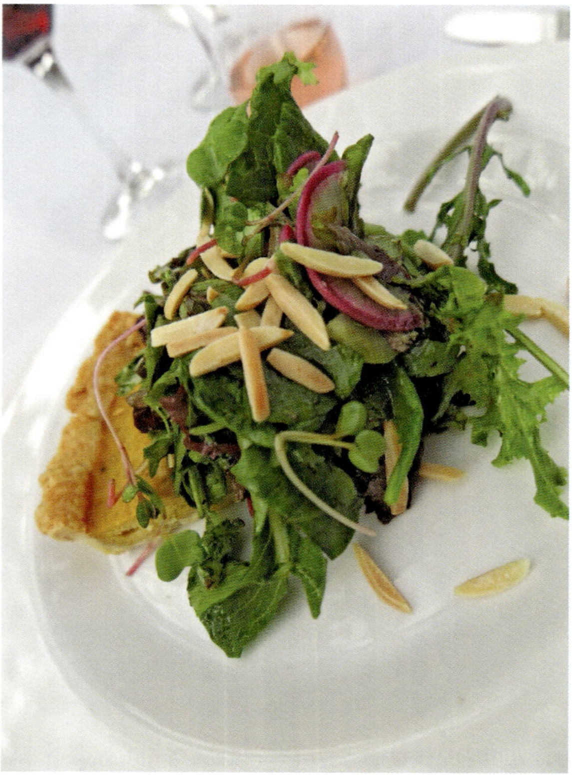

Above: Sautéed vegetable tacos from 29th Street Cafe.

Left: "Roast pumpkin and egg tart with summer vegetable salad, toasted almonds and sage vinaigrette" served at "An Evening Under the Stars."

At Asian Sea Grill, "Signature Dishes" feature "Crispy Duck served with plum sauce" and "Salt and Pepper Prawns." There are almost a dozen "Hibachi Dinner" options with chicken, beef, shrimp, scallops, lobster or a combination. The hibachi choices are also available downtown. Oyster shooters, along with raw and cooked sushi rolls, are presented with delectable appeal. "Dinner Entrée" choices are listed by the sauce or key ingredient in the dish, such as "Sweet and Sour" for pork or chicken or "Hot Garlic Sauce" for a variety of meat and fish options. "Red and Green Curry" and even "Fresh Mango Sauce" are other choices.

The teppanyaki concept has been firing up for some time in Billings, starting when Samurai Japanese Steak and Seafood House, owned by Khanthaly Keutla and her daughter Keomany Moua, opened the branch on Grand Avenue back in 2004. Nowadays, they perform their cooking styles at a Central Avenue location. It was back in 1981 that St. Luke's Episcopal Church helped bring Keutla's family—her husband and four children—to Billings after they fled Laos. Umi Japanese Steakhouse Restaurant was finally opened in the autumn of 2014 by Billy Wong and Andy Chan after many delays. Located in the West Park Promenade, Umi (which means "ocean") brought food from many fathoms away. This restaurant brought Wong and Chan's portfolio to six Umi restaurants nationwide.

For those who love buffets, Shanghai Village, located downtown; China Buffet on Grand; and China Bistro at Shiloh Crossing offer a generous variety of Asian food for those with an appetite. A complete meal from appetizer to soup to dessert can be found.

In recent years, some established Asian restaurants, including Sweet Ginger, Jade Palace and Four Seas, have closed their doors. Sweet Ginger, opened in 2002 by Lin Lin and C.W. Lo on Montana Avenue, shut down after the couple decided to retire. The community felt the loss of the popular restaurant that featured flavors of China and Japan. The Los, longtime restaurateurs who also ran the Great Wall, now own a small store called Lin Lin's Cupboard selling treasures that Lin Lin has collected in a lifetime of travel.

Serving Eastern Indian dishes is the India Grill. In 2013, Bhupinder "Roger" Singh and his cousin Balwinder opened Taste of India on Twenty-fourth Street West after operating downtown for three years. Figuring that customers did not venture downtown because of limited parking, they moved to the former Godfather's Pizza site closer to the West End with plenty of parking. On India Grill's website they advertise, "We offer the most authentic Indian food in Billings. Come enjoy a genuine cultural experience."

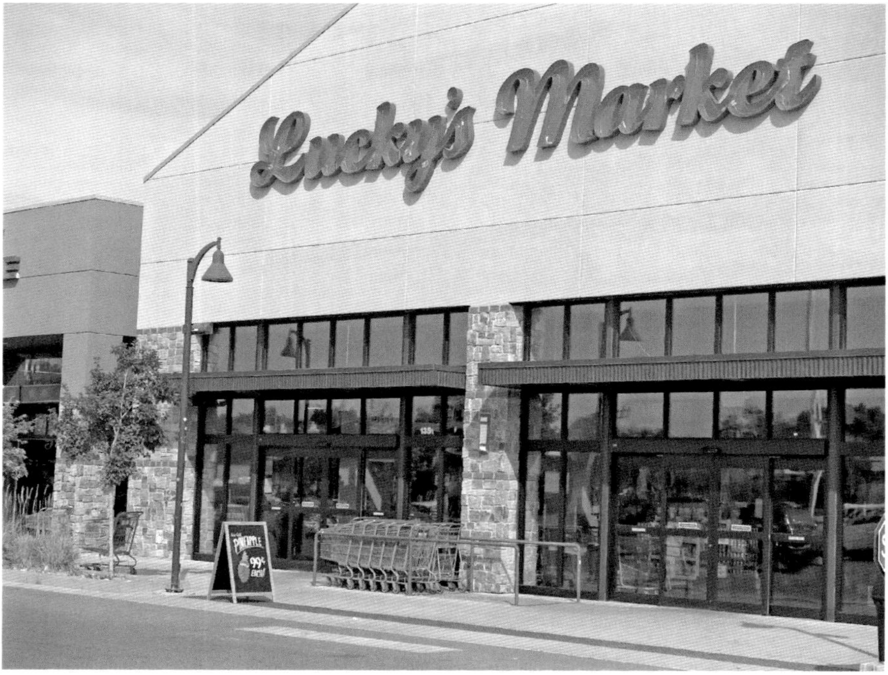

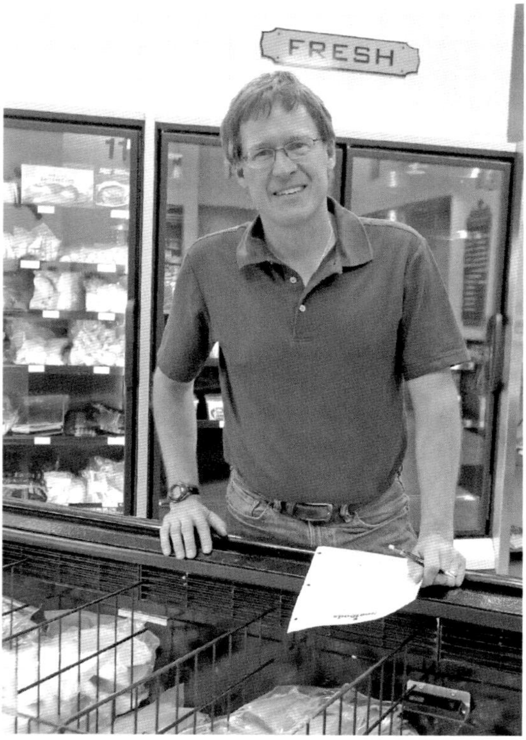

Above: Lucky's Market, a store believing good food should not be a luxury but a right.

Left: Dave Smith, president of Seafoods of the World, takes inventory of frozen fish he sells to the retail and wholesale market.

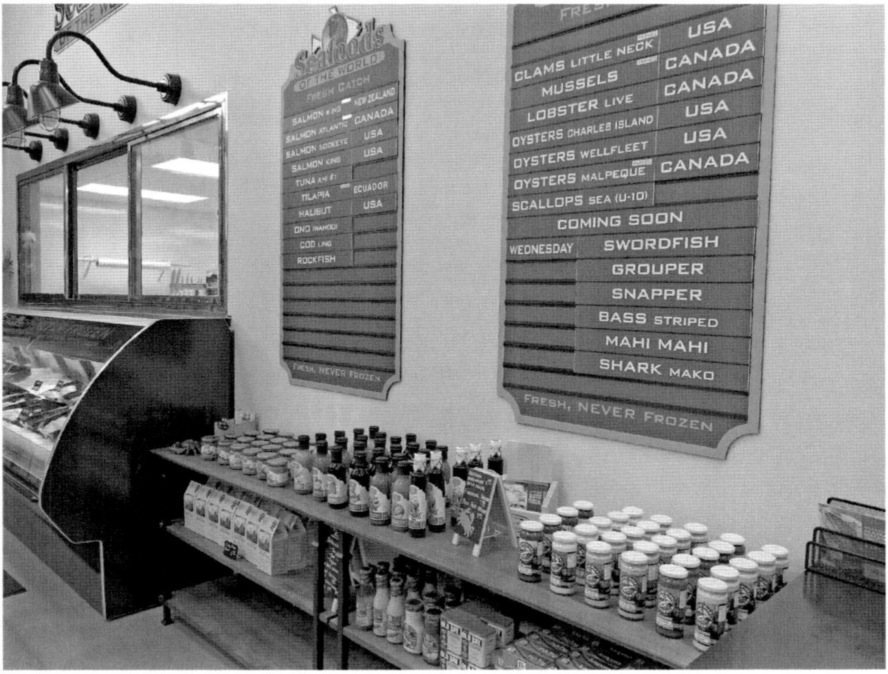

The fresh fish board at Seafoods of the World.

On a flat-screen television, a Bollywood film or the news from India is showing, adding to the ambiance. The food is colorful in sight and taste. From the traditional clay tandoori oven, fish, chicken and lamb emerge along with flatbreads of naan, roti or paratha. Biriyani—basmati rice flavored with saffron and spices—provides the perfect accompaniment to choices of beef, chicken, lamb or seafood cooked freshly with pungent spices.

With the influx of people coming to Billings and traveling through Montana's Trailhead, there has been a demand for Asian flavors. Even grocery stores such as Lucky's Market and Albertsons now offer takeout sushi. Seafoods of the World, a local wholesale/retail importer, sells the makings for creating your own sushi, offering sushi-grade fish flown in daily and a variety of other seafood. While supplying wholesale fish to local restaurants for years, Dave Smith expanded his family's business in the early summer of 2015 by opening up a retail outlet.

The palates of Billings citizens are expanding. With the abundant presence of new Asian restaurants headed by creative and eager entrepreneurs, eastern flavors have now reached Montana's largest city.

Chapter 16

JAVA JOLTS AND STEAM

Being near the Pacific Northwest, it is no wonder that the aromas of coffee have wafted into Billings. The paper cup with a plastic lid held in a sleepy hand has become a normal sighting in these parts. In 1998, Becky Reno was one of the first to catch the jolt of caffeine when she opened City Brew. Here she roasted and brewed some of the first coffee beans. Now she has more than a dozen outlets in Montana, Wyoming and North Dakota.

When walking into or out of City Brew, there is always a cheerful greeting of welcome and a bid of adieu upon leaving. The drive-throughs are always popular in the mornings as Billings wakes itself up and when the weather cools down. The coffee beans support its "Montana born and roasted" logo with names like "Blazing Prairies," "Cool River" and "Crazy Mountains."

At the Seventeenth and Grand Avenue location, there is a wine, gourmet market and tasting bar next door, City Vineyard. One could spend the afternoon sipping wine and beer and then getting a pick-me-up at the coffee shop with a dark brew and a sweet treat.

Off the Leaf Coffee Company joined the coffee scene ten years later by opening a coffee bar. At the 819 Grand location, not only is there ample room to gather or study, but there are also two rooms—one with couches and comfortable seating and the other a boardroom-style space with a projector TV. Outdoor seating puts the coffee sipper atop the stream of traffic on Grand Avenue. The gathering space is open until midnight every night except Friday and Saturday, when a latté or cappuccino can be brewed and steamed until 1:00 a.m. In 2015, Off the Leaf launched its mobile coffee

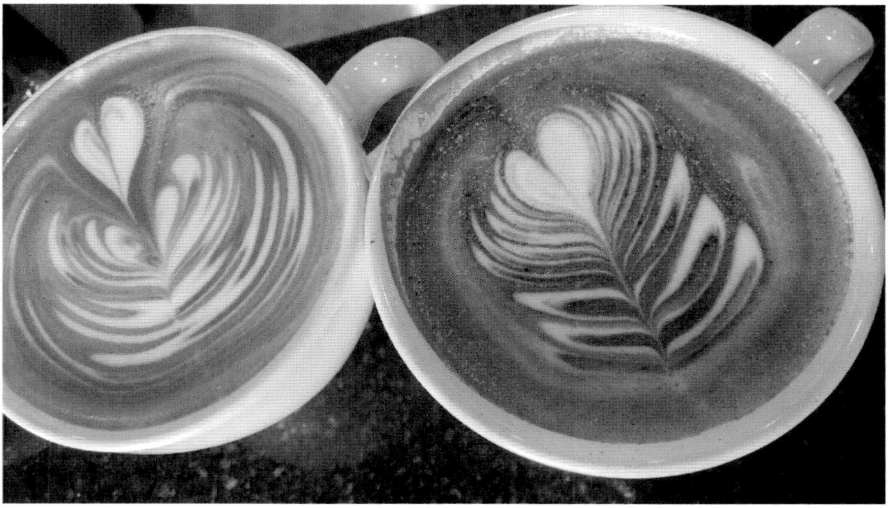

Latté art from Off the Leaf.

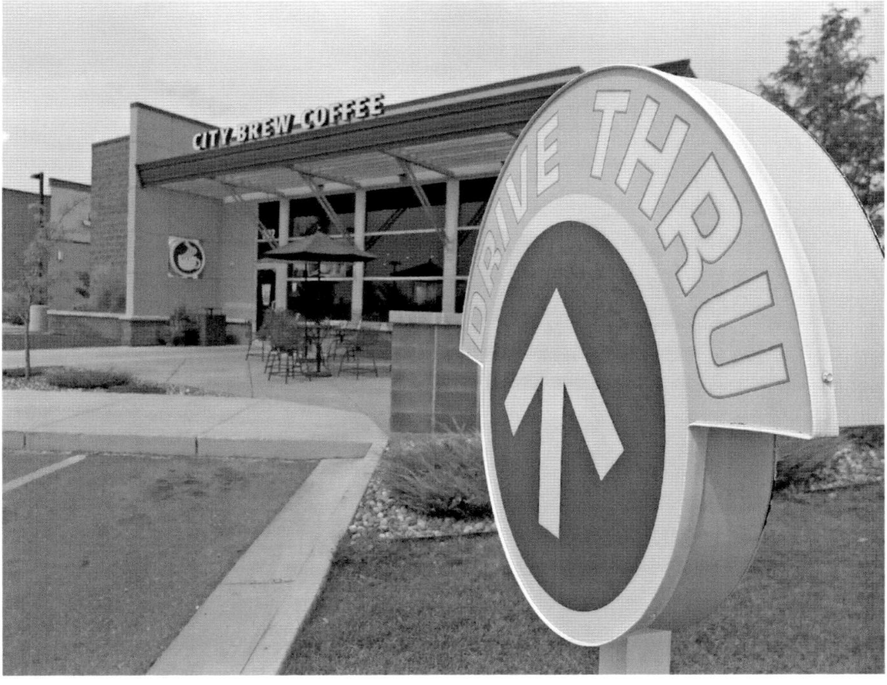

City Brew Coffee drive-through for coffee born and roasted in Montana.

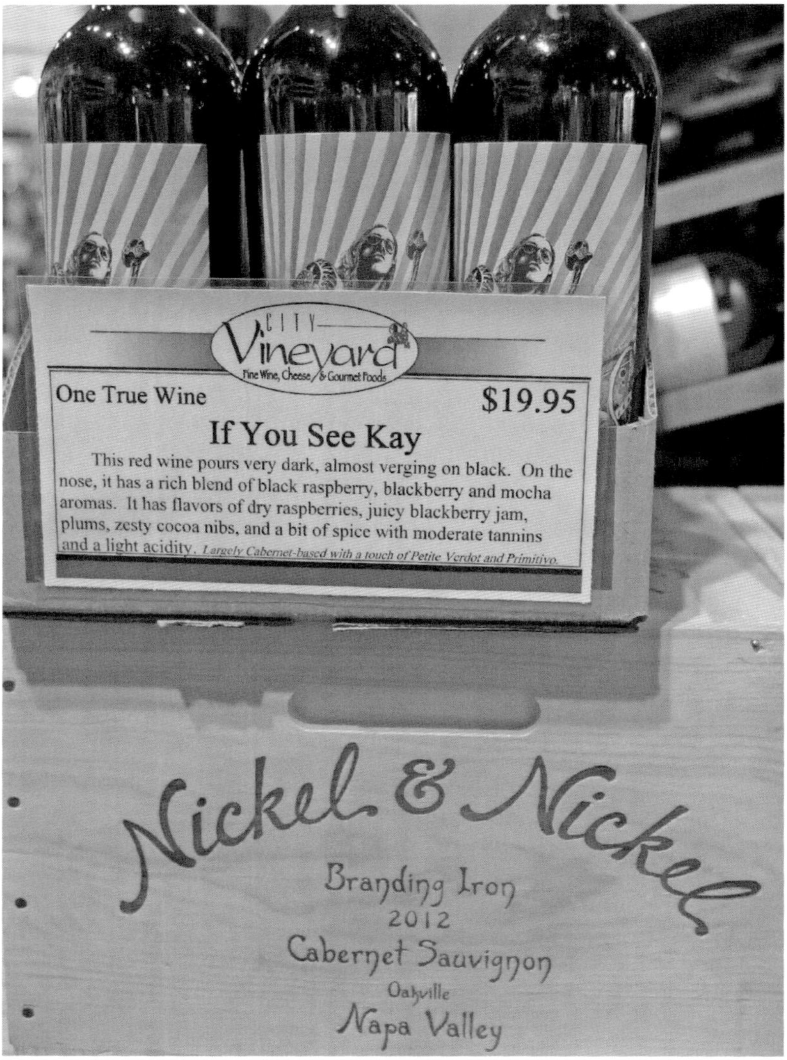

Wine notes from staff at City Vineyard, Fine Wine, Cheese and Gourmet Foods.

bar traveling to entertainment venues, athletic events and private functions. It hopes to open in downtown Billings in the near future and is preparing to launch a bar in Sacramento, California.

For those who want to secure a cup of coffee without leaving their cars, Mountain Mudd Espresso and Revel Coffee Roasters can pass you a cup of Joe just by rolling down your window. At Revel Coffee, Gary Theisen Jr. brews coffee that "eludes perfection." With beans he personally roasts, he is constantly striving to create the perfect cup out of his kiosk found in a parking lot on Grand Avenue. His beans have earned ninety-plus points from *Coffee Review*.

Rock Creek Coffee Roasters provides the best view of Billings' SkyPoint and downtown life through soaring windows. With exposed ducting, hanging ceiling fans, wood counters and tables, a vintage air dominates. There is ample space to linger for work or conversation, but the real heart of the café is found in the back corner, where a working Diedrich coffee roaster sits surrounded by canvas bags of coffee beans. The beans it roasts go into making espresso drinks but also provide for four styles of brewing: Chemex, Aeropress, Hario and French press.

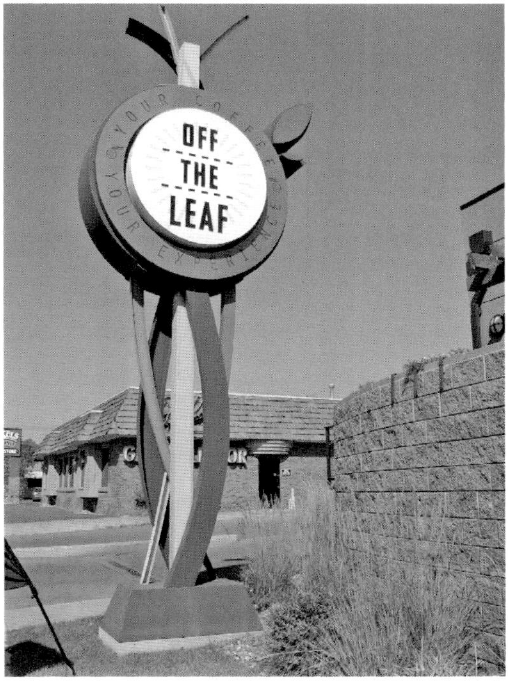

Off the Leaf Coffee Company, established in 2008 at 819 Grand Avenue. *Photo by Deborah Goffena.*

Harper and Madison, owned by Joanie Swords, opened in the hospital corridor neighborhood in 2010, creating an intimate space to serve the cakes and desserts she had created for her past businesses, Poet Street Market and Dancing Oven, both of which she birthed and then sold to other proprietors. The café is filled with details and infused with chic modern touches. Sandwiches are filled with innovative combinations like the "California" with "shaved carrots, sweet bell peppers, onion, avocado, sunflower seeds, cheddar, radish sprouts and an avocado wasabi dressing." Panini include the "Market Club" with "turkey, bacon, avocado, provolone and cilantro cream." The breakfast sandwich special comes wrapped in parchment tied with a string, while the quiche has a tall collar of crust. To accompany the delectable food, a hot cup of coffee brewed from local beans such as those from Revel Coffee Roaster provides the perfect infusion for morning alertness.

In Boston Harbor, owner Cathie Boston brews aromatic teas for improving the spirit and soul. Boston's philosophy is that tea benefits

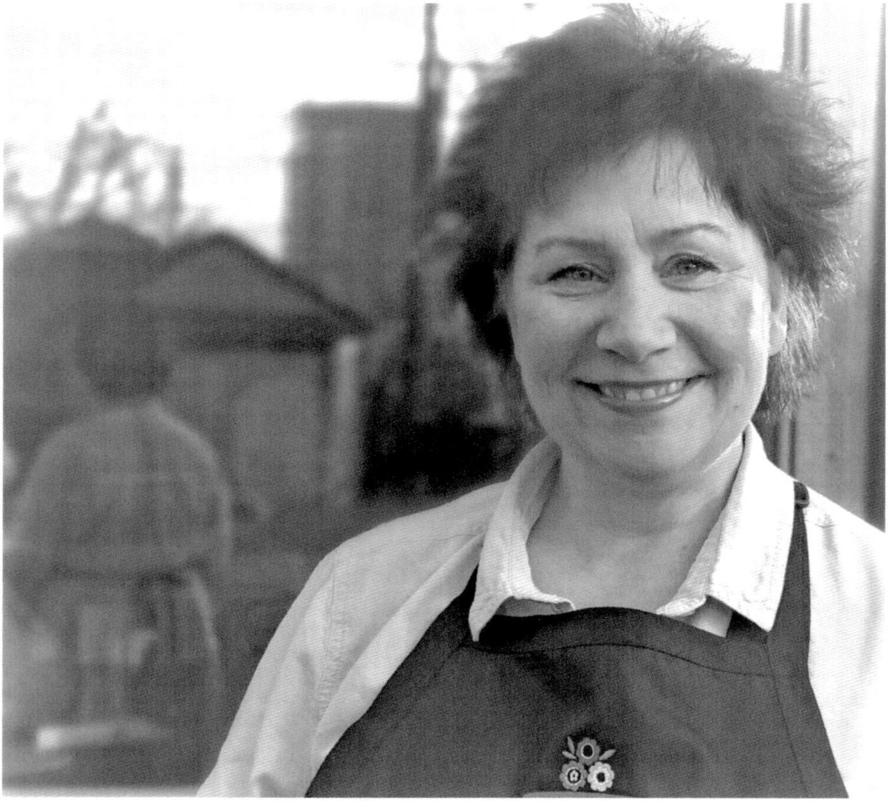

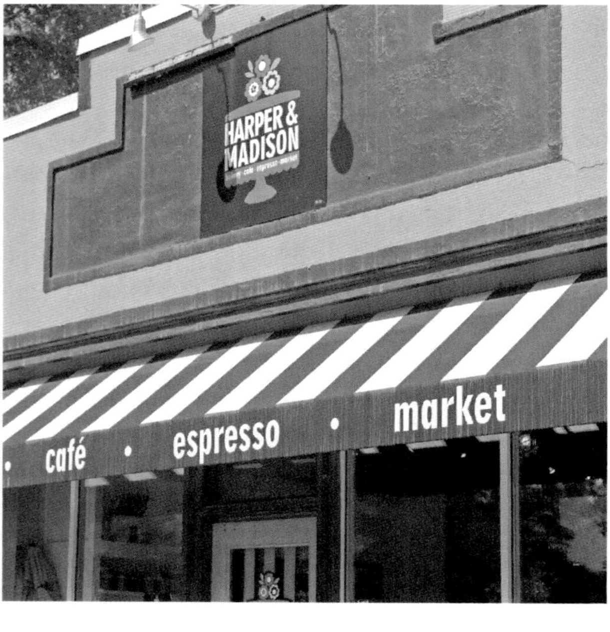

Above: Joanie Swords, owner of Harper and Madison.

Left: Harper and Madison, a neighborhood gem where comfort food and culinary delights are enjoyed.

customers both physically and emotionally. When Boston was diagnosed with an ailment that required surgery in her twenties, a homeopath recommended she stop drinking coffee and cease taking the medication she was on at the time. To her surprise, her health improved. In 2002, Boston opened her tea shop where she sells tea leaves and brews tea to satisfy her passions of healing and tea. Though she has a drive-through, her tearoom is reminiscent of being in someone's parlor. In the back, a brick patio with a rock garden, flowers and a green lawn is the perfect backdrop for iced tea in the summer.

Out in Shiloh Crossing is Tea City and Cupcakes, opened by Jeanne and Cameron Bullard in the summer of 2015. Here they took over the space that Tipsy Cupcake had occupied. The Bullards offer loose-leaf and prepackaged teas and tea accessories for sale, but the real treat is to come here for a cupcake, such as a Red Velvet or Snickers, accompanied by a cup of freshly steeped tea.

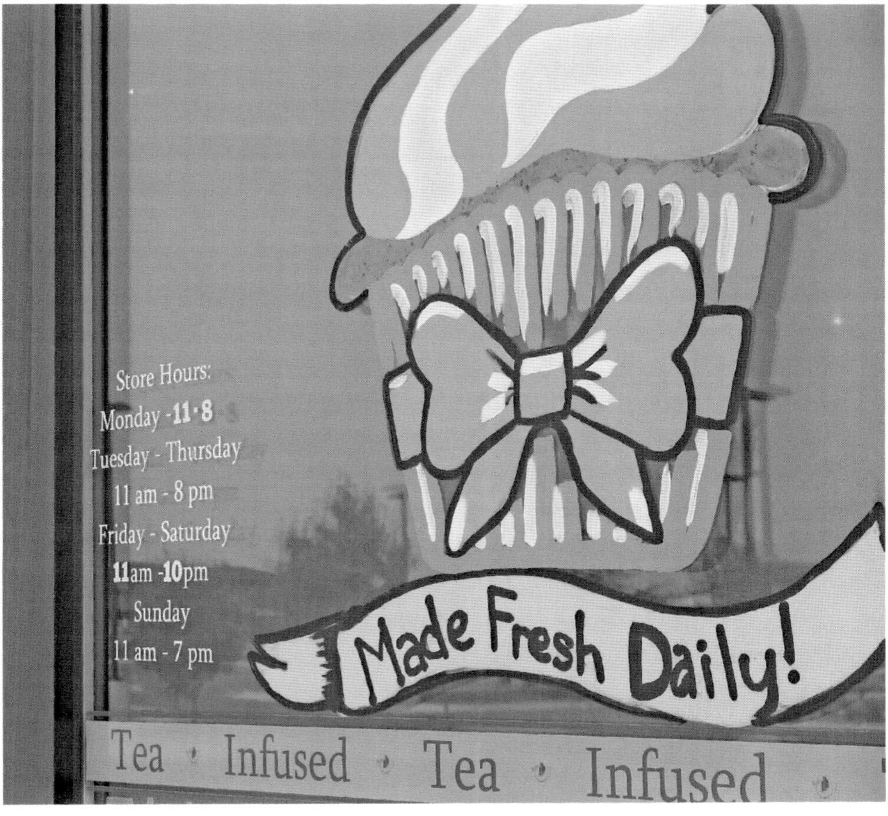

Tea City and Cupcakes, located in Shiloh Crossing.

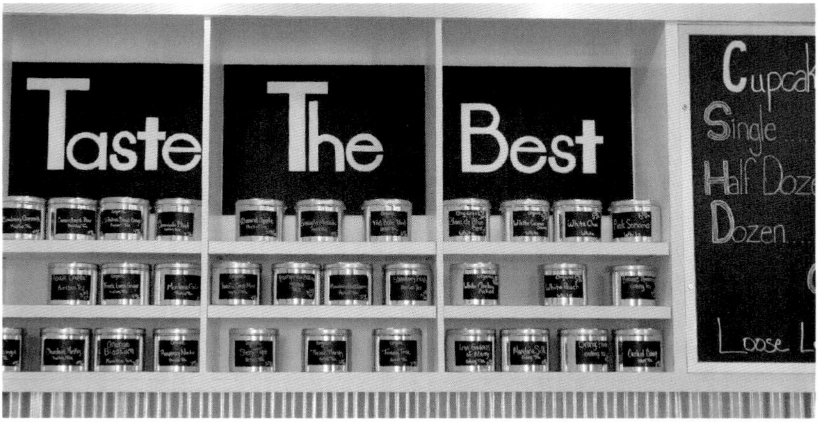

Tea City and Cupcakes offers the finest loose-leaf teas and delectable cupcakes.

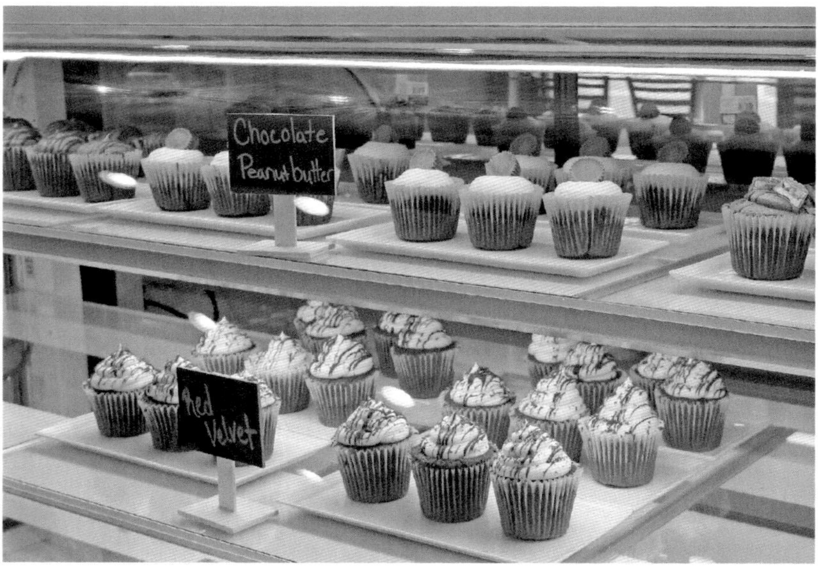

Chocolate Peanut Butter, Red Velvet and Snickers cupcakes found at Tea City and Cupcakes.

Billings has moved aside the percolator for machines with pressurized hot water to pull flavor and caffeine from finely ground coffee beans. The sound of forced steam bubbling into milk to create light fluffy foam is here to stay. Already roasted coffee beans are sprouting java jolt outlets here in Billings. Perhaps soon an espresso can be sipped at every corner, as in European cities and urban centers on the West Coast such as San Francisco, Portland, Seattle and Berkeley.

Chapter 17

SLICE OF PIZZA PIE

Pizza may just be a flatbread topped with tomato sauce and cheese, but it is food that brings people together, tasting so much better when shared. Brought home or to a party, or just enjoyed at the restaurant, just about anyone loves a pizza pie.

Here in Billings, several companies made their start in Big Sky country. Village Inn Pizza Parlor has been a mainstay on Grand Avenue for over thirty years. The dark wood and stone A-frame building serves up not just pizza but also steak, sandwiches and salads. If you are feeling a bit nostalgic, this is the place to come.

MacKenzie River Pizza Company opened in downtown Bozeman in 1993, serving some of the first gourmet pies. Billings has two outlets, one in the Heights and the other located on the West End on Grand Avenue. Sporting a rustic theme, the décor includes carved wood bears, canoes dangling from the wood-beamed ceiling, antlers, buffalo skulls and fish-themed blankets. The pizzas take on names such as "Rancher," "Stockman," "Flathead" and "Branding Iron." One of its most distinctive touches is the addition of Grape-nuts to salads for added crunch. The "Lodgepoles" (breadsticks) feature olive oil, garlic and mozzarella served with a marinara sauce. Servers provide cheerful service. Currently, the company is honing down its menu and launching a new concept: MacKenzie River Pizza, Grill & Pub.

Grains of Montana Restaurant and Bakery's motto is "Fresh baked goodness from our family farm to your family table." In 2005, Kyle and

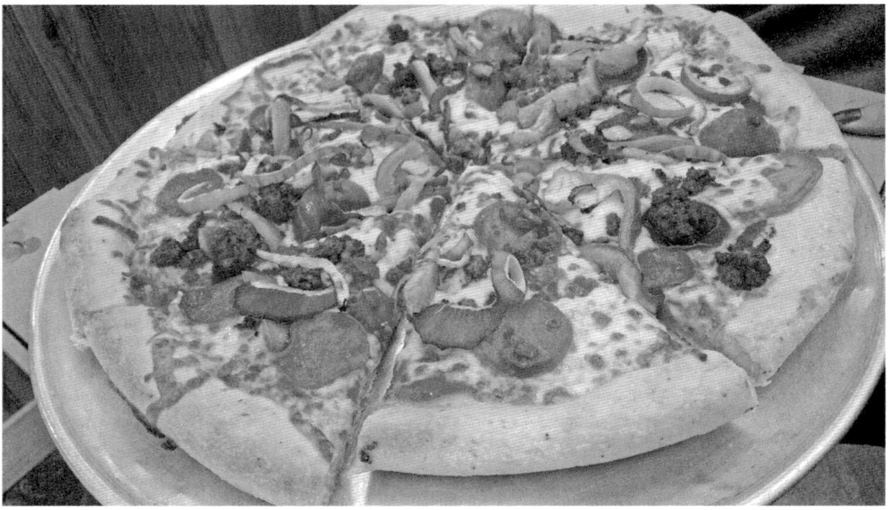

"Rancher Pizza" from MacKenzie River Company with tomato sauce, ground beef, pepperoni, smoky bacon, tomatoes, red onions, green peppers and mozzarella.

Travis Nielsen opened their first facility at 926 Grand Avenue with hopes of expanding nationwide with franchises baking bread and serving food. They process the McNeal Spring wheat they have grown since 1965 on their Nashua, Montana farm. The wheat is milled into flour used in the "Wood Stone Oven Pizzas." The advertised "mouth watering toppings" are approachable with choices such as pepperoni, "BBQ Chicken" and "Four Meat—Italian sausage, Canadian bacon, pepperoni and bacon pile high & pizza sauce." The restaurant has a welcoming fireplace with a cluster of couches and booths by the window where soups, sandwiches and breakfast items such as French toast and pancakes are enjoyed.

Just a few blocks away is Tarantino's Pizzeria. The popular takeout pizza place has branches in Bozeman, Belgrade and Missoula. Its "Grande"- and "Grandioso"-sized pizzas have playful toppings including the "Gyro—Tzatziki sauce, Mozzarella, White Cheddar, Feta, Parmesan, Gyro Meat, Garlic, Fresh Roma Tomatoes, Fresh Basil and Lettuce" and the "Roman Luau—Tomato Basil Sauce, Mozzarella, White Cheddar, Pineapple, Canadian Bacon, and Bacon."

Bullman's Pizza, started in Helena, makes wood-fired pizza in its wood-burning stone oven on the West End. It advertises its pizza to be Neapolitan style with "a lightly crisp, nicely chewy crust with a hint of smoky aroma." Pie Guy Pizzeria, founded by Evan Joda and Steven Nicol, serves ten- to eighteen-inch pizzas at its King Avenue location. The menu is small,

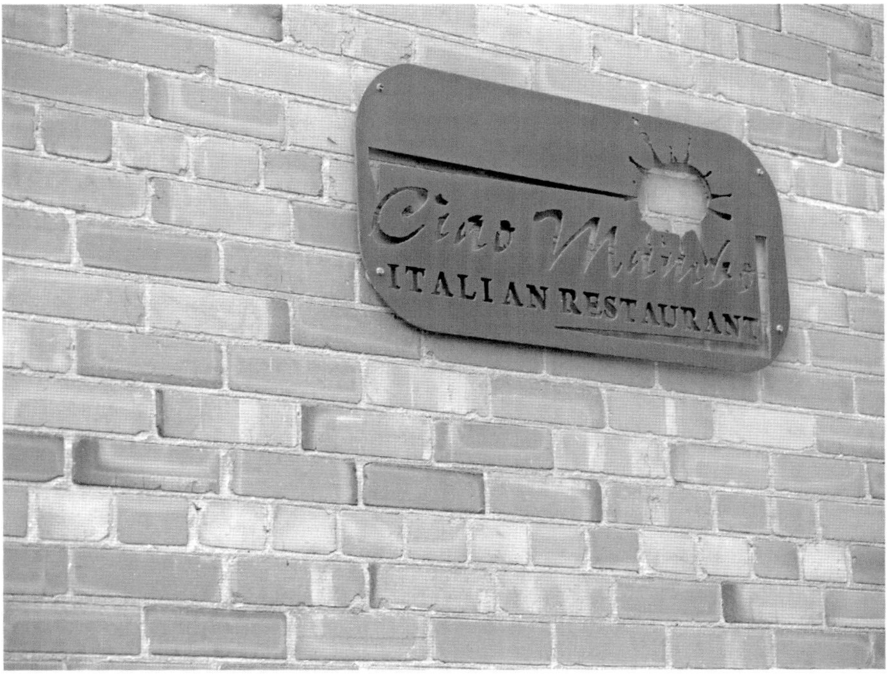

Ciao Mambo, "Where Even the Pasta Is Sexy," is found on Montana Avenue.

featuring chicken wings in the spicy realm and in flavors of garlic or cilantro lime. Pizzas include "The Grail," made with spicy marinara, pepperoni, Italian sausage, bacon, jalapeño and cheddar cheese, and breadsticks called "Styx" are offered plain with pesto or with cinnamon.

Montana Avenue's Ciao Mambo serves up home-style pizza with straightforward toppings such as "pizza rustica—grilled vegetables, goat cheese and housemade tomato sauce" and "pizza volpetti—roasted red potatoes, mozzarella, crispy pancetta and a creamy parmesan sauce."

Pizza brings people together for hearty kinship and dining. The food based on baked dough and then capped with endless possible toppings makes for fun eating.

Chapter 18

SCREAMING FOR ICE CREAM

I have a sweet tooth that saves room for a sugary treat no matter how full I am. After dinner, especially in summer, my dessert of choice is usually a rich, creamy ice cream cone. So when Big Dipper Ice Cream opened downtown, about a mile from where I live, I could not stop screaming for ice cream. Since its opening in April 2015 across from the Northern Hotel, I have not been alone when seeking a cooling reward, as there is usually a line out the door and onto Broadway.

Big Dipper, brainchild of Charlie Beaton, now also has locations in Missoula and a franchise in Helena. These days, the company is co-owned by Bryan Hickey and his wife, Sarah, who grew up in Billings. The mascot, Coneboy—a young boy carrying an ice cream four times his size—is emblazoned on the marquee outside. Inside, a light blue neon sign that says, "Oh Boy" hangs on the wall and greets the customer when ordering at the counter.

The ice cream is made from Meadow Gold cream and comes in a variety of flavors, including "Black Licorice," "Espresso Heath," "Cardamom" and "Green Tea. There are also three daily specials. Big Dipper Ice Cream has elevated the concept of "local" to another level. Caramel Cookie Waffle Swirl (made from the bakery's scratch cookie pieces) and the Espresso Quake Shake (using Rock Creek Coffee Roasters brew) demonstrate Big Dipper's ability to think out of the scoop. The brownies for the sundae options come from Harper and Madison. Angry Hank's Irish Red beer and the Scottish Ale from the Montana Brewing Company make for unique ice cream. Überbrew and Canyon Creek Brewing will provide beer for future specials.

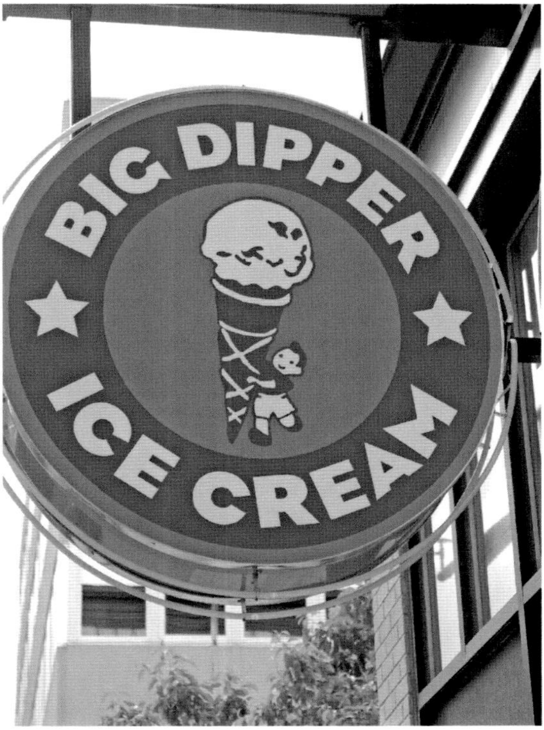

Right: Cone Boy carries a bigger-than-life Big Dipper Ice Cream cone.

Below: Big Dipper Ice Cream serves Montana-made ice cream with flavors such as cardamom and huckleberry.

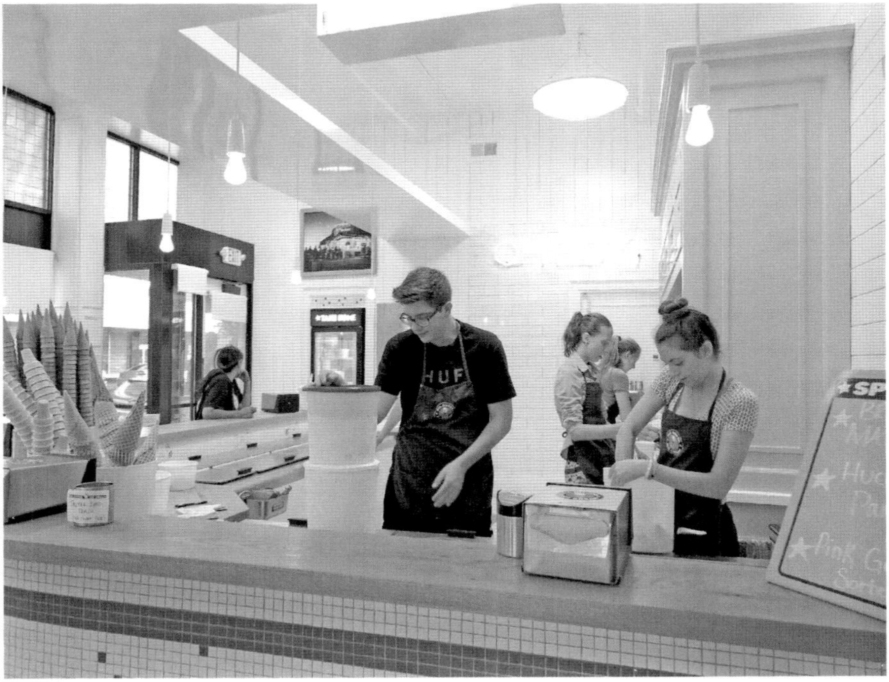

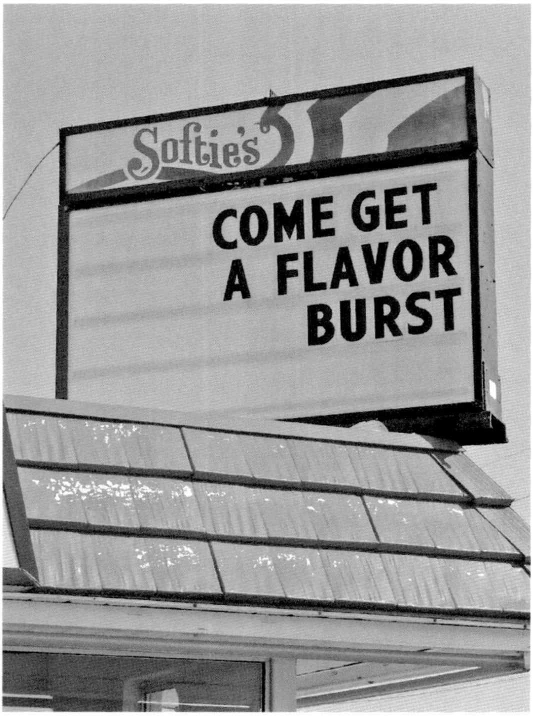

Summer does not officially start until Softie's opens for the season at 2407 Broadwater Avenue. *Photo by Deborah Goffena.*

As with the ice cream, the space is pure, with high ceilings, white tiles and white boards. Blue and white mosaic tiles speckle the floor, while a tall butter-colored mantel unit frames the back wall behind the long, curved counter. A bank of windows affords views of the bustling activity on First Avenue North.

Softie's, a seasonal ice cream shop, located at Twenty-fourth Street West and Broadwater, has been the iconic summer cooling stop for nearly eighteen years. Opened by Mike Glennon, the walk-up kiosk swirls many a soft ice cream onto a cone or into a cup. Dipped cones, chocolate-covered frozen bananas called "monkey tails," slushies, flavor burst with vanilla soft serve edged with various flavors, blitz-it and soft-serve yogurt are some of Softie's specialties. There is no seating, so summer weather encourages getting out of the car, standing in line and then ordering a treat. While you enjoy your ice cream, you probably will run into a neighbor or friend also licking up summer coolness.

Wilcoxson's Ice Cream, a longtime Billings favorite, was established in Livingston over one hundred years ago. At the 114 North Nineteenth Street store, scoops of ice cream in flavors of "Mountain Berry," "Carmel Apple" and "Stuck in a Rut" are scooped up for immediate enjoyment. The ice cream can be purchased in nearly all frozen sections in local grocery stores.

Even more decadent are the serve-yourself ice cream and yogurt outlets. At places such as Spinners, U-Do Yogurt and Billings Best Yogurt, you can create your own ice cream treat, no holds barred. This means you can choose the flavor, dispense the amount you want, spoon on as little or as much topping as you want—choosing among cookie crumbs, sprinkles, candies, fruit and cake chunks—and then drizzle on a finishing sauce of chocolate, caramel or marshmallow, and then perhaps a squirt of whipped cream. The moment of delicious truth comes when your concoction is weighed and a price is placed on your tasty treat.

During the warm months in Billings, crying for ice cream will help squelch your personal summer heat. These days, there are a variety of ice creams and frozen yogurts in flavor and style. I will scream for that.

Chapter 19

CARAMEL COOKIE WAFFLES

THE ICONIC HANDMADE TREAT OF BILLINGS

For nearly twenty-five years, Jan and Judy Boogman have handcrafted Dutch stroopwafels in an unassuming strip mall location on Seventeenth Street at Caramel Cookie Waffles, Artisan Stroopwafels and Cafe. The cookies are so recognizable that on a recent trip out of town, the TSA agent at the airport knew exactly what I had in my carry-on suitcase as a two-pack was scanned through security. The sweet treats often accompany travelers out of Billings, requested by expats living in nearby states or abroad.

On cold mornings, steam obscures the bakery's windows, as the couple press, bake and fill thousands of cookies. Though they have had many opportunities to mechanize and move into a larger space, they have persisted in the original location. Though the wafer is machine-made, the sandwich construction of spreading caramel onto the cookie and the sealing of the wafers are all done by hand.

Two thin waffle-indented golden brown wafers, the diameter of a baseball, sandwich a layer of thick, rich caramel. The cookies are the perfect combination of crunchy crust with a gooey center, combined with just enough sweet richness and spices of cinnamon, cloves and vanilla. The cookie breaks easily when bitten into, and as you chew, the caramel wraps itself around the rich crumbs. Then a symphony of butter and spice rises onto your palate. On the bakery's website, it recommends putting the cookie on top of a cup of warm coffee to let the steam soften the caramel for the ultimate gustatory experience.

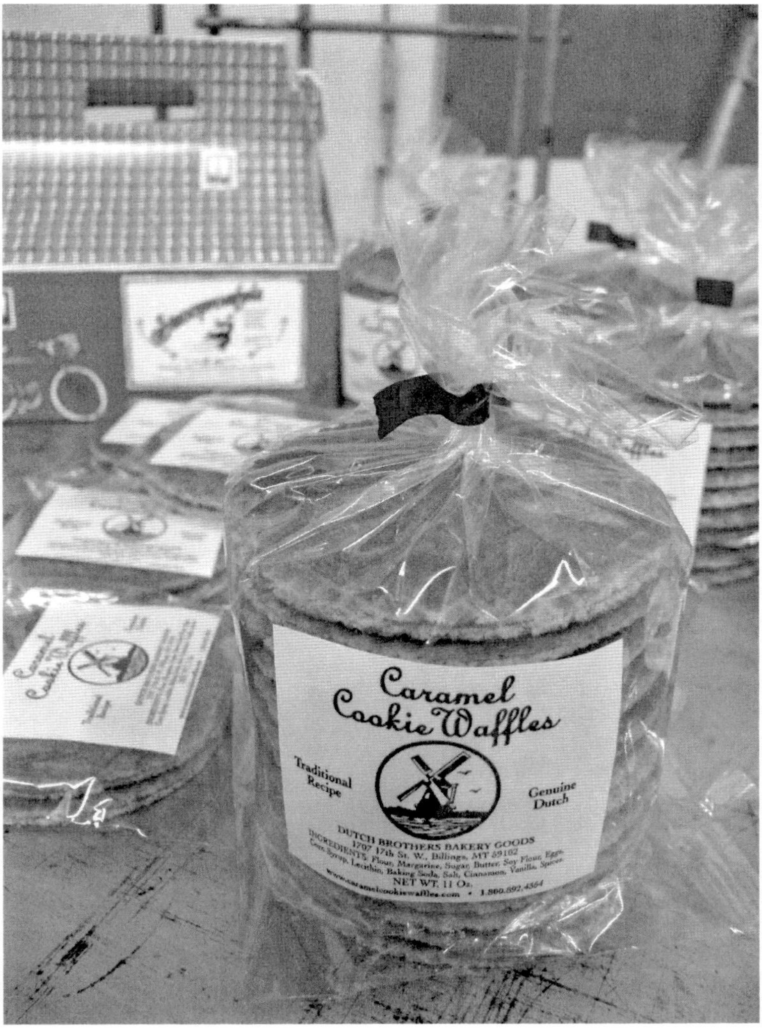

Caramel Cookie Waffles stroopwafels, a traditional Dutch treat, are handmade by the owners, Jan and Judy Boogman. *Photo by Deborah Goffena.*

A fresh batch is made nightly, combining sugar, butter and corn syrup in a sixteen-gallon pot. At 5:00 a.m. the next morning, butter, eggs, flour, sugar and spices are added to an industrial mixer and stirred to a texture that Jan now knows innately. The seasons influence how this dough sets up, so Jan goes by feel and sight, adding extra flour or liquids as needed.

Equipment is pushed in and out of place as each task is completed to make room for subsequent steps. After the mixer is cleaned, it is moved to make room for the dough extruder, a tool much like a pasta maker. The rhythmic clack, whack, grind and squeak repeat, setting a metronomic pace in the workspace. Jan feeds in large pieces of dough, the size of a soccer ball, that he divided up earlier.

As Jan flicks on a small conveyor belt located next to the cookie oven, he calls out, "One minute and we will be going!" Jan stands in front of the oven with an opening at chest level as wide as outstretched arms. Eight iron griddles warm up on a round track perched over fingers of blue flames. Jan places four "dough pillows" on an iron that automatically moves clockwise. The iron closes, cooks, flips over, cooks and opens to reveal golden brown wafers that are lifted off with a spatula. The cookies go on the conveyor belt and, as they travel down, are trimmed with a round mold and split through the middle by a thin wire. The cookie is picked up, split open, coated with caramel and sandwiched back together. No gloves are used, as tactile sensation is important when distributing the caramel evenly onto the cookies. Four thousand cookies later, at around 9:00 a.m., cookie making is complete for the day.

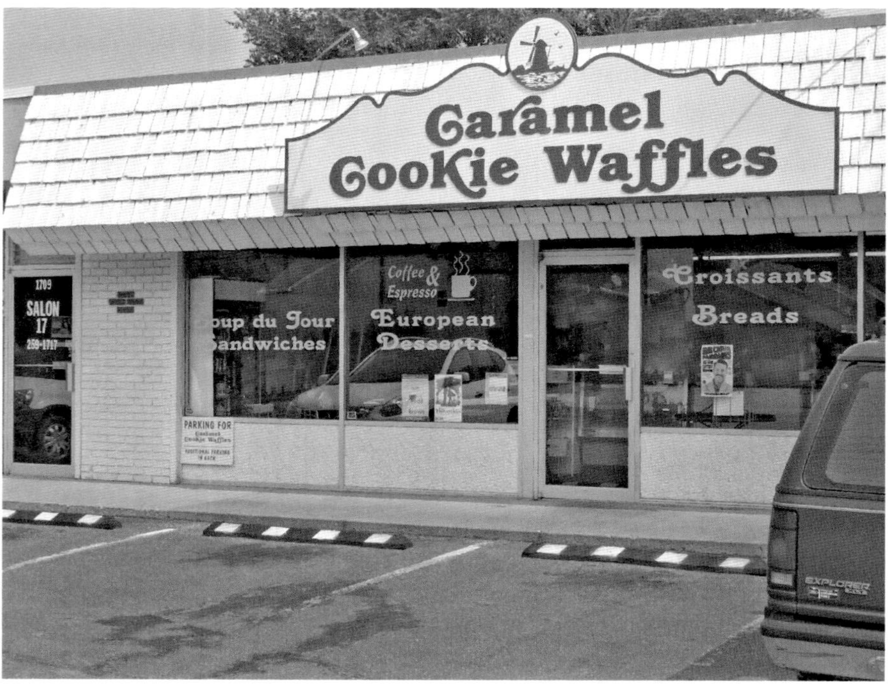

Caramel Cookie Waffles, located at 1701 Seventeenth Street. *Photo by Deborah Goffena.*

Cookies are made freshly throughout the week, with production ramping up during the holidays, when colorful boxes filled with cookies make popular gifts. Aside from the cookies, soups are homemade with stock made from whole chickens. Daily fresh croissants and fruit and cream cheese pastries are baked along with cookies such as "Nainamo bars" and "Oatmeal Haystack Cookies." Judy is famous for her "Dutch Almond Apple Cake" and cheesecakes. Whole wheat and sunflower breads are also baked in house, and a slice always comes with homemade soup that rotates weekly (with the menu posted on caramelcookiewaffles.com).

Caramel Cookie Waffles is the epitome of a neighborhood and family bakery and café. The owners work hard and impart a part of themselves into every item they sell. At lunchtime, there is always a line for their sandwiches and soup. People gather for comfortable conversation at tables in the homey, open space featuring the work of local artists and photographers. This intimate yet approachable café will satisfy the most demanding sweet cravings.

Chapter 20

SPIRITED BILLINGS

BREWERIES, DISTILLERIES AND WINERY

The citizens of Billings will not go thirsty anytime soon as watering holes continue to spring forth. Seven beer breweries are crafting award-winning brews, and now, two distilleries and a winery are fermenting spirited beverages. It began in 1994, when Himmelberger Brewing Company and the Montana Brewing Company came on the scene. Montana Brewing Company made its home on the bottom floor of the 1887 Montana Power Company Building, while Himmelberger, claiming to be the first microbrewery in town, supplied wholesale brew out of a home operation.

Suds-making dates back to 1900, when the Billings Brewing Company opened on Montana Avenue in a three-story brick building. The goal of proprietors Henry Mueller, Louis Best and Phil Grein was to make beer that would make Milwaukee jealous, and they did so until closing their doors in 1959. Bottles from the Billings Brewing Company were recently discovered stashed in the foundation of the old Yellowstone Garage on Montana Avenue during construction of Überbrew.

Überbrew

Is it a coincidence that Mark Hastings is the beer maker at Überbrew? Hastings was the first master brewer for Montana Brewing Company, along with Sam Hoffmann, now of Red Lodge Ales. Hastings also created beer at Sleeping

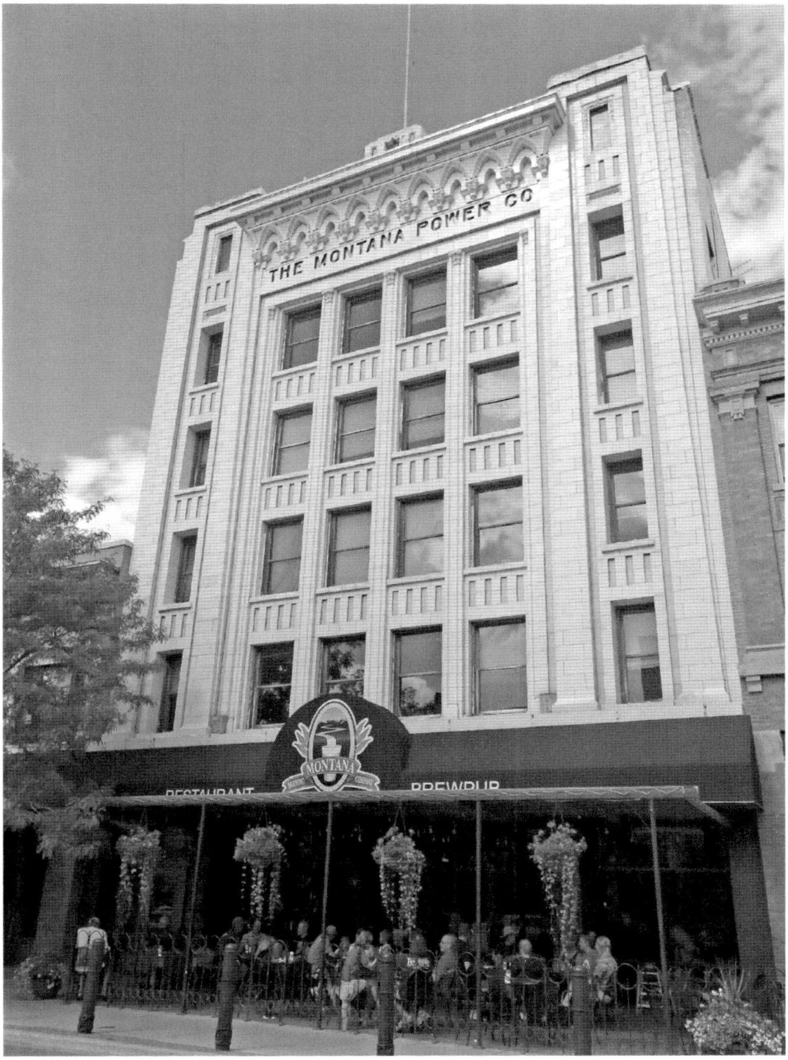

Montana Brewing Company, a small brewery, saloon and restaurant with sidewalk seating.

Giant Brewery (now known as the Lewis and Clark Brewing Company) in Rimrock Mall when the Helena-based business expanded to Billings. Now ensconced at Überbrew, he is fermenting his dream after teaming up with Jason Shroyer in 2012. The pair brews grain and hops in a period building owned by Ken and Sandy Kunkel and John and Joan Grauman. Ken and John, award-winning home brewers, live vicariously through the venture and consider the lease to Hastings and Shroyer a natural fit. The building has tall ceilings for

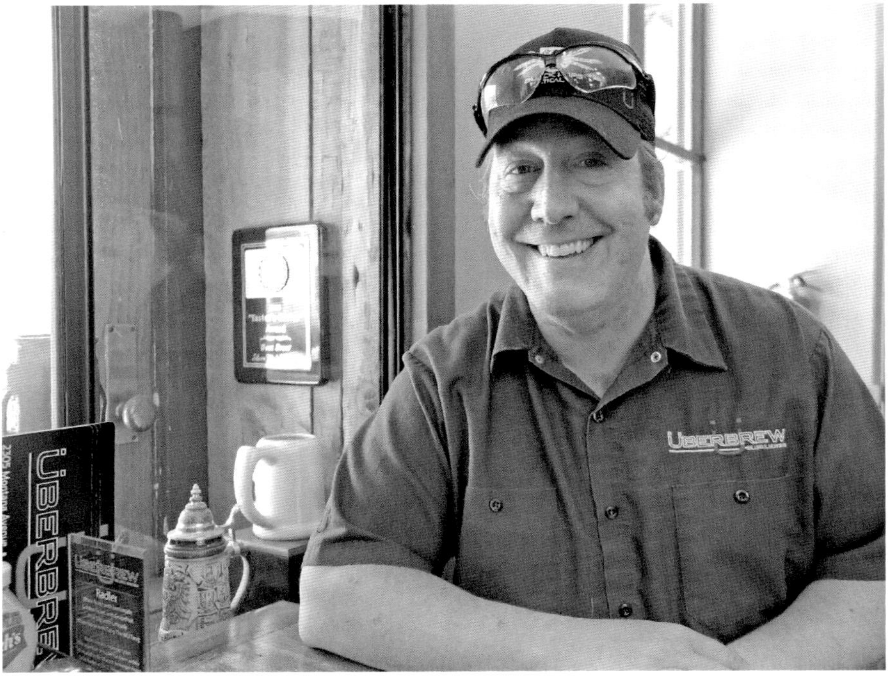

Brewmaster Mark Hastings of Überbrew.

the brewing tanks and skylights for generous natural lighting. Hastings says of the name of his venture, "In the Merriam-Webster Dictionary, *über* is the superlative example of something. Überbrew is the superlative pint of beer." Right now, it appears to be the über situation.

Überbrew is the culmination of years of hard work. While earning a business management degree from the University of Mary, North Dakota, Hastings had studied the success of companies such as Pyramid Breweries, Redhook Brewery and Samuel Adams. He manages the brewing and culinary matters while Shroyer, a home-brewer with a love of music and physics, is handling the business end of things. Hastings admits, "I thought the food was the hardest part." Friendships with local restaurant experts such as the Honakers, Laurent Zirotti, Alan Sparboe and Mike Callahan provided valuable insight. With help from restaurant consultant Sean Nystul, the micropub came to be. Before that, Hastings's resume included experience with MacKenzie River Pizza Company and two years working the front of the house at the Granary.

Überbrew has an extensive menu serving appetizers, from "Smoked Chicken Wings" to "Bacon and Eggs" of "candied brown sugared bacon served with deviled eggs" to a "German Egg Roll" with a fried Bockwurst encased with sauerkraut in an eggroll wrapper. Burgers, sandwiches, sausages and salads are also offered to please all diners. For example, under the burger selection, the "Über burger" with a half pound of meat topped with a hot beer sausage and peppers is balanced with the "Tempeh Burger" made with soy-marinated tempeh.

Hastings focuses on making beers that satisfy the Billings lifestyle. "I spent two years brewing Hefeweizen and brown ale." These days, White Noise and Stand Down Brown are the popular brews. Überbrew's flagship beer, White Noise, described as an "American-style Hefeweizen brewed with imported German malt and hops," was what Hastings believed to be "a good idea of what Billings was like. People work very hard, play very hard here. We wanted to make a lighter thirst quencher."

A couple years after opening, validation of Hastings and Shroyer's efforts arrived when White Noise took second place in the World Beer Cup in Boulder, Colorado. The beer arrived on retail shelves at the end of 2014. Six months later, their English-style ale, Stand Down Brown, was also distributed in bottles. Hastings and Shroyer contracted with Fort Collins Brewery in

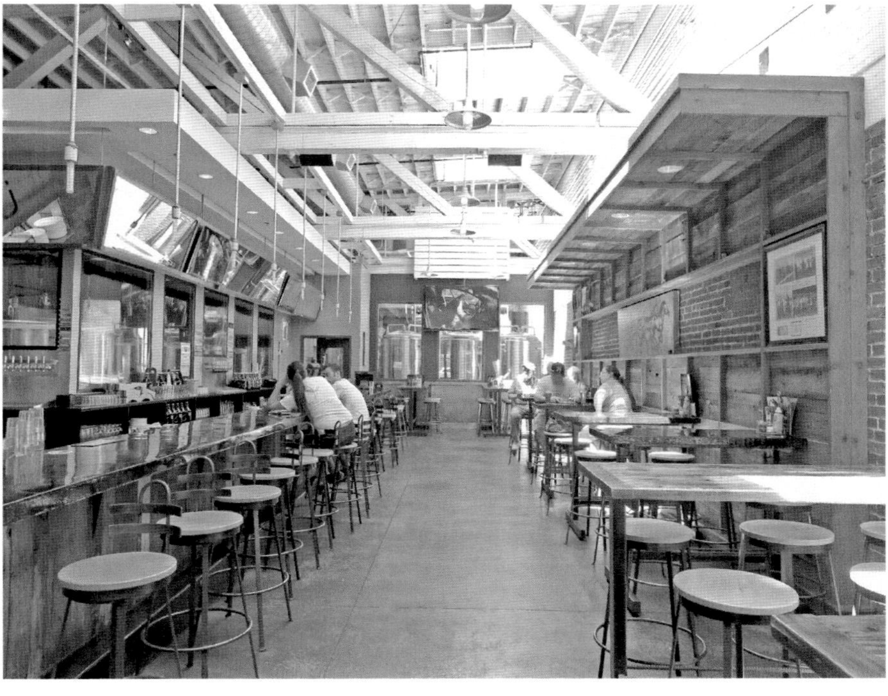

The interior of Überbrew, inside the restored Yellowstone Garage.

Colorado to bottle their beers after crunching the numbers and opting out of building a local bottling facility.

Hastings's vision for the future involves beer agritourism. He sees a "From Grain to Glass" opportunity, much like the travel and learning experiences found in wine country. Currently, there is a "Walking Brewery District Map" available from the Billings Chamber of Commerce for a self-guided tour of the unofficial brewery district with a few historical highlights. The tourist should keep in mind a couple rules set by Montana law, such as a brewery can only serve a customer three pints of beer and taprooms without a liquor license must close by 8:00 p.m.

Yellowstone Valley Brewing Company

The tour outlined by the "Walking Brewery District" from the Billings Chamber of Commerce begins at the "The Garage" or the Yellowstone Valley Brewing Company, which was opened by George Moncure and Jay Shearer in 1997. This venue inside a repurposed auto repair space has also established itself as a great place for music. The stage hosts entertainment four times a week, with a focus on raising money for the community. At "The Garage," beer names take on a fly-fishing theme. Grizzly Wulff Wheat, Wild Fly Ale and Wooley Bugger (Grand Cru) Root Beer, along with Huckle-weizen and Black Widow Oatmeal Stout, have become signature brews. Adjacent to the brewery, the recently launched Spirit of Montana Distilling creates Cliffhanger Vodka and 40 Love Gin, both made with spring water from Froze to Death Plateau Ice Fields above Red Lodge.

Trailhead Spirits and Carter's Brewing

The next stops on the tour—Trailhead Spirits and Carter's Brewing—are all located on Montana Avenue. Found in the Beanery building in the historic Depot complex, Trailhead Spirits produces small-batch handcrafted spirits. Owners Casey and Steffanie McGowan are distilling the spirit created in the 1920s by his uncle Michael Healy, proprietor of the Radio Bar in Butte. With a family farm in Highwood, Montana, just outside Great Falls, growing wheat, barley and oats and Casey's degree in agriculture, the groundwork was laid to venture into this new business. Finally, while on a trip to Portland, Oregon, Casey visited a bar with a wide selection of locally sourced vodkas and realized that there was a market for local spirits here in Billings.

For almost two years, the McGowans navigated the legal obstacle course in their pursuit of a distilling license. By Montana law, they needed a building before they could obtain the license. This meant they had to lease a space, which necessitated keeping their day jobs—his in insurance and hers in marketing. They purchased a custom high-tech distilling system from Hungary with a delivery time of six months; it was to come with five installers. The machine arrived six months late and with a single installer, the owner of the company. At the eleventh hour, immigration issues prevented the entire team from entering the United States. "Eventually, we finally figured out how to put it all together," Casey says. Now, in the back room, a three-hundred-liter hand-hammered copper still with a towering sixteen-plate column designed by Arnold Holstein of Markdorf, Germany, fits into the space like a glove.

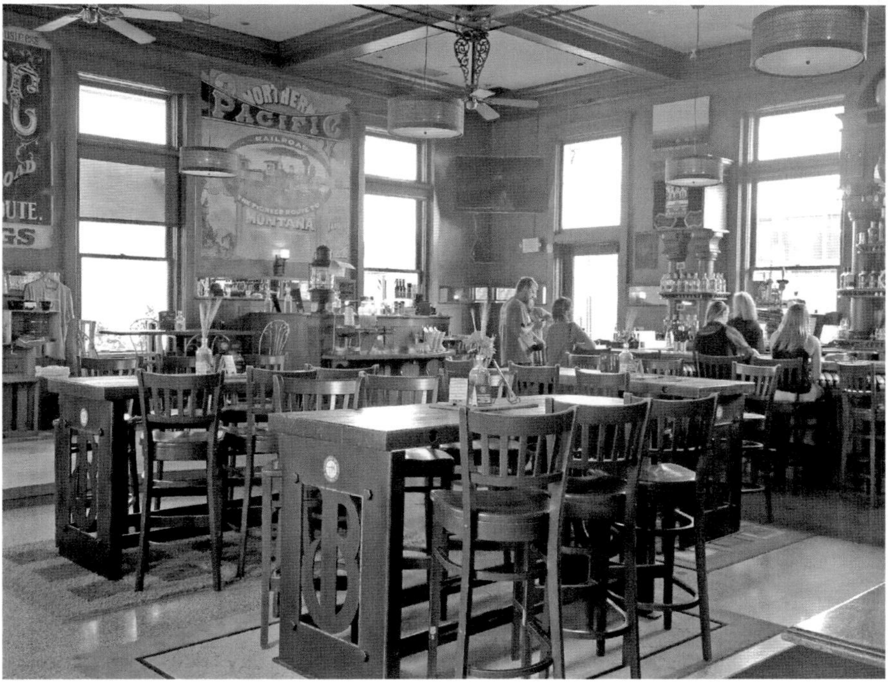

The tasting room of Trailhead Spirits was the original Beanery building, where passengers could find a bite to eat and something to drink.

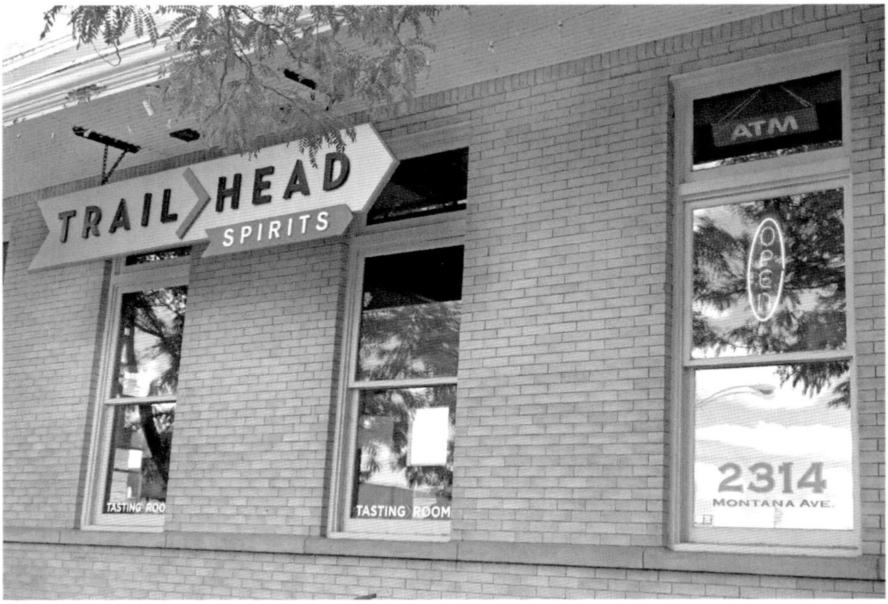

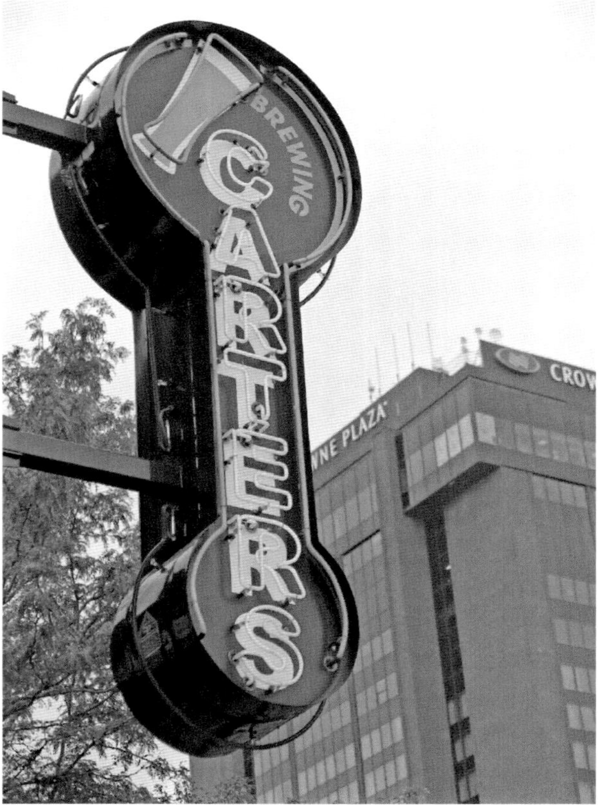

Above: Trailhead Spirits, owned by Casey and Steffanie McGowan, makes vodka and whiskey with grains from their family Highwood, Montana farm.

Left: Carter's Brewing on Montana Avenue next to the railroad tracks.

Under Montana law, distilleries can serve only two ounces of liquor per customer per day. The cocktails they serve, such as the "Vojito" (made with "Great North Vodka, lemonade, strawberries, mint and soda water") and "Big Sky Sage" (composed of "Healy's Gin, orange juice, honey and sage"), are thirst quenching and satisfying. The Great North is short for the Great Northern Railroad and appropriate to their location, given their proximity to the tracks. The gin is named in honor of Casey's uncle. Trailhead Spirits also offers Highwood Rye Malt Whisky and Highwood Chocolate Flavored Whiskey for dessert.

Heading west on Montana Avenue is Carter's Brewing, where brewmaster Michael Ulrich has produced his namesake beer since 2007. Prior to opening his own shop, he was head brewer at the Yellowstone Valley Brewing Company. Around the time of the birth of his first son, Carter James, he opened Carter's Brewing. His train logo honors his son's love of trains and his location adjacent to the iron tracks. His bottles sport names such as Handcar Hefe, Derailed IPA, Train Wreck Imperial IPA and Boxcar Brown Ale.

Angry Hank's Micro Brewery and Himmeberger Brewing Company

Montana native Tim Mohr first opened Angry Hank's Micro Brewery in a defunct gas station in 2006 on First Avenue North. Garage doors opened onto a wood-fenced patio sitting next to one of the busiest downtown thoroughfares. With a degree in business already under his belt, Mohr enrolled at UC-Davis to complete a degree in fermentation science. Returning to Montana, Mohr worked at Red Lodge Ales to gain practical beer-making knowledge. After six years at the First Avenue location, Mohr wanted more space and moved his operation to North Thirtieth Street into an old brick building, which he remodeled. Popular beers include Anger Management, Head Trauma IPA and Street Fighter.

Around the corner from Angry Hank's is Himmelberger Brewing Company, owned by Dennis Himmelberger. For seventeen years, he brewed beer for wholesale purchase out of his home on Custer Avenue. Bursting at the seams, he remodeled the 1911 storefront, six times larger, at 3008 North Thirty-first Street, where he now has room for not only a brewery but also a taproom and coffee shop. His beers take on Big Sky names such as North Forty Amber and Whitewater Wheat.

Though not officially on the brewery map, Pug Mahon's Irish Pub is across the street from Himmelberger and is a popular watering hole, especially on St. Patrick's Day. Claiming to be "Only 4000 miles southwest of Dublin," this well-established restaurant and pub has become famous for its generous "Pork Chop Sandwich" with onion rings and "Meat Pastie" with a filling of beef, potatoes and onions. Rest assured that a tall glass of Guinness Stout can always be secured here.

Montana Brewing Company

Down the street, the Montana Brewing Company features award-winning beers and a large menu. There is a wide variety of burgers, salads, pastas, sandwiches and pizza and a "Mac & Cheese" category featuring shell pasta smothered with cheese sauce and options of rock crab, spicy buffalo chicken and bacon, roast beef and even onions and green peppers (the latter named the "Philly Mac"). Master brewer Evan Taylor is at the helm, making beers with names like Custer's Last Stout, Sharptail Pale Ale, Strawberry Wheat and Indian Cliff IPA. Next door, Hooligan's Sports Bar has one of the largest flat screens in Billings and is a popular hangout on game days. Open daily until 2:00 a.m., there is ample opportunity for late-night dining.

Canyon Creek Brewing

Across town on the West End is Canyon Creek Brewing at 3060 Gabel Road. Opened in 2013, it is the newest taproom and brewery in Billings. Here, Ron Halvig is brewing Cold Creek Scottish, a Scotch ale; O.N.S. (One Night Stand) Blond, a golden ale; and Irish Head Red, an Irish red ale, in the recently built brewery with a copper roof. The tasting room is large and spacious, with two patios, perfect for a summer afternoon's quaffing.

Yellowstone Cellars and Winery

Clint Peck's Yellowstone Cellars and Winery is located in the West End in an industrial space south of Highway 90, near Josephine Crossing. Peck has created what he calls a "bookend" boutique winery, including a tasting room, winery and event space, providing a gathering space for local oenophiles. The winery has hosted many special events and fundraisers and features open mic night on Wednesdays and music on Fridays and Saturdays. Cheese, cold cuts and crackers are available for purchase, and food trucks such as Montana Melt (owned by Danielle and Jason Amundsen) show up to sell gourmet grilled cheese sandwiches.

French oak barrels brim Peck's climate-controlled aging room as he gains momentum in his business. Five years ago, he funded his business by selling his house and Harley Davidson motorcycle. He actually lived in the winery for the first few years. With his background as a cattleman and an agriculture/business journalist, he was well aware of the hard work and perseverance

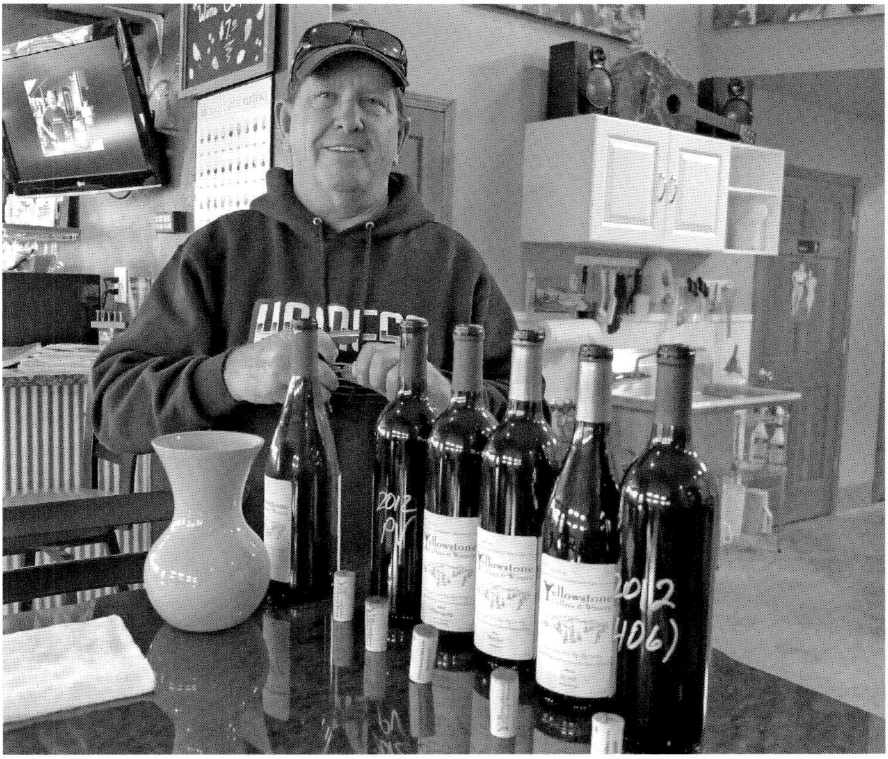

Clint Peck, owner and winemaker of Yellowstone Cellars and Winery.

required to succeed. Peck is always at the winery, working the crowd while working the wine. The grapes are sourced in eastern Washington (Yakima Valley and Rattesnake Hills), and Peck makes several trips in his truck each year to procure fresh product, which is processed in Billings. The annual Grape Stomp and Grape Crush Festival is a celebration of the harvest.

Malbec is his signature wine, with Cabernet Franc, Cabernet Sauvignon and Petit Verdot rounding out his offerings. A few years back, he left a batch of juice making to friends who neglected to label the grapes. In good humor, he named this wine "(406)" for the local area code, and it was a surprise success. The blend was a mix of Merlot, Cabernet Sauvignon and Syrah in unknown proportions. Since the faux pas, Peck continues to make a (406) red blend and enjoys sharing the story behind it. With more than four thousand people on his mailing list, Peck has a loyal following. With his marketing plan maturing along with his wine, he feels comfortable letting his wines age in the bottle before release. Patience has its virtue: *Wine Spectator* awarded Yellowstone Cellars 2010 Malbec a score of eighty-eight.

City Vineyard, Simply Wine, Kennedy's and Bottles and Shots

Good wines can be secured in the Magic City. A handful of specialty wine, beer and spirit stores supply a good range of choices. City Vineyard carries over two thousand different wines along with beers and an excellent selection of cheeses from all over the world. Becky Reno tested the wine business beginning in 1999 and then moved into her current space at Seventeenth Street West and Grand in 2005. Store manager Carolyn Korb has been at the helm of the store and has provided wine and food expertise for years. A wine bar offers the opportunity to explore new wines by the glass or enjoy a bottle of wine with friends, as well as sample a beer.

In Shiloh Crossing, just across the parking lot from Scheels Sporting Goods, is Simply Wine. Sue Rydquist and Stephan Bradley moved here in 2014 to open the wine store and bistro after running their business at Rimrock Mall for three years. The wine bar offers twenty-five wines from the Italian WineEmotion Dispenser and Preservation System from behind a purple- and black-trimmed bar. The color purple sets the tone for the space, along with faux painting and an image of a corkscrew painted by Cindy Smith. The bistro offers panini, salads and cheese to accompany the sips. The store prides itself on having a friendly and

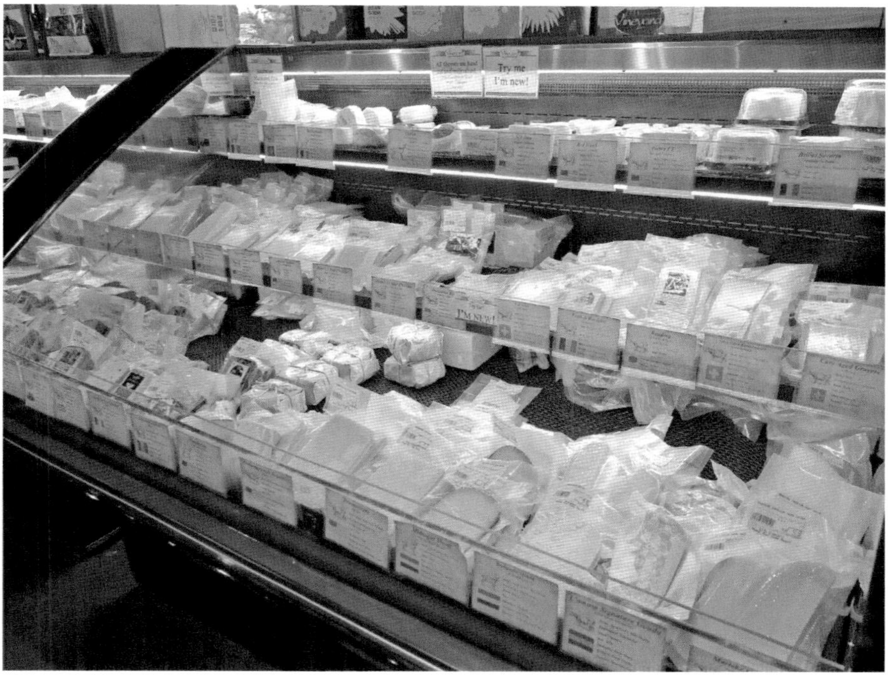

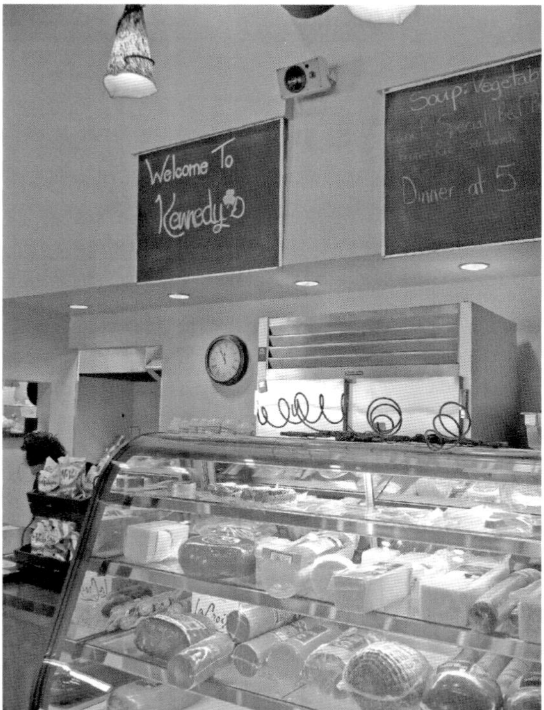

Above: The cheese selection at City Vineyard Wine.

Right: The deli at what is now Kennedy's and was once the Wine Market and Deli, owned by Bill and Mary Kennedy.

helpful staff so customers can "experience wine buying without fear," as expressed in its motto.

Billings natives Bill and Mary Kennedy moved into a new three-thousand-square-foot space in the spring of 2015 to expand the Wine Market and Deli. From their original small storefront, they now had room to start a café with seating and more elbowroom for their catering business. A separate room offers a good selection of wine for purchase. Now renamed Kennedy's, Food, Wine/Beer and Catering, the business extends Bill and Mary's spirit of family, friends and community.

Bottles and Shots Liquor Stores and Club Casino offer wine tastings every Wednesday and Friday evenings. This allows for customers to taste the wines before purchasing. There are two locations, one in the West End and the other in the Heights. They also sell premade Jell-O and pudding shots in a colorful assortment of flavors.

Billings is becoming a "spirited" town. Its population works hard and plays hard and has a thirst that needs quenching. With grain at the heart of local agriculture, brewing and distilling are a logical progression.

Chapter 21

FARE AT THE MONTANAFAIR

Once again, grills and grease are primed to cook up the indulgences that derail diets. As temperatures heighten into the nineties on this second Monday in August, anticipation rises for fare at the MontanaFair held at Metra Park. Though a traditional weeklong agricultural celebration, it is also the annual opportunity to feast on fried or grilled food served on paper plates or sticks or gnaw on a fist-sized turkey leg or lick a bacon ice cream cone. Navigation through the two long rows of food stalls known as the Midway concessions should require the purchase of additional tickets, as eating here is an amusement ride in itself.

The difficulty is planning the strategy of how to attack the stalls. Do we head toward the food we most crave? Appetizer-like foods first? Are we drawn to the most colorful booth or the one with the best slogan? Do we find the food stall with the shortest line or just eat dessert first?

Funnel cake is one of the iconic foods offered at carnivals and fairs. A batter of flour, sugar and egg is poured through a funnel and dripped into hot oil in a swirly spiderlike pattern. The flat cake is dusted with powdered sugar, with or without cinnamon, after being placed on a paper plate. Unlike a doughnut, there is more crispiness than cakiness. The strands of fried dough make for delicious crunchiness. Beth Connaghan comes every year with her daughter Nicole to eat funnel cake for nostalgia's sake. She likes the funnel cakes because they remind her of the beignets she grew up with in New Orleans. "In preparation, I eat salads and super light food for four days. I get a jumpstart so I can

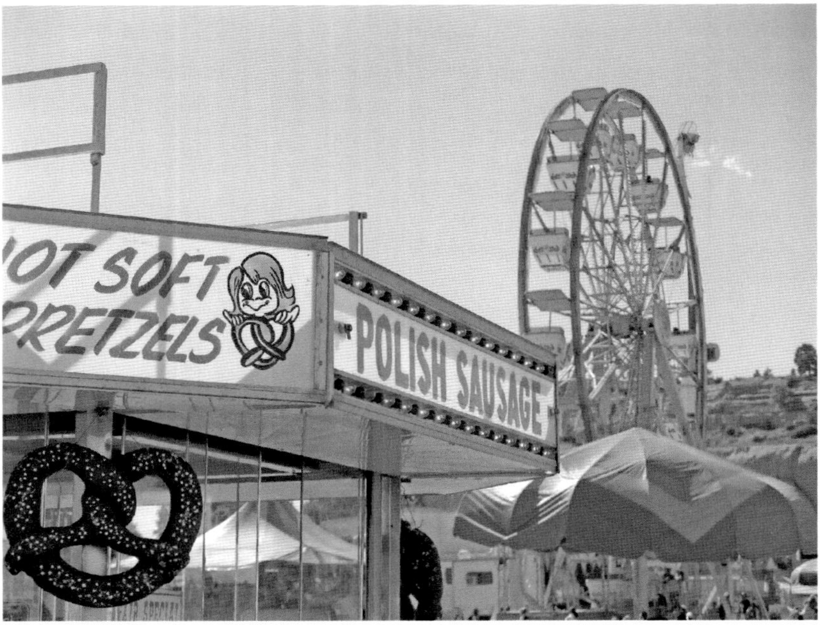

At the MontanaFair, where the Ferris wheel and Polish sausages and pretzels make the world go 'round.

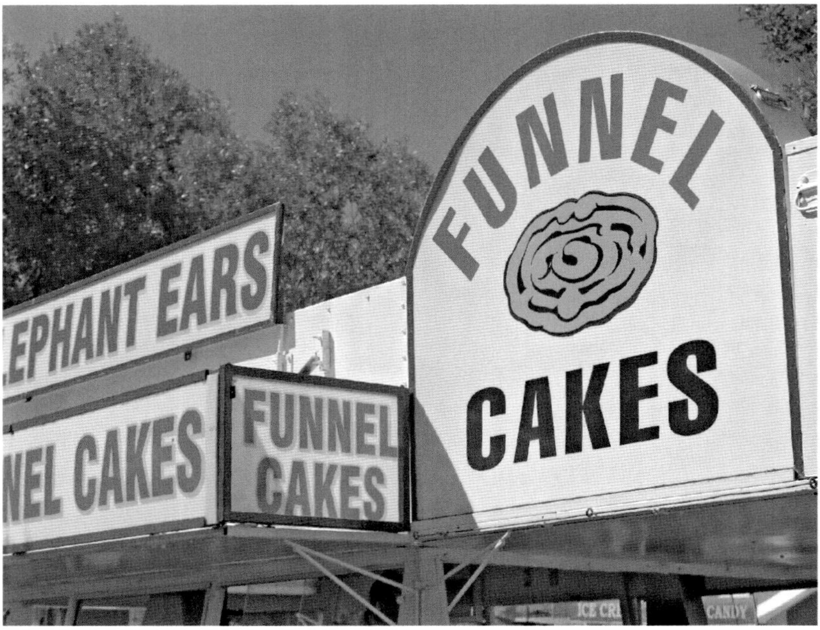

MontanaFair funnel cake concession.

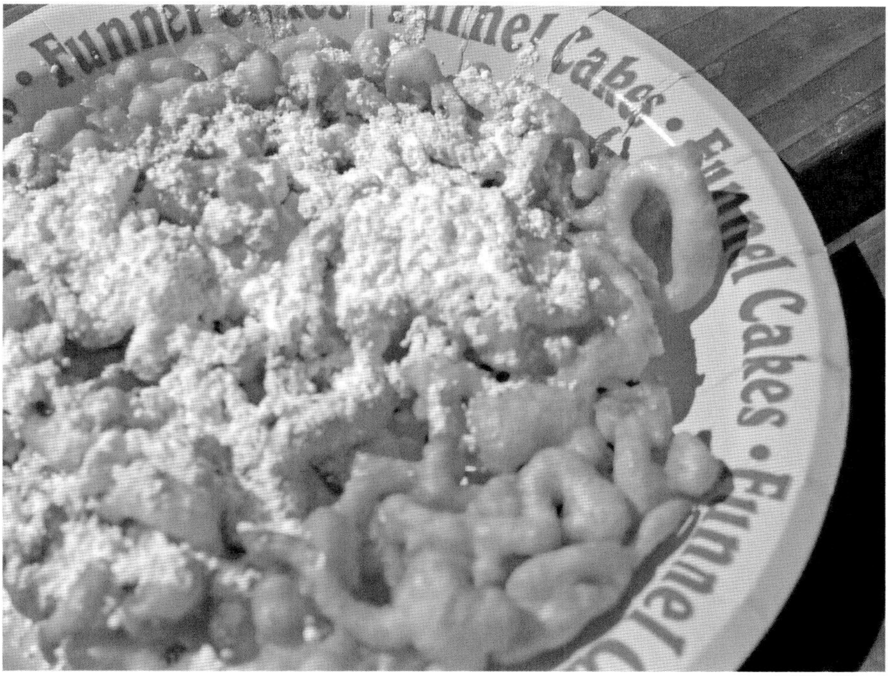

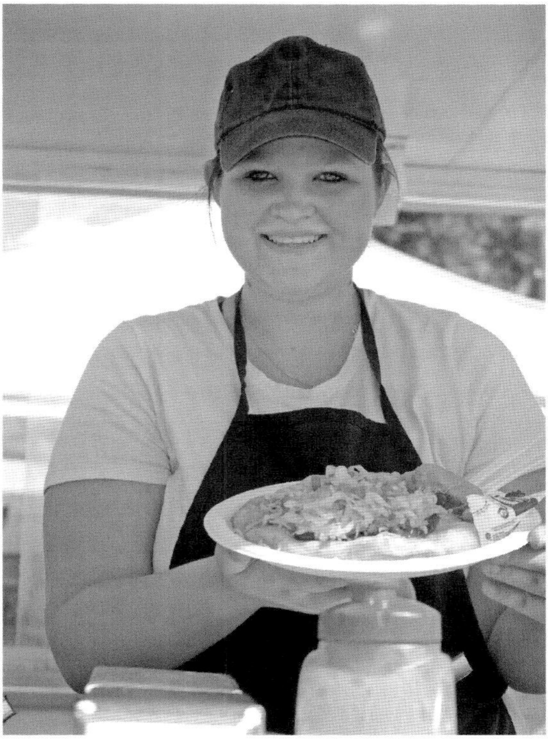

Above: Funnel cake with powdered sugar, a crispy donut freshly fried at the MontanaFair.

Right: Kalie Conklin at the MontanaFair serving up an Indian taco with chili con carne, cheese, onions, lettuce, tomato and salsa with Tabasco sauce.

add calories," Connaghan said of her tactics. Her other indulgence is the foot-long corn dog.

For those who want fried dough, an elephant ear will please the sweet tooth, while the Indian fried bread satisfies the savory palate. The elephant ear is served with the same adornments as the funnel cake, while the Indian fried bread serves as the base of a taco. Of course, it can be eaten plain or with that sweet white dust: powdered sugar. Topped with chili con carne, cheese, lettuce, tomatoes, onions and sour cream with the option of salsa and hot sauce, the combination is the mainstay of events such as the Crow

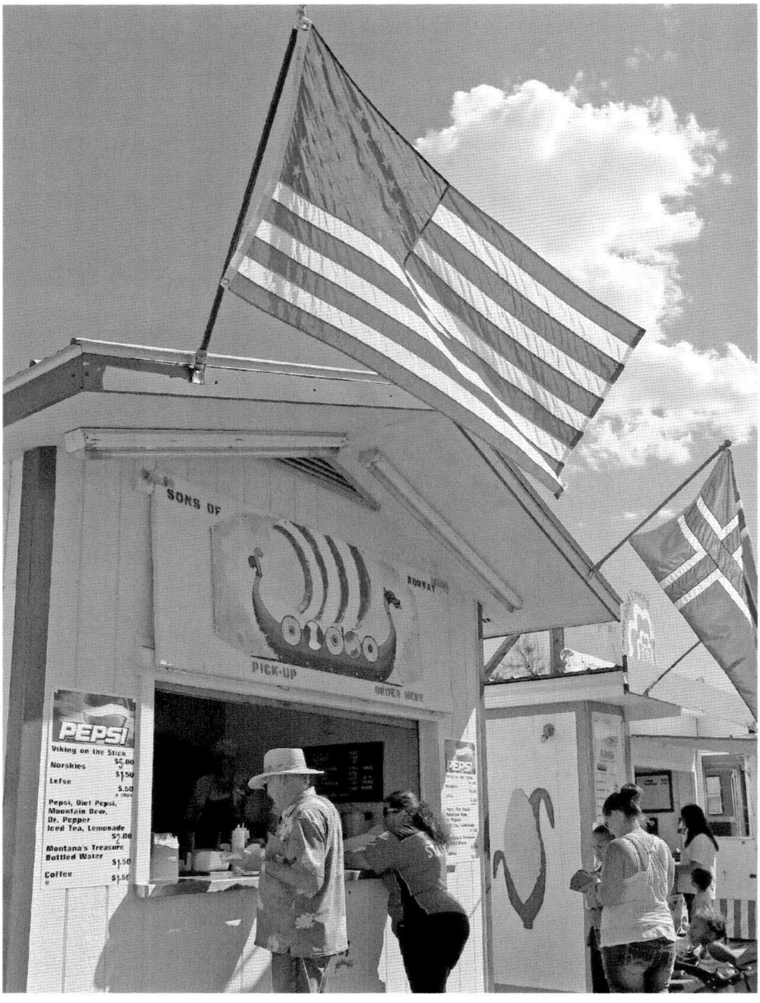

"Viking on a Stick" is one of the most popular items at the MontanaFair.

Fair Celebration. At this gathering, variations are many, with combinations of meats and other additions. Vendors build up reputations and become personal favorites for those who attend.

As the crooning of the country singer fades into the grind of the Ferris wheel and surging organ tones, the smell of grease melds with aromas of grilled meat, French fries and onion rings. There are over half a dozen corn dog stalls with red letters emblazoned with "Hot Dog on a Stick" and "Footlong Corndogs," inviting the world to step up and secure the other symbolic food of the fair. The hot dog coated with a thick batter of cornmeal on a

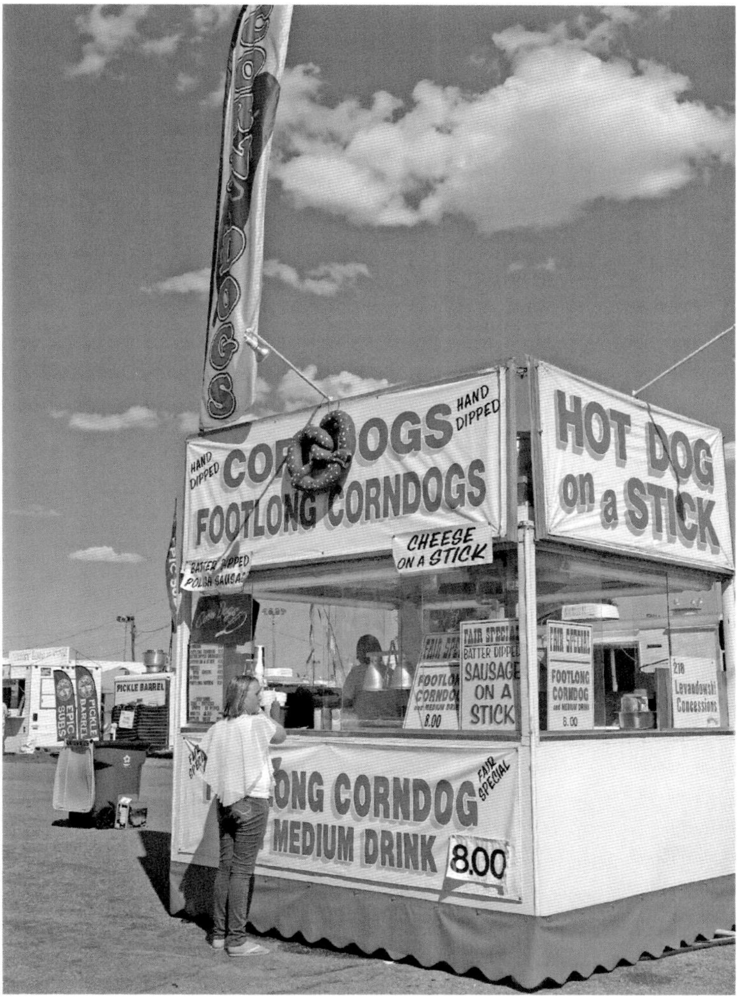

A MontanaFair corn dog stand, where the foot-long corn dog and cheese on a stick can be found.

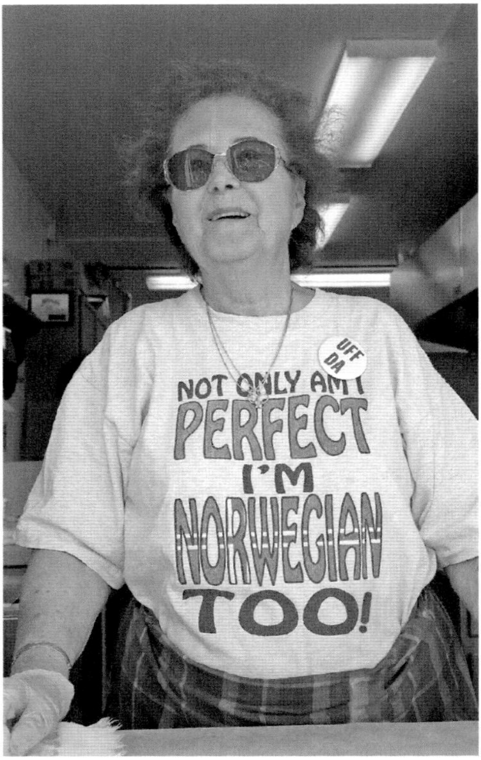

Dolores Baldry has run the Sons of Norway booth, selling "Norskies" and "Viking on a Stick," for thirty years.

stick is fried to golden brown. Then, to enjoy it at its best, it must be doused with mustard and ketchup.

Thirty years ago, Dolores Baldry and her late husband, Rodney, brought the Sons of Norway stall to the MontanaFair. "Viking on a Stick" is a Norwegian meatball shaped into a thick sausage around a stick, battered and then fried. Ole Berg, who came with his wife, Linda, stated that mustard was the best condiment for the Viking. On this day, they ordered "Norskies," the Norwegian version of fried bread with powdered sugar. Linda shared, "My husband is Norwegian. We have lived in Billings for thirty-five years, and we come here every year to the Sons of Norway." Here one can also taste *lefsee*, a thin potato pancake spread with butter.

The bread theme, especially the fried version, dominates at the fair, from funnel cake to elephant ears to Indian bread to the "Norskies," and then to the non-fried rendition, the king-sized pretzel. The food stall Ben Yay's plays on the pronunciation of the French name, *beignets*, for the fried pastries made popular in New Orleans Creole cuisine. More battered and fried desserts include the fried Twinkies, Snickers and ice cream. A light and fluffy pancake-like flour egg mixture encases the goodies.

The stall with the name Guttbusters captures the authentic spirit of fun gluttony at the fair. Guttbusters offers "Cow Pies": specialty burgers of grilled Angus sealed in a special press, battered in light tempura and then fried, making them crispy on the outside. The menu includes the "Flyin Hawaiian," "Ranchero," "Buckin Bronco" and "All American." "The Ranchero" includes mild chili, pepper jack cheese and a ranch sauce, while the "Buckin Bronco" has sharp cheddar cheese and smoky barbecue sauce.

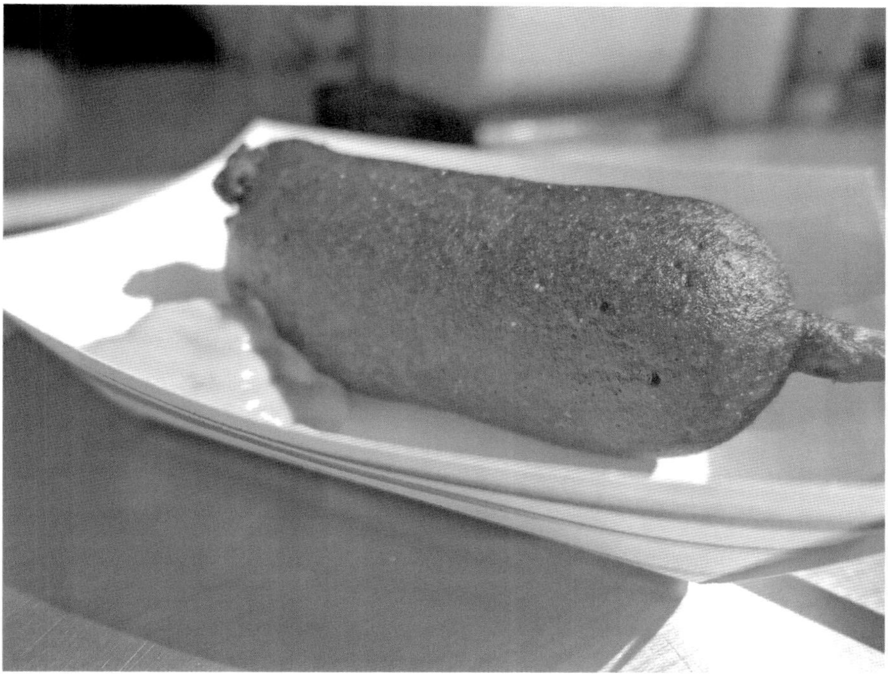

MontanaFair required eating: a corn dog with mustard.

Just to the side of the order window, the cartoon of a cow chewing on grass stands tall, with a shovel in one hand and a cow pie in the other. The letters "GB" are tattooed on one of his bulging biceps. "You ain't been to Montana til you've tried a Cowpie!"

Other food on a stick includes chicken on a stick, cheese on a stick and even s'mores on a stick. Technically, cotton candy could be viewed as being on a stick. Caramel apples usually come on a stick. Corn can come on a stick, but then a smoked turkey leg has its own stick: the bone. Even bacon can come on a skewer. Candied bacon ice cream, while not on a stick, can be had in a convenient cone.

Though teriyaki chicken, fresh squeezed lemonade and chocolate-dipped strawberries can also be appropriated, they possess a lesser degree of sinfulness. Perhaps it is a blessing that the temperatures are up, as it might help visitors sweat out a few of the calories after grazing through the food concessions at the MontanaFair.

FINAL NOTES FOR SAVORING

The restaurant scene in Montana's largest city is growing by leaps and bounds as the population approaches 150,000 people. Franchised food chains have proliferated, supported by a hungry transient population from Wyoming arriving to shop tax-free, while conventioneers and traveling athletes from all around Montana fill tables with eager diners. Franchises provide familiar, if less adventurous, food options and are attractive to investors looking for an easier startup without having to create a restaurant from scratch.

Fortunately, these days, locally owned shops and cafés provide tasty alternatives. I could now confidently offer a food tour in Billings. For instance, in downtown a decade ago, I would have been hard-pressed to find more than a dozen good places to explore. Now there is a martini bar, an ice cream store, a wine restaurant, a brewery or three, a coffee roasting company, two cupcake shops, a fancy cake store and half a dozen special dining rooms. Greek, Irish, Mexican, Chinese, Thai, Japanese and Vietnamese flavors can now be explored. We even have an intimate movie theater that serves refreshments, including wine and beer. Given these options, and with an enlarging sphere of local eateries, the question of "Where to eat?" is easily answered.

Though franchises and chain eateries dominate the avenues and shopping centers in the West End and in the Heights, privately owned enterprises have managed to stand out in the repetition of franchising. Hard work and perseverance fuel the success of these private restaurants and cafés. The

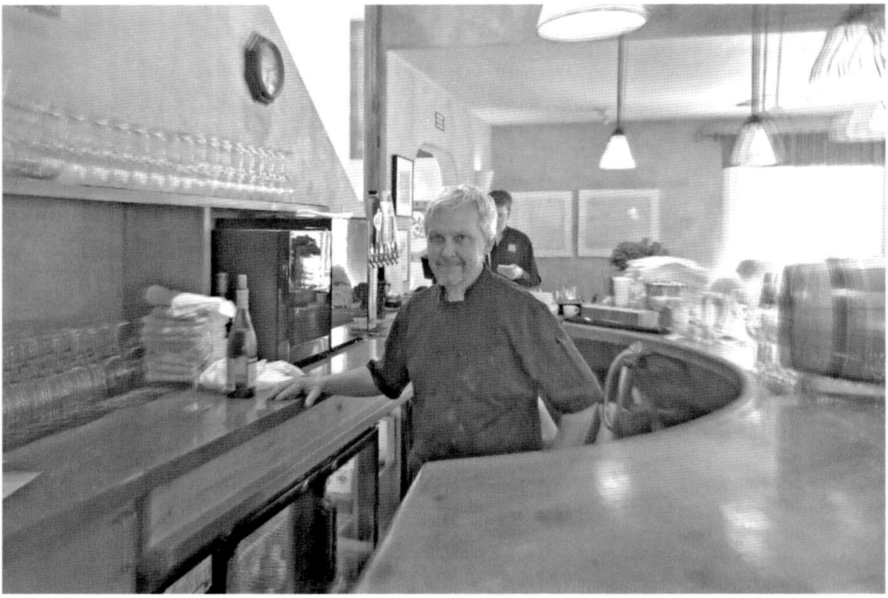

Executive Chef James Honaker of Bistro Enzo.

enterprises tend to come and go, like the wind, but the strong and dedicated survive and prosper.

Dotted around town, there are unique enterprises started by innovative and passionate chefs. These specific examples illustrate the diversity of food found in everything from strip malls to old manor houses. Executive Chef James Honaker established Bistro Enzo with Laurent Zirotti in 1998 and continues to serve fresh Italian, French and Asian fare from his Mediterranean-style restaurant, located in a strip mall. In another strip mall is a cozy breakfast and lunch place. Misty and Kenneth Miller run Red Rooster Cafe on Broadwater and Fifteenth, providing a sense of home. Sheer curtains cover the windows, rooster-themed plates hang on the wall and fresh flowers in canning jars color the table settings. Homemade jars of jams in assorted flavors are offered for sale. The breakfasts are hearty, from chicken fried steak to pancakes to omelets and burritos, but the treasures are Misty's fruit and cream pies and cakes.

Juliano's Restaurant was opened by Carl Kurokawa in 1995. Twenty years later, he is still serving Asian-inspired food out of the carriage house of "the Castle," a historic manor house. On the industrial east side of downtown, Mary Jackson seized the opportunity to open a small restaurant where she serves up Montana-style fried fish at Crazy

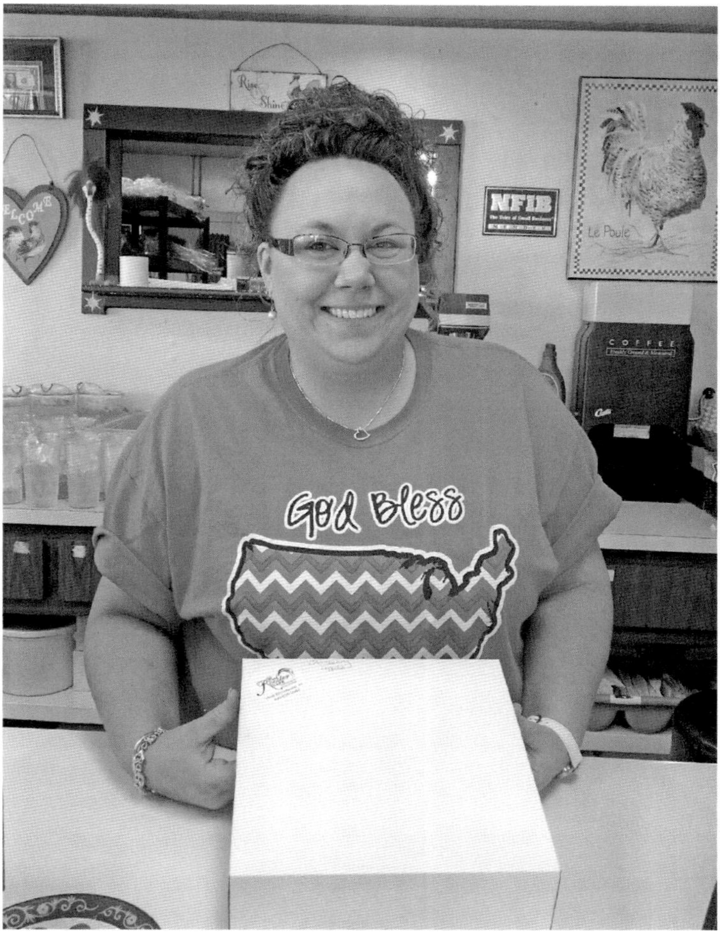

Misty Miller, owner of Red Rooster Cafe, offers up a cranberry apple pie.

Mary's Fish and Chips. Both the portions and personality are large, with Jackson often singing verse while she cooks. Her humor and enthusiasm enhance the daily flown-in fresh seafood she serves in the small space of her restaurant. The culinary school graduate and former cook at Red Rooster Cafe now sings a Janis Joplin or Garth Brooks tune as she fries up your meal. Everyone is treated like family.

There are many others who have stirred, grilled or braised their way into Billings' culinary landscape, and in this book, I had the opportunity to tell their stories and share their dreams and hopes for the future of food in our city. They are the ones who are paving the path to our appreciation of offerings while integrating the foods and tastes from around the world.

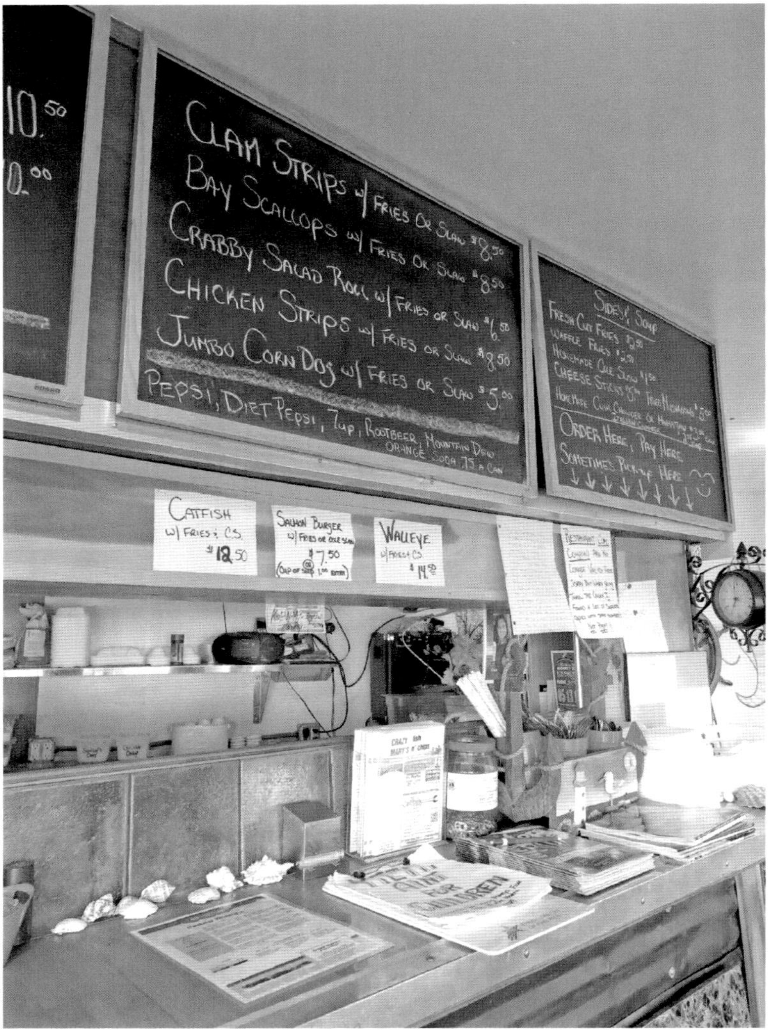

Crazy Mary's Fish and Chips is homemade and fresh.

The most recent restaurant to open in Billings at press time is Local Kitchen & Bar, with chef Travis Stimpson and owners John and Meagan Heenan. After opening on September 29, 2015, reservations are impossible to obtain, which demonstrates the hunger Billings has for new flavors. With an eclectic menu that offers "Bison Hash," "Poutine," "Vegetarian Salisbury" and "Skirt Steak," along with wood-fired pizzas, the restaurant should have something for everyone. On its website, it proclaims "Local" is not just a name but means "getting involved in the community and giving back. We believe that simply buying produce doesn't make you a truly local restaurant. Local covers more ground than that."

On Grand Avenue, between Thirteenth and Seventeenth Streets West, there is a culinary crucible igniting. On the west side of this "hood" is Lucky's Market, anchoring the West Park Promenade, where Umi Japanese Steakhouse, U-Do Yogurt, Red Robin, Panda Express and Chipotle are found. Kitty corner and across the street are City Brew for an espresso drink and City Vineyard for wine and gourmet food. Traveling east into a

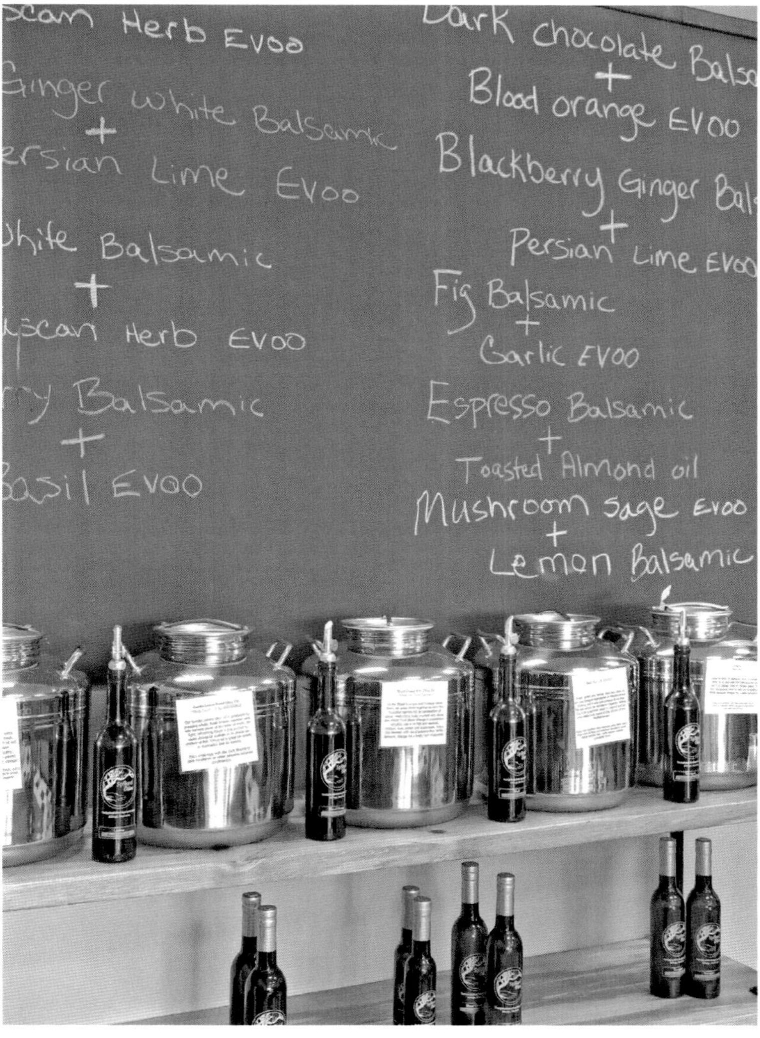

Suggested oil and vinegar combinations at the Spike Olive, where tastings are offered.

strip mall bordering Seventeenth, Spiked Olive sells oils and vinegars from around the world and has taken residence next to Sugar and Spice, where cookies are made from scratch. Two doors down from Fancy Sushi Asian Fusion is the Ranch House Meat Company, a family-owned business selling quality meats. All these outlets are within walking distance of locally owned Van's Evergreen IGA and Albertsons supermarket and across the street from the State Liquor Store.

Local historian Joyce Jensen also speaks of the progress: "Many decades ago, when I was just a kid, Billings had fine dining establishments, but almost none welcomed kids. My dad loved eating out. So our usual place was the Beanery at the Depot, where kids were welcome. As we grew older, Wong Village became our spot. What a change since those times. So many to choose from now! Fine food is available in every part of our city." Most restaurants now offer specific menus for children, and with new restaurants coming into town, the young of Billings will be exposed to a broad range of cuisine, perhaps expanding their perspective to a larger worldview.

Jeff Bosche, the technical director for Billings Studio Theater, never cooks, dining out every night, so he is living the change. His nightly prowls in search of international food were not even possible in years past. Though Bosche may alter his schedule, he mostly keeps to a regular pattern. On Monday and Thursday nights, he seeks out the familiar at Old Chicago Pizza or ventures to the Hog Wild Cafe for comfort food. Other nights he goes to Cham Thai, Los Mayas Mexican Restaurant and A Taste of Asia. On the weekends, Cafe Mabels in Laurel for Mexican food and Siam Thai are his restaurants of choice. However, Bosche is conversant in several dozen restaurants in Billings and is proud of the advances our city has made on the culinary front.

Love of food and community has propelled events such as the Montana State University–Billings Foundation Wine and Food Festival, the Strawberry Festival that features a sixty-plus-foot-long shortcake kicking off summer for twenty-four years and now the Taste of Billings–Summer at the Billings Depot that features local chefs.

From humble beginnings, the MSUB Foundation Wine and Food Festival has expanded to a six-day event with cooking classes, wine seminars, a massive tasting event on Friday and an auction on Saturday night. Through the years, the festival has hosted celebrity chefs, wine experts and cookbook authors such as Raghavan Iyer, George Geary, Elizabeth Andoh, Leslie Sbrocco, Christy Rost, Bernard Guillas and so many more. An army of more than three hundred volunteers makes the event happen, and the proceeds go toward scholarships for needy students.

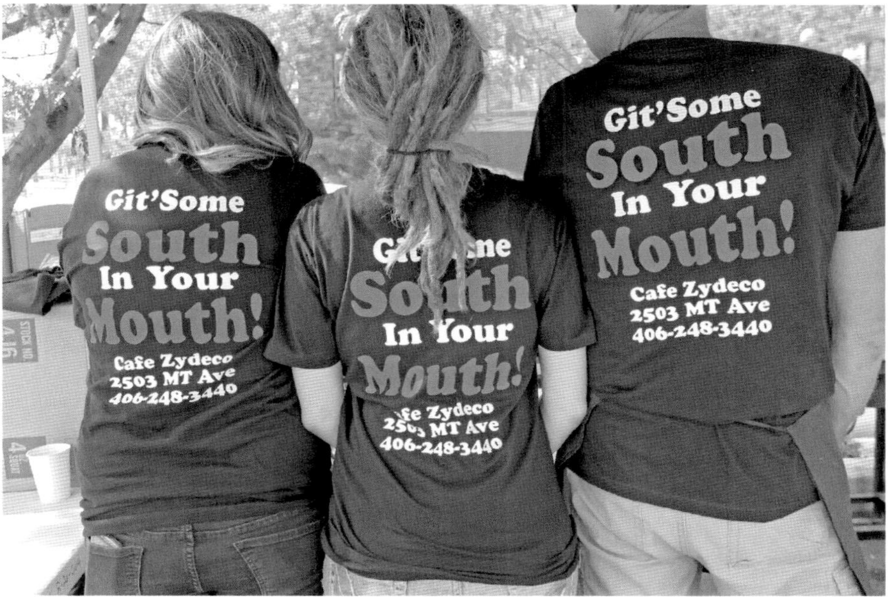

At the Taste of Summer at the Billings Depot, Café Zydeco serves up shrimp étouffée and spicy T-shirts.

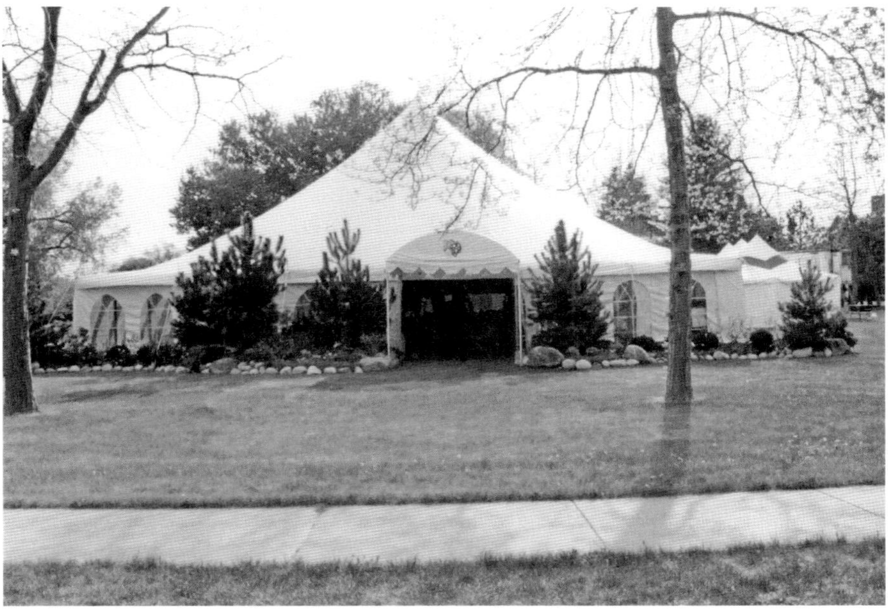

The tent for the Eastern Montana College (now Montana State University–Billings) Wine Festival in 1993. *Courtesy of MSU-Billings Foundation.*

The Strawberry Festival started twenty-four years ago. It takes place downtown under SkyPoint with a pancake breakfast in the morning to kick off shopping at over one hundred "Arts, Crafts, Food, and Cool Stuff Booths," as promoted on the Downtown Billings website. Two stages provide entertainment, but the highlight is eating the gigantic strawberry shortcake and being greeted by "Ziggy" Ziegler, the Strawberry Man.

In 2015, the fourth annual Taste of Billings–Summer at the Billings Depot brought together fifteen Billings restaurants and chefs for unlimited wine, locally crafted beers and sodas. Food was offered by TEN at the Northern, Bin 119, the Rex, Commons 1882, Lilac, Jakes, Montana Brewing Company, Überbrew, Cafe Italia, Bull Mountain Grille, Fancy Sushi, Don Luis, Dickey's BBQ, Stacked and Cafe Zydeco. Attendees kept cool under water mist while they sampled food from booths set up in the parking lot between the Depot and Carter's Brewery and listened to music played by the Clintons. A great summer night for all the senses!

As Montana's Trailhead, Billings is quickly becoming the focal point of a food revolution encompassing the passion of the people and the natural resources of the region. Billings food has a delicious future.

BIBLIOGRAPHY

Art House Cinema & Pub. arthousebillings.com.

Beef for Foodservice Professionals. "Previous Beef Backer Awards, 2007 National Beef Backer Winners." www.beeffoodservice.com/previousbeefbackerawards.aspx.

Bennoit, Kathleen Anne, and Corby Skinner. "Walkers American Grill in Billings." *Distinctly Montana*, April 4, 2006.

Benoit, Zach. "Montana Made Spirits Growing in Popularity." *Billings Gazette*, January 3, 2015.

Billings Gazette. "The Cattle Company—Rimrock Mall—1995–1997." March 30, 2014.

———. "40 Under Forty: Antonia Craighill, owner, Velvet Cravings." February 4, 2014.

———. "40 Under Forty: Sean Graves, Owner, Montana Brewing Co., Hooligan's, The Vig." February 2, 2014.

———. "Yellowstone Valley Farmers' Market." billingsgazette.com/places/yellowstone-valley-farmers-market/business_4000005367.htm.

Bismarck Tribune. "Billings Woman Helps Friend Launch Thai Food Trailer on Bakken's Fringe." In *Billings Gazette*, July 6, 2014.

Bonanza Health Foods. "Your Gold Mine in Nutrition." bonanzahealthfoods.net/about-us.

Boston Harbor. www.bostonharbormt.com.

Bottles and Shots. www.bottlesandshots.com.

Burgess, Dave. "New Building Houses City Vineyard and City Brew." *Western Business*, November 2005.

Caramel Cookie Waffles. caramelcookiewaffles.com.

Carter's Brewing. www.cartersbrewing.com/1952.html.

Chun, Janean. "Wilcoxson's Ice Cream CEO Matt Schaeffer Sparks Social Media Firestorm, Claims Innocence." *Huffington Post*, September 27, 2012.

Cioffi, Chris. "Überbrew Gets Second in World Beer Championships." *Billings Gazette*, April 14, 2014.

City Brew. citybrew.com.

City Vineyard. www.cityvineyardwine.com.

CJ's Bar and Grill. cjsbarandgrill.com.

Davis, Seabring. "Dining Out: Cosmopolitan Cuisine at TEN, the Newly Restored Northern Hotel in Billings Offers All the Elements of an Urban Retreat at Its Upscale Downtown Restaurant." *Big Sky Journal*, July 2014.

Falstad, Jan. "Billings Brewer Mixes It Up with Missouri Bourbon Maker Over Who Gets to Be Yellowstone Finest." *Billings Gazette*, April 17, 2004.

———. "Craving Leads 'Crazy Mary' to Open Fish and Chips Shop." *Billings Gazette*, January 19, 2014.

———. "Downtown Breweries, Two Breweries Tackle Major Expansions." September 1, 2011.

———. "Former Store Site to Be Steakhouse." *Billings Gazette*, November 13, 2009.

———. "Have You Heard: Celebrating a Century of Frozen Fun." *Billings Gazette*, March 11, 2012.

———. "Have You Heard: Master Chef Ditches Retirement to Cook in Laurel." *Billings Gazette*, March 17, 2013.

———. "Have You Heard: New Family-Run Restaurant Has Japanese Steak, Seafood." *Billings Gazette*, April 13, 2004.

———. "Have You Heard: Serving Up New Tennis Courts, Dining Choices around Town." *Billings Gazette*, March 12, 2012.

———. "LIGHTS, CAMERA, BISON: Travel Channel Turns 'Steak Paradise' Lens on Cuisine from The Rex." *Billings Gazette*, September 16, 2012.

———. "Livingston Publisher Decides to Buy 6 Small Newspapers." *Billings Gazette*, October 7, 2000.

———. "Montana Upstart Business Going National with String of 400 Franchise Restaurants." *Billings Gazette*, October 8, 2005.

———. "North Broadway Building Houses Travel Café Sold." *Billings Gazette*, January 5, 2011.

———. "Pouring It On: Thirst for Craft Beers Prompts a Boom in Billings Brew pubs." *Billings Gazette*, April 29, 2012.

———. "A Year in Business: A Boom in Hotel Rooms, a Grocery Chain Leaves Town, West End Continues to Fill In." *Billings Gazette*, December 31, 2006.

The Garage at Yellowstone Valley Brewing Company. www.yellowstonevalleybrew.com/index.html.

Good Earth Market Co-op. "Danly Farms, Laurel, MT." goodearthmarket.coop/learn-more/local-producers/local-producers-spotlight/local-producersdanly-farms-llc.

———. "History." goodearthmarket.coop/the-co-op/history.

———. "2014 Annual Report Meeting." goodearthmarket.coop/the-co-op/annual-report.

Hagenbruger, James. "Good Earth Struggles with Success." *Billings Gazette*, July 13, 2003.

Harper and Madison. www.harperandmadison.com.

Healy, Mark. "A Montana Loophole Leaves a Bitter Taste with Bar Owners." *New York Times*, April 20, 2013.

Hinsley, Libby, and Kira Pascoe. "Farmers' Markets, Enriching Communities Across Montana." Environmental Studies Program, University of Montana. Study conducted in collaboration with the Alternative Energy Resources Organization (AERO), the Montana Department of Agriculture and the University of Montana Environmental Studies Program, December 2002.

Howard, Tom. "Attitude Adjustment: Angry Hank's Microbrewery Just Might Improve Your Mood." *Billings Gazette*, August 12, 2012.

———. "For the Health of It: Gluten-Free Products Are a Fast-Growing Segment in Food." *Billings Gazette*, April 1, 2014.

India Grill. www.billingsindiagrill.com.

Jamie's American Road Trip. "Cornish Cowboy Pasties." www.channel4.com/programmes/jamies-american-road-trip/articles/all/cornish-cowboy-pasties-recipe.

Kemmick, Ed. "Doc Harper's Adds a Splash to Downtown Billings." Last Best News, January 22, 2015. lastbestnews.com/site/2015/01/doc-harpers-adds-a-splash-to-downton-billings.

———. "Make Some Noise: Uberbrew Bottling Popular Wheat Beer." Last Best News, November 13, 2014. lastbestnews.com/site/2014/11/make-some-noise-uberbrew-bottling-popular-wheat-beer.

Koernig, Olivia. "Billings Chop House Partners Almost Have the Table Set." *Billings Gazette*, June 16, 2007.

Lilac, Modern American Cooking. www.lilacmt.com.

Local Kitchen & Bar 59102. localbillings.com.

MacKenzie River Pizza Company. www.mackenzieriverpizza.com.

Manta. Montana Harvest Natural Food. www.manta.com/c/mm5y6c7/montana-harvest-natural-food.

Market Wine and Deli. www.winemarketanddeli.com.

Mary's Health Foods. www.maryshealthfoods.net.

Meyers, Christine. "Thai Dishes at Their Best in Family Operation." *Billings Gazette*, August 8, 2002.

Montana Organic Association. "Danly Farms, LLC." www.montanaorganicassociation.org/directory.htm#d.

MSU Billings Foundation Wine and Food Festival program. "2015 Guest Chefs." www.winefoodfestival.com/participants/guest-chefs.

Muzzleloader and Powderhorn Lounge. powderhornlounge.com.

Niedermeier, Jordon. "Stacked Restaurant Opens Up Shop in Downtown Billings." *Billings Gazette*, June 29, 2015.

Northern Hotel. www.northernhotel.com.

Off the Leaf. offtheleaf.com.

Olson, Erik. "Have You Heard: Kennedy's Moving Wine Shop, Opening Restaurant." *Billings Gazette*, May 17, 2015.

———. "Have You Heard: South Side Eatery Fieldhouse in Midst of Updates." *Billings Gazette*, August 23, 2015.

———. "Shaken or Stirred: Doc Harper's Martini Bar Set to Make a Splash Downtown." *Billings Gazette*, January 18, 2015.

———. "Umi Japanese Steakhouse Opens at West Park Promenade." *Billings Gazette*, October 9, 2014.

PR Web. "TEN Executive Chef Invited to World Gourmet Society Festival." February 26, 2015. www.prweb.com/releases/2015World-Gourmet-Society/02Festival-TEN/prweb12545406.htm.

Pug Mahon Irish Pub Menu. www.billingsgazette.com/app/enjoy/dining/menus/pugs_menu.html.

Pulis, Dana. "Making Progress: Good Earth Market Aims for Feb. 19 Opening." *Billings Gazette*, January 7, 2006.

Red Robin. "Chef Brad Halsten Serves Up Success with the Blackened Sabbath Burger as Red Robin's 'Best of the Bash' Winner at the Food Network South Beach Wine & Food Festival." www.redrobin.com/newsroom/article/662.

Rib and Chop House. ribandchophouse.com.

Scotty's Table, an American Bistro. scottystable.net.

Simply Wine. www.simplywinestore.com.
Tode, Laura. "Teen Culinary Experts to Compete." *Billings Gazette*, April 8, 2008.
Visit Billings. "Walking Brewery District." www.visitbillings.com/pdf/CVB_BreweryTourMap.pdf.
Walkers American Grill and Tapas Bar. www.walkersgrill.com.
Webb, Jaci. "Adding a Generous Amount of Heart, Maplethorpe of the Rex Brings Together Top Culinary Artists for 'Over the Top' Meal. *Billings Gazette*, May 11, 2012.
———. "Good Eats: Drunken Noodles at Lemon Grass." *Billings Gazette*, October 18, 2013.
———. "Good Eats: Scotch Ale at Canyon Creek Brewing." *Billings Gazette*, January 10, 2014
———. "Meet the Chef: Stella Ziegler at Stella's Kitchen and Bakery." *Billings Gazette*, June 22, 2012.
———. "Out in the Fresh Field: After Whirlwind Opening of his Cafe, Harman Set for Library's Food for Thought." *Billings Gazette*, June 1, 2012.
———. "We All Scream for Ice Cream." *Billings Gazette*, June 29, 2012.
———. "YelCo 52: Main Street Holds the Title as Busiest Street in Montana." *Billings Gazette*, September 6, 2014.
Woodcock, James. "Tao New Asian." *Billings Gazette*, July 24, 2015.
Yellowstone Cellars and Winery. www.yellowstonecellars.com.

INDEX

F

G

H

I

J

S

T

U

ABOUT THE AUTHOR

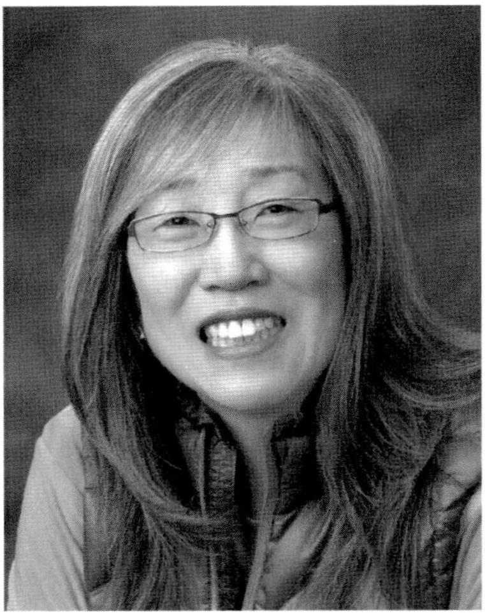

Stella Fong writes, cooks and plays in Billings, Montana. For sixteen years, she has called Montana's Trailhead (once also known as the Magic City) home after relocating from San Diego, California. Fong shares her love of food and adventure through her contributions to *Yellowstone Valley Woman Magazine*, *Big Sky Journal*, *Blue Water Sailing*, *Western Art and Architecture* and *Magic Magazine*. Online, her blog postings and stories can be found at thelastbestplates.com, lastbestnews.com, vinography.com and stellafong.com. Her articles have also appeared in *Cooking Light*, *Fine Cooking* and the *Washington Post*. Through her food and wine classes she teaches for the Montana State University–Billings Foundation, she continues to bring flavor and knowledge. For years, she taught cooking classes for Sur La Table, Williams Sonoma, Gelson's Super Market, Macy's Cellars and Great News! Cooking School. Fong contributed to some of the first Sunday Suppers at the Good Earth and one of the first Farm-to-Table Dinners in the region at Danly Farms with Chefs Tom Nelson and Shane Weigel. She recently completed her first book, *Historic Restaurants of Billings*, which was published by Arcadia Publishing.